Sustainable Development in Western Europe: Coming to Terms with Agenda 21

edited by

Tim O'Riordan and Heather Voisey

FRANK CASS

LONDON • PORTLAND, OR

First published in 1997 in Great Britain by
FRANK CASS & CO. LTD.
Newbury House, 900 Eastern Avenue
London IG2 7HH. England

and in the United States of America by
FRANK CASS
c/o ISBS
5804 N.E. Hassalo Street
Portland, Oregon 97213-3644

British Library Cataloguing in Publication Data

A catalogue record for this book is available from
the British Library

ISBN 0-7146-4830-2 (cloth)
0-7146-4376-9 (paperback)

Library of Congress Cataloging in Publication Data

A catalog record for this book is available from
the Library of Congress

This group of studies first appeared in a Special Issue:
'Sustainable Development in Western Europe: Coming to
Terms with Agenda 21' of *Environnental Politics*, Vol.6, No.1,
published by Frank Cass & Co. Ltd.

Printed in Great Britain by
Antony Rowe Ltd., Chippenham, Wiltshire

Contents

The Political Economy of Sustainable Development

TIM O'RIORDAN and HEATHER VOISEY

This introductory essay sets out the research which produced the following collection of articles. The aim of the research was to develop further a theory of the institutional responsiveness triggered by the Agenda 21 exercise, by examining the extent to which sustainable development may be regarded as an energising force in its own right. The research concludes that this transition has to be assisted by a myriad of institutional changes that are not in themselves directly promoted by the sustainable development agenda. Nevertheless there are distinctive features of sustainable development that clearly create important and continuing institutional change. This introductory essay summarises those conclusions in a broad theoretical context.

What follows is an essay on the institutional dynamics of the transition towards sustainable development, together with five case studies of how that transition is taking place. The research published here was financed by the Human Dimensions of Environmental Change Programme of the European Commission, administered by Directorate-General (DG) XII. The aim of this research was to develop further a theory of the institutional responsiveness triggered by the Agenda 21 (A21) exercise, by examining the extent to which sustainable development may be regarded as an energising force in its own right. The research concludes that this transition has to be assisted by a myriad of institutional changes that are not in themselves directly promoted by the sustainable development agenda. Nevertheless there are distinctive features of sustainable development that clearly create important and continuing institutional change. This

Professor Tim O'Riordan is an Associate Director of the Centre for Social and Economic Research on the Global Environment (CSERGE), University of East Anglia, Norwich. Heather Voisey is a Research Associate also at CSERGE, University of East Anglia. The research on which these contributions are based was funded by DG XII of the Commission of the European Communities. The authors gratefully acknowledge the support and encouragement of the Directorate-General and its staff.

introductory essay summarises those conclusions in a broad theoretical context.

The case studies that follow cover the United Kingdom, Norway, Germany, Portugal, Greece and the European Commission itself. The selection was made because: the UK has the most explicit response to A21 of any member state, Norway and Germany have long-standing responses to the environmental agenda but are less progressive in this context, and the two Mediterranean nations represent developing economies assisted in their growth and competitiveness by European Community funds, and illustrate the emergence of environmental and sustainability policies. Thus we also look at how the Commission itself is fairing, given its ambiguous and contradictory role in both promoting economic growth and in safeguarding sustainable societies. This is a paradox that has not, as yet, been resolved. The research indicates that sustainable development as an organising force in the socio-economic dynamics of these countries institutional structures is having its effect, both in changing perceptions and valuation procedures and in reconstituting governmental structures.

Contemplating Sustainable Development

Sustainable development ought to mean the creation of a society and an economy that can come to terms with the life-support limits of the planet. That in turn suggests that sustainable development can only be maintained by a global society that fully recognises that it cannot expand its population numbers and its economy indefinitely, and that collective self-interest lies in co-operating towards a more socially just economy, as well as competing within it. No-one knows what such an economy or society would look like, what its democratic and judicial institutions would resemble, and what signals would exist to indicate that nature's tolerances were being reached or breached. Habermas [1994] and O'Mahoney and Skillington [1996] for example see such a society developing outside of the formal administrative system in patterns of interactive networks.

To begin with, therefore, the current approach to sustainable development can only be a chimera, a theoretical position that attracts attention, stimulates debate, and raises awareness about the scope and interconnecting complexities of the changes that will have to be made in the transition to a less unsustainable world. This is the phase we are in now. Very little has been achieved to change course, and the institutions of social and economic order have yet to respond in any meaningful way. But a beginning has been made, and that beginning in itself has brought with it some institutional changes. It is these that we shall be studying in this report, for these changes indicate both the nature of the response and the impediments to further progress. These early changes also clarify what further institutional adjustments will be desirable to continue the transition, what they might look like, and how they might be achieved.

Looking across the formidably treacherous terrain of the early phases of this transition the distant prospect does not look very inviting to many late twentieth century citizens. Most, if not all, are embedded in an outlook and way of life that is at cross purposes with that vision of sustainable development. Individuals will be have to act as socially responsible citizens, not self-gratifying consumers, and to care for their neighbours near and far. The amount of waste created to produce any useful item will have to be cut by at least half and preferably more. Energy and materials usage will also have to be reduced by almost as much per unit of value used. Prices will reflect the full ecological and social 'footprint' of economic activity, and the precautionary principle will become the holy grail of management and science. Equity issues, notably the improvement of the well-being of both ecosystems critically endangered, and human populations threatened, by unmanageable catastrophe, will come to dominate efficiency rules in the determination of valuation, risk avoidance and cost benefit analysis. Citizens will have to 'get involved' in the process of governance, in order to have a say in the next phase of the transition. The sustainable policy will be a collectivist polity, indentured to tending the global commons.

That is one vision, and one that may not appear to be palatable for many who contemplate it. The difficulty with sustainable development lies not just in its ambiguity: there is a real issue of democratic probity at stake. If a majority honestly does not want to pay what it sees as 'the price' for sustainable development, who is to deny them their legitimate wish?

Of course the middle horizon may look like that. It obviously depends enormously on what the pathways on the near horizon create. In any case, outlooks may change in the process. What may appear alienating and uninviting today may become part of the civic culture tomorrow, just as computer games might have been viewed as awesome by 19th century youngsters had they envisioned it without the social and technological preparation to embrace it. Until we embark on the journey, we will not know how we may become transformed by our experience. But transformed we must inevitably be if we are to explore a less non-sustainable age. Indeed this is the central message of the report. Institutional innovation of a procedural and orientational kind may prove to be the most significant aspect of institutional response in that it should lead to a more general preparedness to 'give and take' on the road to a fairer and more liveable world. Yet to create the climate for such a vital transition will first require organisational reform of a more conventional kind. This, we believe, is what is happening.

Envisioning Sustainable Development

There are almost as many definitions of sustainable development as there are writers who contemplate it. The very ambiguity of the term allows interests from many different walks of life to debate it and to seek to achieve it. Because sustainable development is seen as a 'good thing' so it is stretched to accommodate almost any unrequited social goal. As Lele [*1991: 613*] wryly remarked:

> Sustainable development is a 'metafix' that will unite everybody from the profit-minded industrialist and risk minimising subsistence farmer to the equity seeking social worker, the pollution-concerned or wildlife loving First Worder, the growth maximising policy maker, the goal orientated bureaucrat, and, therefore, the vote counting politician.

Sustainable development is a neo-renaissance idea that covers the whole of human endeavour and planetary survival. Who could possibly oppose it? The roundtables that have sprung up in a number of countries survive because members, gathered from different sectors of society, have a wish to reach some form of consensus, no matter how unsatisfactory that may be from their starting point. The very continuation of such roundtables is a form of institutional commitment to a process that is seen to be good and worthwhile, even when progress is painful and the language unintelligible. Sustainable development is a socially motivating force where we are not at all sure where we will end up but we keep on trying, because we perceive our long-term survival is at stake. This may prove to be the most important driver towards envisioning sustainable futures.

In an interesting experiment, Nagpal and Foltz [*1995*] solicited the imaginings of 52 people from 34 countries in five languages on how they envisioned the future. What they found was an enormous pressure of social concern for the future of their children as well as for the plight of present generations less fortunate than they were. Equally interesting was the apparent psychological difficulty of jumping too far from the here and now into a world where the main strands of personal identity appear too disconnected and chaotic. Nagpal and Foltz [*1995: 159*] observe:

> People's visions for the future are frequently coloured by their nostalgia for the past. People mourn the passing of former days, but simultaneously express longing for a future free of restrictive cultural traditions. Thus, visions often reflect a struggle between shrugging off the burden of custom and the effort to keep traditions alive as an anchor against the tides of change.

Their essays also reveal a deep contradiction in the role of the state. People who advocate a local focus, community empowerment and collective responsibility through individual enlightenment, see the state as a potential facilitator and protector of the peace. Those who favour eco-efficiency look to more international frameworks to guide competitiveness into more socially beneficial ways, yet still unleash all the best in scientific innovation and enterprise. It may be possible to reconcile the two, by adjusting the role of the state towards one of an international 'broker' for global agreements on trade, competitiveness and regulation, and a local 'facilitator' of communal self-reliance and consensus building. Such a combination would mean the reconciliation of the two great forces that may prove to be the most important influences on the sustainability transition over the next generation, namely 'globalisation' and 'localisation'. 'Globalisation' is a process fostered by the almost unrestrainable forces of technological and managerial advance, information advances, and the ubiquitousness of knowledge, capital flight and capital investment. 'Localisation' is the supposed antidote: the shift towards greater control over local lives and natural worlds. The result is the uneasy relationship between the inexorable process of homogeneity, and the politics of heterogeneity emphasising locality.

Nagpal and Foltz [*1995: 169*] sum up this dilemma:

> The paradox we face is: how do we help the poor if their survival is repeatedly put at risk by those who say they wish to help them, but whose primary concern is capital accumulation and exploitation of raw materials? There exists a far reaching force of importing alien models of consumption and behaviour – in sum changing indigenous cultures – with no purpose other than foisting the western market model on these peoples ... or to make these people useful tools for enriching others.

There we have it: what is sustainable development actually for? If it is for the gradual victory of capitalism in some eco-moderated form, then equity and cultural identity objectives get short shrift. If the objective is greater social justice, a more effective sharing of the global commons, and respect for community identity at a local level, then much of the case for eco-efficiency based as it is on quasi-market principles will be treated with circumspection.

Envisioning sustainable futures will mean, at the very least, clarifying these underlying value premises. It will also entail discovering why such value premises are formed and through what revelations they may be accommodated into larger and more coherent wholes. That in turn opens up the dilemma that sustainable development has to be visualised at various scales of space and time, culture and economy, ecosystem and bio-geochemical-flux. We do not have ready institutional nor psychological means of co-ordinating these scales of envisioning. We appear to be temperamentally and constitutionally capable of connecting only a small number of these scales at a time. If it is to progress, the sustainability transition will have to include learning how we connect up scales of perception and consequence that are almost unnatural to us now.

Four Interpretations of Sustainable Development

The organising idea of sustainable development is so hospitable to various interests it is possible for us to pick on four significantly differing perspectives, as summarised in Figure 1. Each, we believe, shapes the position of key players to the debate. The first, namely that of *reliable and continuous wealth creation*, is by far the most powerful at present. In essence it is primarily focused on sustained economic growth, predicated on low inflation, declining levels of public expenditure relative to wealth creation, falling unemployment, and rising rates of investment in technology and industrial innovation. In short it is the classical economist's agenda for reliable and prolonged growth, the mainstay of any electoral mandate. Of importance for this analysis, is that this picture is shared by all political parties. Also of significance is that this view does not take environmental quality as such into account, and hence it is not supported by green accounts or sustainability indicators. But these dimensions are beginning to force their way into the attention span of central and local government policy analysts, and business accountants. The influence of these more qualitative and socially sensitive indicators is still very weak. This is mostly because the idea is too new to be effective, and partly because the applicability of such indicators in policy terms is still lacking.

The second definition applies to the notion of *stewardship*, trusteeship for the planet and future generations, and the notion of shared development for mutual gain. Here the muddle in the concept of sustainable development becomes more evident. For example, treaties and laws promoting the cause of free trade and open competition between nation states rarely take into account distributional consequences for long term environmental protection or social well-being amongst the poor or marginalised. Cruz and his colleagues [*1996: 8*] point out that both economic development as such, and trade opportunities in particular, only promote the cause of sustainable development if politics are addressed across a wide arena of social and economic issues, and are not confined to macro-economic policy. In a similar vein Durbin [*1995: 16–17*] points out that the signing of the Uruguay Round in 1993 will yield possibly an additional $23 billion in

FIGURE 1
FOUR COMPONENTS OF SUSTAINABLE DEVELOPMENT

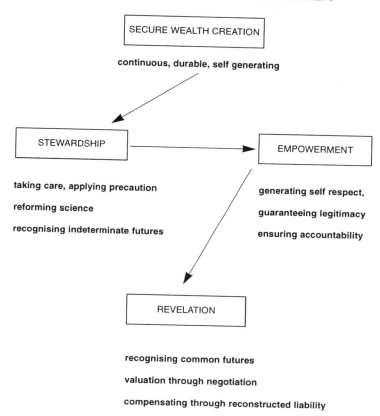

trade, of which the rich North will accrue $14.7 billion, and Africa will actually lose $2.7 billion. The issue is not, however, free trade versus environmentalism. The whole future of sustainable development in this second, developmental sense, is bound up with the huge complexities of North–South political and economic relations.

The third perspective, namely that of *cultural justice*, is a very different one. This is based on the view that sustainable development is a confidence trick that mainstream environmentalists have fallen for. Wolfgang Sachs [*1993*] is the most articulate advocate. Environmentalists, he proclaims, have lost their way and have become as much a force of domination as the very interests they once opposed. The current debate on global ecology, he asserts, is 'largely devoid of any consideration of power relations, cultural authenticity or moral choice; instead it rather promotes the aspirations of a rising eco-cracy to manage nature and regulate people worldwide. Ironically, a movement which once invited people to humility has produced experts who succumb to the temptation of hubris' [*1993: i*]. Sachs speaks for those who believe that the self reliance, cultural and social-ecological justice dimensions to sustainable development have been hijacked by those who originally rose to protect them.

The fourth dimension is the *visioning process* that helps to reveal the other three positions and seek a reconciliation between the complementary roles of globalisation and localisation. Visioning is becoming popular because it sounds attractive, educational and vaguely democratic. In fact it is a technique that remains largely untried, and very difficult to do well in a world that is not ready to transfer real power to local groups and well-intentioned sustainability initiatives. Nevertheless, the device of creating mechanisms through which citizens groups can visualise how a more sustainable future might map out, and be more aware of the consequences of their own ideology for the well being of others, has merit. So we place it in our lexicon of prerequisites for the sustainability transition.

Tentatively we argue that there is a kind of evolutionary staging in the transition to sustainable development. The growth paradigm remains the primary positional focus. No democratically elected government can seriously challenge the vista of real material gain for its electorate. Where environmental threats loom, the promised growth is the basis for technological innovation and regulatory belt-tightening. This is the classic accommodative mode: business is nearly 'as usual' with a green tinge that still promises new investment and jobs. The stewardship mode enters slowly but stealthily. It is apparent in the obvious sense of biodiversity protection and enhancement. But the concern for people as future 'green citizens', at home and abroad, is very much part of this line of argument. As the sustainable development evolution unfolds, look out for stewardship encompassing citizen care as much as environmental care. The focus on best business practice and environmental awareness for a more considerate future generation will too intensify.

The social justice and empowerment motifs, outlined in our third stage of evolution will take longer. It will necessarily regain an element of 'green accounting' and 'citizen stewardship' before it takes root. But it may, paradoxically, take root at the local level of informal activism rather than through formal state structures. Hence the lubrication of visioning. Putting all this in a slightly different way, these four interpretations of sustainable development, each of which is essential to its achievement, and each of which cannot be identified in the absence of the others, are complementary and conditional perspectives of any transitional pathway.

- *markets* refer to arrangements in the competitive economy ensuring that ecological and social tolerances to expansion and change are not exceeded. Though the mechanism of control may also be regulatory, the process of implementation is competitive and market driven;

- *regulations* apply to patterns of control and guidance imposed either by the state in the form of legal rules, or various formal restrictions, or by collective action supported by voluntary agreements or legal norms;

- *equity* relates to distributional fairness in dealing with both non-human and human life but mainly the latter, and encompasses both rights and duties towards future as well as present generations and ecosystems. Within equity will be legal norms that guide such institutional arrangements as monitoring, protecting, evaluating and compensating, either in cash or in kind;

- *revelation* encompasses the idea of capturing the spirit of communal obligation and citizenship. It is a processes of discourse and negotiation towards consensus that shows that common interests have been recognised.

According to various conceptual analyses, for the most part undertaken by economic theorists, potential scientists and sociologists, each of these four components of the sustainability transition contain attributes that resonate and are interdependent. To follow this, it is necessary to break down each component along seven dimensions, as follows: myths of nature, or views of natural tolerances; social values, or view of social tolerances; policy orientations, or performances of policy instruments; distributional arrangements; generating consensus, ideas on how to reach acceptable negotiated outcomes; intergenerational responsibilities, or views on the rights and needs for future generations; and liability arrangements, or the basis of compensation. In diagrammatic form, the pattern of discourse around sustainable development might look as in Figure 2.

One can see that there are many variations of a possible sustainability transition by means that are seemingly coherent in goals but inherently diverse in approach. This suggests there can be no commonly accepted definition of sustainable development, nor can there be any collective position as to which institutional means or forms are best able to facilitate the transition. By producing this table, one does not have to assume that the differing strands of outlook and values are conflicting to the point of immobility in the transition. Indeed, one should argue that *all* parts of the discourse are associated in any tolerated transition, for it is only by weaving these different strands together into new institutional arrangements that a truly democratic transfer towards sustainability can be determined.

FIGURE 2
PATTERN OF DISCOURSE AROUND SUSTAINABLE DEVELOPMENT

	Market	Regulatory	Equity	Revelatory
myths of nature	expandable limits	precautionary limits	breached limits	negotiated limits
social values	enterprise	protection of vulnerable	citizenship	community
policy orientations	price signals	rules to contracts	equality of opportunity	inclusion
distributional arrangements	markets	by agents of rule-makers	by democracy	by negotiation
generating consent	compensation	by agreed rules	negotiation and compensation	by reasoned discourse
intergenerationality	future looks after itself	future helped by present	future planned by present	future envisioned
liability	spread losses	fine redistribution	burden-sharing	by negotiation

O'Neill [1996] regards expanding civic awareness and obligational perspectives as central to any institutional transition. He seeks a neo-Aristotelean order of political and social associations which enable every citizen to act virtuously and live happily while limiting the power of the market and restraining the regulatory interventionism of the state. O'Neill regards this necessary decentralisation, or informal subsidiarity, as a necessary background to the fettering of both the market and the state.

On the basis of the argument above, any institutional adaptation for the sustainability transition may be summarised as follows: it must reflect all the levels of discourse outlined in Figure 2; it must be seen to be responsive to identifiable visions of a more ecologically protective and fair future state; it must be created by negotiated consent, and when that consent cannot be guaranteed, then by understanding and tolerance; it must be measurable, set in parameters that have ecological and social references, and linked to agreed norms and targets; and it must be carried out according to agreed rules and norms, both of a formal and informal kind, located in markets, in regulatory practices, in the law, and in social values.

If sustainable development is non-threatening, the four visions outlined above can emerge side by side. They are articulated by different interests, but can cross over in the discourse of, say, sustainability indicators, green accounting and regulation. The tension is most obvious is when the discussants are institutionalised, as for example in the UK Round Table on Sustainable Development. Here the transformation is too raw and the level of understanding too recent to permit effective dialogue. Respect for legitimate positions is beginning to occur, but at too slow a pace to permit the kind of progressive institutional innovation so essential for the true sustainability transition.

This is why the research that follows places so much attention on the intricacies of the variables outlined in the table, namely:

* *policy integration*, utilising fresh perspectives on the social valuation of environmental capital, calling on stewardship;

* *roundtables and environmental fora* to allow citizens to discuss in a context of openness and, mutual respect, calling on empowerment;

* *green accounting and eco-taxation* reforms;

* *changing interpretations of the state and civil society*, via a healthy re-analysis of globalisation and integrationalism on the one hand, and localism and empowerment on the other, a tension that is challenging legal norms of differential rights (to make wealth and to ensure individual and cultural security);

* *changing attitudes within the business community* regarding the social as well as economic role of commercial operations, favouring care and training of employees and responsiveness to local economies and environments; and

* *shifts in educational curricula and practices*, beyond the classroom walls with community projects and participatory activism, so that schools and universities become two-way learning laboratories.

These are the zones where the most important institutional innovations should occur if the transitional pathways envisaged in the table are to progress peacefully and equitably. In the light of where matters were, say a generation ago, there is just enough of a dynamic in these active zones to be sure that sustainable development is an organising force for institutional responsiveness.

Objectives

The original objectives of this project were to extend earlier work on institutional adjustment to climate change in selected European countries and in the Community itself [*O'Riordan and Jäger, 1996*], to the response to A21. This is the sustainable development audit signed by all countries following the United Nations Conference on Environment and Development in June 1992. The theory and implications of institutional adaptation are analysed extensively in O'Riordan and Jäger [*1996: 87–101*].

Specifically for this project, the aim was to develop a fuller understanding of the political dynamics associated with the organising focus that is sustainable development. To do this, the project team sought to examine a number of indicators of both policy shift, including policy integration, and structural or positional adjustment in the pattern of forces guiding and co-ordinating policy. These organisational and procedural modulations are associated with a host of actors and agencies including government departments, and non-departmental public bodies, regulatory agencies, business, local government, the voluntary sector, communities and citizens.

Throughout our assessment we were influenced by the conclusions of the climate politics study [*1996: 351–60*]. These observations suggested that the following themes should be addressed in any future analysis of institutional dynamics in response to global environmental change initiatives. First, institutional adjustment takes place in a number of policy arenas, working co-operatively, but not necessarily with the same set of political triggers. Thus response to sustainable development can and should come in a number of guises. Secondly, robust institutional adjustment has to be backed by the economic ministries and economic policy strategies. Tackling the roots of macro-economic philosophy with an environmental agenda will fail, unless the two approaches can be made to reinforce one another. And finally, because policy networks are constantly coalescing and fissuring, the most successful institutional adjustments require linkages of policy coalitions, fresh groupings of interests whose unequivocally co-operative support buttresses a number of policy innovators and executors at a variety of levels of action. For sustainable development, such coalitions have to shape a common political space, and combine economic, social and environmental interests. Therefore, the project team approached this task by searching for 'policy indicators' that might herald a shift towards more sustainable pattern of economic development and social welfare.

As a means of identifying how far any country studied has moved in its institutional re-design for the transition to sustainable development, we proposed eight 'indicators' for testing response and adaptation:

(1) *the language and meaning* of sustainable development as expressed in official document and popular discussion during the early years of the debate over sustainable development;

(2) *the scope for policy integration* where heretofore policies were neither united nor mutually reinforcing;

(3) *the nature of inter-departmental co-ordination* promoting and reflecting these new policy alliances;

(4) *the role of legislative (parliamentary) surveillance* of both policy integration and administrative cohesion, including improved means of identifying targets and performance indicators;

(5) *the compilation of environmental and social indicators* of quality of life and ecological tolerance as a basis for legitimising action, and evaluating the sustainability transition;

(6) *the creation of 'green' accounts* covering indicators of resource depletion, environmental disruption, price incompatibilities, inappropriate subsidies, and measures of human welfare and social justice, coupled to tentative moves towards ecological tax reform;

(7) *the involvement of the business community* in addressing sustainability through full cost accounting, internal housekeeping, full regulatory compliance, product stewardship, supply chain audits, and sustainability awareness-raising for shareholders and customers; and

(8) *the emergence of local action*, along the lines of Local Agenda 21 (LA21), to bring about a locally responsive version of all the above points, set in a drive for fresh democratic mandates.

Findings

The overall conclusion of this study is that sustainable development is a very important organising force for political, social and economic response, covering far more than environmental problems, and destined to evolve into a broader social agenda as Europe continues both to federate and to decentralise. Its influence will be shaped by political and economic processes that will evolve, mostly independently, from the sustainability transition. But its significance as an organising force depends ultimately on its own identifying focus. To date that crucial aspect of institutional response is only embryonically discernible, and even then only in a fragmentary way.

There are two fundamental challenges to the progress of sustainable development in Europe. The first is the lack of an intrinsic policy focus that channels the pattern of political, social and economic change in the specific direction of economic durability, precautionary stewardship and citizen empowerment as a unifying transitional engine. The second is the potential incompatibility between the economic and technological forces of economic globalisation, as seen in the drive towards international competitiveness, freedom of trade and movement generally, and privatisation of former state-supported responsibilities in both business and social services. All this is predicated on the principles of growth through innovation and comparative advantage in an ever-increasing economic and cultural homogeneity. Set against this is a call for self reliance, for community ideology, for cultural tolerance and for 'people-centred' means of debating and reconciling future choices for sustainable development. This line of analysis supports localism, cultural variety, collective identity and a sense of community control over the nature of change.

At all levels of government, European Commission, nation-state, regional, and local, this tension between competitive globalisation and empowering localisation is beginning to emerge in the politics of the sustainability transition. At present these tensions are made manifest in the dismay over the closing of factories and local services in the name of 'efficiency', in the debate over the funding of services such as schools, post-school training, social care, prison and probation services, health care and pensions provision, and in the emergence of a host of new socially concerned self-help groups around such heretofore neglected issues as health, domestic violence, rights of asylum, and drug addiction. The evidence is beginning to emerge that active groups have little faith in the ability of government at any level to handle such issues in a comprehensive and caring manner. Hence the shift towards civic activism, political disobedience, and collective efforts to achieve greater measures of security in local economies.

The research team regard these 'empowering' moves as a vital aspect of any sustainability transition. And it also believes that many social and political movements are in place to promote this objective. But there is no conscious connection between the two in any sustainable development agenda. This is a lost piece of institutional innovation, whose non-appearance is all the more alarming because of its significance.

Language

In terms of language, the phrase 'sustainable development' has caused some difficulty of translation. In some cases (Greek, Irish) the wording had to be invented. In all cases the translation adopted in formal treaties reflected national biases in interpretation of sustainable development. The British liked the notion of continuity and reliability, the Germans stewardship, the Greeks life support, the Portuguese something akin to self perpetuation and the Norwegians 'being upheld' by self-generating investment. There may be no agreement as to language, but in the Portuguese and Norwegian texts there is an innovative sense of the Brundtland Commission notion of self-limiting and self-perpetuating closed loop economies. This is mostly theoretic at present. The core concept of sustainability remains in terms that prefer the language of continuation and stewardship.

As for the European Commission, the language of Article 2 of the Maastricht Treaty is a classic example of politically ambiguous draftmanship. The final wording was 'harmonious and balanced development of economic activities, sustainable and non-inflationary growth respecting the environment'. As Haigh [1996: 90] puts it: 'while the intention to introduce the Brundtland concept underlies the wording, it is arguable that the combination with another, quite different, intention has resulted in wording that is either meaningless or at best ambiguous.' The Commission is currently seeking to clarify the wording for the Intergovernmental Conference with reference to 'making environmental protection more effective and coherent at the level of the union, with a view to sustainable development' [European Council, 1996: 4]. This interprets sustainable development as an environmental quality objective rather than a social justice or empowering device. One can hardly expect anything different but this is not a sufficient response.

Policy Integration

Policy integration requires a common evaluative yardstick, coalitions of supportive interests, and a machinery of execution that co-ordinates a host of governmental and non-governmental actors. Such conditions are rare, despite the current trend towards policy coalitions and interest groups realignments. One cannot expect much movement here, except where there is genuine policy ambiguity and an overwhelming political demand to get things done. Transport policy which touches the interrelated areas of public health, economic decline in urban centres, pedestrian and cyclist safety and road-related damage to wildlife sites, is one such arena.

The evidence emerging from this study is that effective policy integration is not taking place. There are various institutional innovations, including co-ordinating cabinet-level committees, interdepartmental working groups around environmental valuation and green accounting, so-called 'green-ministers', and important new combinations of interests across business, environmental, consumer and justice groupings. But none of this has any serious political or administrative force at present.

In the Commission, the legal requirement under Section 130(r) of the Maastricht Treaty, namely to integrate environmental considerations into other policy arenas, has little administrative or even political effect. Again, movement is taking place for reasons other than those of policy integration, notably in agriculture and energy. As David Wilkinson shows in his analysis of Commission responses, there are institutional innovations in the form of an Integration Unit in DG XI (the DG responsible for environmental matters generally), for 'integration correspondents' within each DG, for environmental appraisals of various policy moves, and for an internal management accounting system. In practice, however, little of this has any practical effect. DGs are not attuned to thinking laterally or environmentally. Sharing of responsibility may be a European ideal, but it has yet to become part of the highly sectorised and self-protecting administrative culture of Brussels. However, the European Parliament has used the integration clause to require much greater environmental accountability for the area of Cohesion and Structural Adjustment Funds, and this certainly is a policy innovation. Adjustments at this level can have significant national impacts on progress towards sustainability. The Portuguese and Greek case studies both contain examples where cohesion funds were used to promote economic development in a palpably non-sustainable manner.

The ultimate barrier to sustainability lies in the lack of encouragement from the top, namely the prime minister or president, the unwillingness of the main economic departments (finance, industry, employment, energy, transport) to address sustainable development within of the mainstream economics focus, and the relative political weakness of the environment ministries. From this perspective, it is hardly surprising, but not helpful, that responsibility for sustainable development rests with the environment ministries. They may seek to co-ordinate, but they have no effective power. No prime minister, not even Mrs Brundtland herself, when in power places sustainable development high on their political priorities, They may like to talk a language of stewardship and empowerment but they do not carry it out.

Inter-departmental Consultation

Any departmental policy requires clearance and support from related departments. So inter-departmental working groups are the coinage of administration discourse. In the name of sustainable development there is movement on green accounting in the form of shadow accounts by statisticians, sustainability indicators of varying degrees of sophistication, and economic valuation of environmental change. At present most of this is in the form of data gathering and seminars on valuation techniques. There is little in the way of discernible policy shift in any of the countries studied with regard to improved use of sustainability accounting methodologies. But this is not to say all this effort is wasted. Far from it. It is actually a vital part of institutional adaptation in the transition. We perceive the early stages of this all-important relationship in the European Environment Agency, in the Department of the Environment in Britain, in the Organisation for Economic Co-operation and Development (OECD) and in the Commission's work on eco-taxation. But without high level political encouragement, this is still embryonic.

The research team concludes that there is a small, but discernable, culture shift taking place in the bureaucracy of official ministries. Officials are beginning to think in a precautionary manner, in the long term, in a language of ecological economics and risk management, and through more integrated structures of accounting and assessment. The newer administrators are especially interested and sensitive to these developments. There are huge structural and attitudinal blocks to this process, make no mistake about it. But the pace of movement is both exacting and progressive. We regard this as a very important form of institutional innovation.

Legislative Surveillance

This, by contrast, is the least active arena of institutional innovation. The various national parliaments and the European Parliament have not been able to organise or undertake any meaningful audit function of national or departmental responses to A21. There is frankly no political push for this, nor any established mechanism to make it work well. Parliamentary surveillance is very much a matter for the legislators and their committee structures, as well as perceived responsiveness of the administrative departments and the states of law. Without formal 'duties of care', and in the absence of any co-ordinating committee structure, parliamentary surveillance is always likely to be wanting. The UK's House of Lords looked at the issue of sustainable development, but this was an episodic affair which is unlikely to be repeated in the foreseeable future. In any case its scope was limited to the contents of the strategy report prepared after Rio, and its influence on the policy process was barely discernible. Legislatures have to be prepared to return to a topic many times if they want to be effective. There is, as yet, no stomach for this with regard to sustainable development, at least in national governments. The European Parliament, however, appears to be more aggressive with a much more focused interest in the 'integration' remit of Article 130(r), and it is intensifying its demands for more specific performance targets through which to evaluate the effectiveness of the various Environmental Action Programmes.

Sustainability Indicators

The OECD is pioneering an approach to sustainability indicators, and this is having an influence on the European Environment Agency, the Norwegian Environment Ministry and the UK's Department of the Environment. Greece has no formal indicators, nor does Portugal. The Commission is considering this, but nothing official has emerged. It may do so in the run up to the Sixth Environment Action Programme now that the European

Environmental Agency has commissioned a study on sustainability performance with regard to targets.

Despite this apparent sluggishness, many official statistical organisations are analysing the scope for more comprehensive indicators of performance towards set environmental goals. In this early stage in the evolution, most of the indicators are either economic or ecological in character. The social dimension, notably in the all-important area of empowerment, is notably missing. Until there is a distinct move in this direction, the role of such indicators will primarily be evaluative for environmental quality change rather than sustainable development in its rounded form. The pioneering British study of national sustainability indicators is nevertheless an important start. This study combined the speculations of statisticians and policy analysts across the sweep of Whitehall. It created bodies of data, and interpretations of trends, that no single department would have recognised if working entirely on its own. It also created a shift in policy, notably towards more social cost pricing of private road vehicles. The fact that the study is published, with a request for its collaborative improvement in future editions, is a good example of institutional dynamics that probably will be copied elsewhere in Europe, and certainly in the European Environment Agency.

Green Accounting

There is a lot of interest in green accounting methodology in the World Bank, the United Nations and the OECD. This is where the models are being developed, not in national economic departments. Only the Department of the Environment in the UK, out of the countries studied, is seriously pursuing green accounting, and there is an interdepartmental working group co-operating with the Treasury in the process. This work, has no specific policy significance as yet, but it is early days. In Norway non-governmental organisations have allied themselves with the local authorities and the environment ministry to establish a network of commentators promoting more sustainable consumption. Still it is not clear precisely what that means, but at least it is a relatively high profile Norwegian institutional innovation in this area. The Norwegians have also a 'green book' of embryonic green accounts, mostly environmental protection experiments, and a Green Tax Commission to examine the scope for eco-taxation. Neither the Portuguese nor the Greeks have developed green accounts. In both countries the environment ministries have responsibilities for public works and infrastructure investment. So these are neither politically nor administratively conducive conditions for green accounting to be developed at present. The Commission remains silent on the issue, but who knows what is going on in the bowels of DG III.

Business and Sustainable Development

Europe-wide, business is beginning to adopt the mode of eco-efficiency [*Easterbrook, 1996; Fussler and James, 1996*]. This is the auditing of business practice to minimise waste and resource abuse, and to concentrate on housekeeping measures that help to make a company more profitable yet less environmentally harmful. This drive is especially noticeable amongst the larger corporations whose chief executives are influenced by public image, cost saving measures, the need for a competitive edge, and the growth of regulations on environmental auditing and product stewardship. This is an area that is more voluntaristic than regulated, but only to a point. The growth of more open government, the surveillance of company accounts, the increasing move towards voluntary regulatory compacts under the eco-auditing schemes, and the introduction of more environmentally and socially concerned younger recruits have helped to promote this trend.

In Norway, Germany, and the UK, the business community has mobilised sufficiently to be a new institutional force in the progress to sustainable development. It is cautiously supportive of moves towards greater environmental accountability and encouraging of shifts towards a greater duty of care. But, paradoxically, it also forms significant political impediments to innovations such as green taxation and green accounting. So, like everything else in this report, a institutional innovation is very much at an early stage, with a contradictory influence between structure and procedure. One can hardly expect anything different in a highly ambiguous policy arena.

LA21

This is the implementation of A21 at local level, as set out in Chapter 28, by local government and other stakeholders at this level. By the end of 1996, all local authorities are supposed to give an account of how they have moved, or are preparing to move towards, sustainable development, in the form of their own LA21. The crucial element to this process is that consultation with the community has to occur as the starting point to action. The success of this initiative lies in its ability to capture the imagination, to promote action amongst community groups that would not otherwise have been stimulated, or involved, and to give local action and ingenuity a place on the international stage. LA21 should be about more than action, it is about involving and empowering to create the structures which will perpetuate locally responsive action and create a shared vision of the future. The research team found that by far the most vibrant institutional innovations were taking place at this level, most noticeably in the UK, and to a lesser extent at this time in Germany and Norway. In Greece and Portugal the constitutional arrangements for local autonomy in local government are not suitably developed for LA21 initiatives. It thus may be some time yet before LA21 takes off.

Although there is evidence for visioning and community participation there is also a great potential for linking environmental, social and economic agendas, as most local government environmental policy still follows more traditional environmental protection lines. Such activities include: waste reduction, energy efficiency, preventing air and water pollution, and nature conservation. LA21 moves beyond these activities to new ways of planning, discussing, delivering, and evaluating progress on environmental, social, economic and political objectives. There are a number of highlights of this initiative so far.

First, full eco-audits are emerging in about a third of local authorities in the UK, less in Germany and Norway. Secondly, there is a serious attempt to enable partnerships to form between local government and the business and voluntary sectors. Thirdly, environmental co-ordinators are being employed to act as facilitators within local authorities, and between them and the wider community. Fourthly, there is a revaluation of the relationship between central and local government, with a strong political move towards greater local autonomy, and for cross-sectoral policy initiatives. This is connected to a shift towards political decentralisation and a move to more sustainable development resonates with a wider forces for change. And finally, there is evidence of the beginning of a serious effort at local governance in the form of environmental fora which are involving people and interests in a common vision of local areas, and the mobilisation of local groups and people to work towards achieving these visions. This aspect contains the potential for real change in behaviour, attitudes and goals.

LA21 could be the grass-root catalyst for serious institutional innovation in the areas of discourse and action suggested in Figure 2. It is by far the most appropriate forum for informal community initiatives in job trading, credit unions, civic protest, and educational reform. It is also the basis for both empowerment and revelation through such devices as visioning and co-ordinated round-tables. The key is the internal mobilisation of collective self respect amongst local authorities and their stakeholder alliances in the context of a need for more political autonomy, a greater sense of democratic proximity, and a voice in the noisy clamour of the globalisation-localisation accommodation process. This is bound to be a highly active area for institutional innovation in the next stages of the sustainability transition.

The European Community and Sustainable Development

This essay has already pointed to the fundamental ambiguity and legal muddle in the division between integration and sustainability at the local level. At present legal norms promote the interests of a competitive single market at the expense of any right to self determination of sustainable futures at the local level. This means that unless there is wider civic awareness, there will always be a legal fudge, and the local cultural aspects of sustainability may forever be secondary in Community law. Yet, paradoxically, Community law is also adopting a 'deminimus' approach to local and national diversity via its subsidiarity principles.

This dilemma is not insurmountable. To begin with both legal and political rules applying to unanimous and majority voting suggest that protectionist positions on national and local autonomy will have political and legal support. Furthermore, moral principles underlying the activities of the European Court of Justice allows individuals to claim the benefits of Community rates before national courts. This would include the promotion of more local autonomy if that could be shown to be in the interest of balanced and harmonious development and sustainable and non-inflationary growth. It will all depend on the evolving liberalisation of community legal principles in favour of greater individual and environmental rights, coupled with the freedom and ability to use a variety of courts for arbitration.

The record of spending in both Community Cohesion and Structural Funds, and investments in the new federal states of former East Germany, shows that the economic development paradigm is still dominant. In these cases there is no formal procedure for guaranteeing stewardship, let alone public participation in project planning. Cohesion Funds have been almost exclusively directed to transport and water supply supply/treatment works, large capital investment with huge environmental side effects. There may be an institutional basis in the form of integration, but there appears to be no political will.

Perspective

Sustainable development is a deliberately ambiguous concept that means conservatism and liberalism in proportions commensurate with the general drift of social and political change. This is its staying power. Its organising focus emphasises more ecological and human-sensitive accounting, the application of a precautionary duty of care, and the scope for civic activism at local level. This provides it with a distinctive role in the evolution of human and natural well-being.

Institutional innovation is a permanent feature of the human condition. What is relevant here is the relationship between general trends of institutional change, promoted by a host of factors: laws, treaties, intervention, to communication, value change, and civic protest. Such change is, by definition, continuous and unpredictable. Then there is the specific change promoted by sustainable development. Here the picture is more variable, with some very distinct moves in the form of policy integration, indicators and targets, and local initiatives. The contradictions between open markets and social democratic principles favouring protection of individual and natural rights have become more sharply defined. This is the area in which the next phase of sustainable development will evolve. For that to be effective, the mood of the body politic will have to shift to favour greater local autonomy and greater collective responsibilities for a variety of rights and obligations to the vulnerable and the unborn. The law will follow attitude shift, but it need not be far behind. The key lies in the juxtaposition of reconstruction of the basic principles of growth, with the flowering of the application of stewardship, and the cry for greater local control over our futures. It is possible that this somewhat more ideal juxtaposition will take off in the next decade. If so, it will be due to institutional innovation spurred by sustainable development that we record in the papers that follow.

REFERENCES

Cruz, W., Murasinghe, M. and J. Warford (1996), 'Greening Development: Environmental Implications of Economic Policies', *Environment*, Vol.38, No.5, pp.6–12.
Durbin, A. (1995), 'Trade and the environment: the North/South Divide', *Environment*, Vol.37, No.7, pp.16–24.
Easterbrook, G. (1996), *A Moment on the Earth: The Coming Age of Environmental Optimism*, Harmondsworth, Middlesex: Penguin Books.
European Council (1996), *Presidency Conclusions*, Brussels: European Commission.
Fussler, C. and P. James (1996), *Driving Eco-Innovation: A Breakthrough Discipline for Innovation and Sustainability*, London: Pitman Publishing.
Goodland, R. (1995), 'The Concept of Environmental Sustainability', *Annual Review of Ecological Systems*, Vol.26, pp.1–24.
Habermas, J. (1994), 'Three Normative Models of Democracy', *Constellations*, Vol.1, No.1, pp.1–10.
Haigh, N. (1996), "Sustainable Development" in the European Union Treaties', *International Environmental Affairs*, Vol.8, No.3, pp.87–91.
Lele, S. (1991), 'Sustainable Development: A Critical Review', *World Development*, Vol.19, No.6, pp.607–21.
Nagpal, T. and C. Foltz (eds.) (1995), *Choosing Our Future: Visions of a Sustainable World*, Washington DC: World Resources Institute.
O'Mahoney, P. and T. Skillington (1996), 'Sustainable Development as an Organising Principle for Discursive Democracy?', *Sustainable Development*, Vol.4, pp.42–51.
O'Neill, J. (1996), 'Cost Benefit Analysis, Rationality and the Plurality of Values', *The Ecologist*, Vol.26, No.3, pp.98–103.
O'Riordan, T. and J. Jäger (eds.) (1996), *Politics of Climate Change: A European Perspective*, London: Routledge.
Sachs. W (ed.) (1993), *Global Ecology. A New Arena of Political Conflict*, London: Zed Books.

Acronyms

A21   Agenda 21

DG   Directorate-General

LA21   Local Agenda 21

OECD   Organisation for Economic Co-operation and Development

Governing Institutions for Sustainable Development: The United Kingdom's National Level Approach

HEATHER VOISEY and TIM O'RIORDAN

Despite the fact that the UK is prompt in discharging its documentary commitments with regard to Agenda 21, real signs of lasting commitment and progress, or their lack, can only be seen with regard to institutional change. There are institutional mechanisms and tools emerging in many policy areas. Those highlighted are: policy integration, performance indicators and monitoring mechanisms, and eco-taxation. However, these represent only the beginnings of the institutional adjustment necessary for sustainable development to be implemented. In short, although it is possible to point to material change in line with international commitments, the current response has produced little in the way of policy realignment and new administrative cultures. It is suggested that this is because of a number of reasons. First, there is no clear consensus on the definition of sustainable development. Secondly, administrative and regulatory cultures are operating conservatively and incrementally. Thirdly, meddling with the tax regime, is practically difficult and politically contentious. Fourthly, the pattern of responses is currently lacking the coherence that effective political leadership could bring. And finally, mechanisms for transparency, accountability and public participation are still not forthcoming.

This study will outline the nature of the UK's response to Agenda 21 (A21) and the signs of a movement towards a more sustainable society from an institutional point of view.[1] In doing so it shall attempt to answer the following questions. Is there a clear and consensual definition or vision of sustainable development? Are there institutional structures and mechanisms in place for the implementation of sustainable development? Are there any signs of change in administrative cultures within government? Is there any

Professor Timothy O'Riordan is an Associate Director of the Centre for Social and Economic Research on the Global Environment (CSERGE), University of East Anglia, Norwich. Heather Voisey is a Research Associate also at CSERGE, University of East Anglia. The authors would like to thank Andy Jordan, Derek Osborne, John Hobson, and the members of the project group for their comments and assistance in the writing of this contribution.

coherence to the responses so far? And, in terms of institutional innovation what progress has been made on three crucial indicators: policy integration, indicators and monitoring of the sustainability process, and eco-taxation?

This analysis will look first at how the concept of sustainable development is defined, arguing that there are three separate but interlinked approaches within policy-making in the UK. It subsequently looks at the two processes framing the UK's response to the United Nations Conference on Environment and Development (UNCED) and A21: the White Paper [*HM Government, 1990*] process, which was the first comprehensive statement of environmental policy in the UK; and the Sustainable Development Strategy [*HM Government, 1994a*] which guides the UK's response to sustainable development until 2012. A final section will look at recent progress towards sustainable development's implementation in the key areas of: economic instruments, green accounting, the new Environment Agency, business, and the Local A21 (LA21) initiative. The main observation of this study is that although some progress in implementing A21 is observable in terms of policy innovation and institutional change, it is slow and uncertain because there is not sufficient political momentum at national level.

Defining Sustainable Development

To paraphrase Sachs [*1993: 9*]: definitions tacitly shape the perception of problems, highlight certain solutions and consign others to oblivion; they feature certain types of social actors, marginalising others, and certain types of social transformation, degrading others. Sustainable development tends to be defined and conceptualised in three ways in the UK. The first two appear in much of the government's documentation on sustainable development and the environment. All three are based on the most publicised definition of sustainable development, that of the Brundtland Commission, namely: 'development which meets the needs of the present without compromising the ability of future generations to meet their own needs' [*World Commission on Environment and Development, 1987: 8*].

The first definition of sustainable development is framed in economic terms and is an extension of academic debate among economists.[2] This approach seeks to use interventions in market prices and in regulatory mechanisms to correct the imperfections of under-valuation of polluting discharges, over-depletion of non-renewable resources, and pollution damage to sites or species of aesthetic or biological significance. It is not a comprehensive statement of sustainable development, more an attempt at fine-tuning to create a more ecologically sensitive market economy. The second definition discusses the concept in the language of development, calls attention to the North–South divide, and issues of intra-generational equity, poverty and population growth. The way forward is in helping developing economies to grow in accordance with environmental protection objectives, so that economic growth is not hindered by environmental degradation. Here the underlying rationale is still capitalist and developmental. The third approach is emerging at present in the literature of Non-Governmental Organisations (NGOs) and local government initiatives to implement LA21.[3] This approach to the conceptualisation of sustainable development emphasises the local social structures that will be implementing it and are affected by it. As such it focuses on public participation, local involvement, and sees the concept as a social transition as much as an environmental one. However, it is not currently an influential interpretation at national level. Let us consider these three in more detail.

Internationally the concept of sustainable development has been on the agenda since the 1987 Brundtland report. As part of the government's belated response to it, in 1989 the Department of the Environment (DoE) produced *Sustaining Our Common Future*, which prioritised economic development, and highlighted the problems of developed countries with regard to environmental degradation resulting from growing populations and poverty. Despite claiming that: 'the Government is making sustainable development an integral part of its domestic and international policies' [*HM Government, 1990: 47*] and declaring its support for the principle of sustainable development, the subsequent White Paper: *This Common Inheritance* [*HM Government, 1990*], confined discussion to a few sentences tucked away in the 'world environment' section, or referred vaguely to 'sustainable growth'. The White Paper's continued emphasis on economic growth and development in its discussion of sustainable development, indicates a very 'weak' definition of the concept. It also pointed to the battle being fought by the DoE to assert environmental principles and concepts against the strong economic concerns of the Cabinet and committee structures

At the time of the White Paper, Chris Patten, then Secretary of State for the Environment, in a bid to strengthen the Department's influence in this area, stated that the basis for environmental policy was 'stewardship', to preserve and enhance, moving away from purely environmental protection towards sustainable development [*HM Government, 1990: 10*]. Despite this, environmental degradation was still perceived as a problem to be solved either by international diplomacy or existing national institutions. In the first, second and third DoE reviews of progress towards the targets of the White Paper, the concept of sustainable development was referred to only in the context of aid programs to developing countries, or in response to the European Union's (EU) Fifth Environmental Action Programme [*HM Government, 1991; 1992; 1994b*].

The document *Sustainable Development: the UK's Strategy*, published in 1994 as part of the government's response to UNCED, says that: '[t]he challenge of sustainable development is to find ways of enhancing total wealth while using common natural resources prudently, so that renewable resources can be conserved and non-renewables used at a rate which considers the needs of future generations' [*HM Government, 1994a: 33*]. However, it was notable that it contained no discussion of sustainable development as a concept and therefore no new thinking, stating only that it was 'difficult to define', hence the tendency to rely on the Brundtland definition. In the UK at present, sustainable development is defined narrowly with little recognition of the implications for wider society and individual behaviour, and the radical agenda of equity, democracy, and empowerment. However, these elements are being explored tentatively at the local level within the local/NGO definition of sustainable development. The lack of debate at national level is a barrier to institutional change and therefore the implementation of A21 and ultimately the principles of sustainability. The following sections, although not referring again explicitly to this lack of debate, illustrate that without broad and open debate and discussion on sustainability there is neither the required understanding of the concept, nor the impetus or opportunity for action.

The 1990 White Paper

The 1990 White Paper: *This Common Inheritance* was produced in response to the rapid greening of UK politics in the late 1980s [*HM Government, 1990*]. It set out the UK's environmental strategy until the year 2000 as prior to this the UK had no coherent policy strategy on the environment. However, even before its publication there were indications within Whitehall that Patten was losing the battle and the potentially innovative and ambitious document would be compromised. This was largely because of Prime Ministerial wariness and opposition from other departments keen to protect their policy areas from DoE encroachment.

The White Paper's key innovations were largely institutional, centred on Whitehall, and primarily of a policy co-ordinating nature. In fact the next Environment Secretary, Michael Hesletine, claimed that the government had put in place 'some of the most sophisticated machinery to be found anywhere in the world for integrating environment and other policies' (quoted in *Green Alliance [1995a: 539]*). As discussed below, this machinery has had some teething troubles. On the negative side, the White Paper suffers from short-termism and lack of vision, with very little in the way of targets, deadlines, firm commitments, and new initiatives. Much of it was simply a restatement of established policy, and actions the government was already committed to under various EU Directives. Promises of hard targets and binding timetables were substituted for reviews, studies and consideration, few of which have yet to be realised seven years later, despite the government's assertions to the contrary. No attempts were made to tackle issues, such as enforcement inconsistencies, or the administrative weakness of the DoE. In many areas, such as agriculture, energy or transport, little or nothing was envisaged in terms of policy change. However, despite the criticisms, the ray of hope for environmentalists was that it had been produced at all, and that its existence appeared to create a documentary process against which government policy and action could be measured and assessed annually.

Since 1990 five reviews of the White Paper have been produced. The first, published in September 1991 [*HM Government, 1991*] added little to the original White Paper, announcing almost nothing new whilst reiterating what had already been promised and not delivered so far. One small but significant introduction, however, was the listing beside each progress report on each measure the responsible department; a victory in the continuous battle waged by DoE officials to share accountability among the departments. By the second review in September 1992 [*HM Government*] the environment lobby's expectations were not high, deservedly so. Although, there was innovation for policy integration in the requirement that papers produced for cabinet and ministerial committees should, where possible, cover significant environmental costs and benefits, evidence of this occurring is not yet forthcoming. The third review in the White Paper process was published in May 1994 [*HM Government, 1994b*]. At this stage any remaining followers of the process could not have been surprised by the lack of initiatives, the reduction in the number, and extension of deadlines, the disappearance of commitments made in previous documents and the number of pledges for action not included or weakened. The fourth and fifth reviews published in March 1995 and 1996 respectively [*HM Government, 1995a; HM Government, 1996a*] are combined updates of activities resulting from the White Paper, and the Sustainable Development Strategy [*HM Government, 1994a*] and shall be discussed later.

The White Paper process appears to have missed the opportunity to address issues such as green taxation, the link between the environment, economic and social policies, and real institutional reform. It represents no strategic assessment of the needs of future society in environmental terms and lacks commitment to those measures it has considered. The opportunity for more accountability and openness was ignored. As the below discussion indicates having the mechanisms in place is all very well but there needs to be political commitment to ensure that they work, otherwise there is no impetus to take environmental considerations into account in more than a mechanical way, to alter, crucially for long-term progress, departmental cultures. Evidence given to the House of Lords Select Committee on Sustainable Development (HOLSCSD) [1995] highlights the importance of greater transparency in the process which would create greater external surveillance opportunities. An important part of this process is a strong critical voice from the environment lobby, in the form of NGOs and individuals, but at present this is floundering on the disappointing White Paper process and their failure to comprehensively to address it [Green Alliance, 1995a].

Four main institutional innovations were introduced through the White Paper process. So far, it appears that they have had little real effect in terms of integrating environmental considerations into other policy areas, and even less with regard to sustainable development, as the following brief analysis will show. However, it is important to note that these form a significant institutional structure for the implementation of sustainable development in the future. Although they have not fulfilled their potential, mainly as a result of a lack of co-operation from other ministries, their continued existence does represent progress in terms of policy integration that can be built on.

Ministerial Committees

The White Paper announced that the co-ordination of action on the environment within Whitehall would be undertaken by two committees. Initially these had co-ordinated the production of the White Paper but were subsequently retained to implement it. Secrecy and a lack of accountability has characterised their activities, and they have rarely met, supposedly because there are few serious disputes for them to deal with: 'although it is fair to argue that if the [DoE] was pushing a radical agenda there would be rather more disputes to deal with than at present' [Green Alliance, 1995a: 540]. In 1992 the most important of these committees, the cabinet committee, was disbanded and the new Ministerial Committee on the Environment (EDE) created. Its chairman is the leader of the House of Lords, not the Prime Minister as previously, denoting a significant loss to the prestige of the Committee and lessening of its political influence. Nevertheless, it is regarded as the most important forum for cross-sectoral policy-making, and the resolution of inter-departmental conflicts concerning the environment, apart from the Cabinet. However it has its limitations in that it cannot supersede the policies of other departments. Its existence and operations are very difficult to monitor and surrounded by secrecy. In practice the EDE is an ineffective institutional device, mainly due to the continued territorial preoccupation of the other departments who are uncomfortable with the environmental agenda of the relatively new

DoE. There is hostility, particularly from the 'economic' departments, at interference in their policy arenas. Yet, the fact that there is a cabinet committee on the environment at this level, which the policy arenas of health and education do not have, suggests that it is considered politically important, thereby increasing the relative status of the DoE and its ability to encourage greater policy integration.

Green Ministers

Green Ministers in each department are nominally responsible for greenhouse-keeping matters, the annual reports, and the co-ordination of environmental initiatives between departments. However, to date they have had little impact on departmental policy in these areas. Their status is either low, or it is one responsibility among a multitude for the respective Secretary of State. They are supposed to meet as a committee to facilitate policy integration, constituting the second ministerial committee announced in the White Paper, under the chairmanship of the Secretary of State for the Environment, but do so infrequently, meeting just twice last year [*ENDS, 1996a*]. They have no power to make major policy decisions and remain focused on internal issues [*Hill and Jordan, 1993*]. One of the main reasons for their creation was to deflect from the DoE the focus of public attention, criticisms and queries over environmental matters when other departments' policies were involved. However, this has not happened. They are rarely the focus of lobbying and questions in Parliament so little pressure is put upon them to take a more visible or productive position. This is not aided by a refusal to publish the minutes of their meetings, and provide information on attendance and frequency of meetings.

The low public profile of Green Ministers in respect to sustainable development policies has been recently noted by HOLSCSD [*1995*], who felt that their reported role, compared to actual achievements and responsibilities, had been misrepresented to such an extent that it could undermine confidence in the government's institutional mechanisms for implementing environmental and sustainability policies entirely. However, they do seem to be re-evaluating their role in relation to the public, probably in response to this criticism and increasingly frequent questions in Parliament from the Opposition party on the green performance of all departments. In January 1996 the Green Ministers announced that they would be publishing in 1997 a number of case studies to illustrate departments' good environmental practice [*HC Debates, 1996a*]. This could herald a higher public profile for Green Ministers in the future. Although the EDE will remain the formal forum of policy discussion on environment-related topics, the Green Ministers will continue to meet to 'discuss in a relatively informal way emerging issues of common interest' and there will be a broadening of the range of these issues [HM Government, 1995b: 20]. Whether this facilitates further policy integration and illustrates good practice remains to be seen.

Annual Departmental Reporting

Analyses of the new system of annual reporting by Whitehall departments, in the wake of the White Paper, have shown a noticeably poor level of environmental content [Green Alliance, 1991; 1992]. Reports in the main fail even to reflect departmental action on the White Papers commitments. Virtually no other targets against which future performance could be assessed are produced and almost no hard data is presented. However some progress is observable in the most recent reports. For example, the recent Department of Transport (DTp) [1995: i] report includes minimisation of the impact on the environment in its guiding principles, and refers to the environment throughout rather than consigning it to just one chapter as in many reports. Although, this is not a statement of support for sustainable development, but an adaptation of the language to departmental objectives, it is at least an acknowledgement that the issues need to be addressed. It also appears that inter-departmental meetings set up to discuss the environmental content of reports have led to improved communications and debate, and so have proved to be a positive integration mechanism [Hill, 1996].

Beyond the rhetoric, a detailed look at the reports in terms of progress on environmental targets, illustrates that little real action is underway. After three years, the overall improvement in energy efficiency is just six per cent (the aim is 15 per cent by 2000), with some departments still investing no effort in this area. Carbon dioxide emissions per m^2 have done slightly better, with an eight per cent decline over those years, although some departments continue to increase emissions, for example, Health recorded a 76 per cent increase [ENDS, 1995a]. It should be noted, however, that this mechanism helps to formalise the involvement of the DoE in other departments' policy-making, and allows a greater amount of transparency in departmental environmental performance.

Guideline Documents

The document Policy Appraisal and the Environment [DoE, 1991] was published as a guide to civil servants, setting out how departments could assess the environmental impacts of their policies in a systematic way. The intention being to encourage all government departments to undertake such an exercise at an early stage in decision-making. However, it was in danger of being emasculated before it began as some departments claimed that their policies had no environmental impacts and so implementation was not necessary. It also came under criticism for its focus on monetary valuation techniques, and starting with the policy as a given, rather than assessing whether the proposed policy was the appropriate solution to the problem. By summer 1993 it appeared to have disappeared without trace into the opaqueness of Whitehall decision-making, but pressure was exerted to produce some evidence of implementation when 12 environmental groups wrote to the Secretary of State for the Environment complaining that there was no published environmental policy appraisal for several major policy decisions, including the roads programme.

The DoE subsequently published *Environmental Appraisal in Government Departments [1994]* consisting of a number of brief case studies illustrating how the principles of environmental appraisal have been applied in a number of government departments. It indicates that departments are taking such techniques more seriously than previously, but that there is little actual policy change or integration. It appears that putting the guidance into practice has been problematic, with training for civil servants being less than systematic. There is a lack of expertise and resources to undertake the appraisal adequately, and it is perceived to not be easily accessible or operational [*Hill, 1996*]. The deficiencies of this second document, particularly in terms of comprehensiveness and projects covered, are evidence of a number of underlying issues: departmental expertise is still evolving; the Treasury is suspicious of some of the economic tools available; and there is a need to widen the scope of these tools and reports to embrace social policy, industrial strategy, international relations, education and health, or even to move beyond what is effectively *project* appraisal. A third report on policy appraisal, looking at the influence of the 1991 document on decision-making within Whitehall, due to be published soon, has already been delayed a year. This will be useful if it can help to solve some of the problems that are being experienced in the implementation of the present guidance.

In the meantime *A Guide to Risk Assessment and Risk Management for Environmental Protection [DoE, 1995a]* has been published. This aims to contribute to the practices of the previous documents, by setting out a more structured approach to risk assessment. The benefits of this approach are described as: reducing disputes over judgements of risk; identifying areas of poor information and uncertainty which could open up the decision-making arena to the precautionary principle; and greater transparency. Significantly, this document clarifies government ideas on the precautionary principle, accepting perceptions of risk as the basis for policy-making in conditions of uncertainty, and the role of monitoring in determining the accuracy of risk assessments.

The mechanism of policy appraisal is potentially the most important in terms of policy integration. The potential is for a less *ad hoc*, more explicit, structured and transparent tool to be established for policy analysis and use in decision-making. Such a mechanism would enable clearer comparisons between the decisions of different departments and policy arenas, and with this the move of departmental cultures towards greater environmental awareness should follow. However, recent questions in Parliament by the Opposition to Ministers have revealed that no policy in any department received an environmental appraisal in 1995, and requests for full copies of the case-studies contained in the second report were not available for examination.

Sustainable Development: The UK Strategy

Sustainable Development, the UK Strategy [*HM Government, 1994a*] was produced to meet the government's commitment, made at Rio in 1992, to produce a national strategy for implementing sustainable development in the period until the year 2012, as outlined by A21. This was the first national response submitted to the United Nations Commission on Sustainable Development (CSD) in 1994 and was the subject of a presentation made by UK officials at its Third Session in May 1995.

The Strategy was criticised on publication by the environmental lobby for having no targets or clear vision of the future, no sense of urgency, and no inspirational capacity. Although it exhorted action from many other groups and stakeholders, commitments to action by the government itself were lacking. Criticism centred on the lack of any real position and action on the international front, the *ad hoc* consultation process and ineffective institutional arrangements. The high point was the acceptance of the principle of demand management by Whitehall, particularly by the DTp where a change in policy substance has occurred breaking the deadlock between it and the DoE. When John Gummer was appointed as Secretary of State for the Environment in 1993, the inter-departmental battles required to produce a strong Strategy were seen as a test of his skills and influence [*Green Alliance, 1993*]. The appearance of the Strategy, the cautious acceptance of demand management, and the subsequent publication of sustainability indicators [*DoE and Government Statistical Service, 1996*] represents a significant victory for the DoE. It is debatable whether any other Environment Minister could have achieved as much in the same time.

Policy integration in Whitehall does not, nevertheless, appear to have moved any further. There is no role mentioned or explored for the Treasury, and nothing of substance, beyond the landfill tax, is suggested in terms of the economic mechanisms. Although, the aim was for it to present a broader approach than the White Paper its only innovation was the creation of new institutional machinery, this time 'external' to departments.

The Panel

The British Government Panel on Sustainable Development has now published two reports, in January 1995 and 1996. It has a roaming brief to advise the government on topic areas of its own choosing, and it has access to all Ministers and the machinery of government. Its terms of reference are: to keep in view general sustainability issues at home and abroad; to identify major problems or opportunities likely to arise; to monitor progress; and, to consider questions of priority.

Both reports have highlighted a number of subjects, chosen for their topicality and general interest, which the Panel is monitoring, providing specific recommendations on only some at present. The initial list of subjects was: environmental pricing and economic instruments; environmental education and training; the depletion of fish stocks; ozone depletion; technology transfer; reform of the Common Agricultural Policy; climate change; and transport. The first report indicated that the initial two topics have long-term significance for sustainable development and urged the government to give these areas higher priority. On the next two topics the recommendation was essentially that the government should be more proactive, particularly in the international arena. The other topics were considered in less detail and comments focus on the Panel's expression of intent to monitor these areas and to look at them in the future.

The second report updated the concerns of the first, and selected four further topics which it considered should have higher priority in government policy. In particular it commended progress on: the establishment of targets and sustainable development indicators; economic instruments; and environmental education. It did, however, feel that more could be done on: establishing targets for agriculture and transport, reiterating the recent evidence of the HOLSCSD report [*1995*]; creating a favourable tax environment for energy saving and conservation devices; international action on the depletion of fish stocks; and more ambitious targets for climate change after the year 2000. In terms of new topics it highlighted the need for: the development of more comprehensive systems of national accounts which consider social and environmental change; discussions and action on genetically engineered organisms; a national forest strategy; and a new research strategy for the disposal of radioactive waste. In general it continued to put pressure on the government for action, building on the recommendations of other agencies, whilst recognising that some progress is being made.

The government's formal response to both these reports [*HM*

Government 1995c; 1996b] was both cautious and non-committal, reiterating the government's major achievements, mostly already laid out in the White Paper process. It has promised nothing new as a result of the Panel's reports, but welcomes the Panel's role in stimulating debate and defining priorities for the government. The Panel is gaining respect for its consistent critical but constructive approach to the government's policies on sustainable development, it appears now to be carving its own niche, and adding its voice to the chorus of other actors in this policy arena evaluating government policy. The real influence of this Panel is, however, difficult to judge. Its success in winning political support and action depends on the personal influence of its members, something which is practically impossible to gauge.

The UK Round Table on Sustainable Development

The Round Table meets around four times a year and had its inaugural meeting on 23 January 1995. Its role is described as that of 'driving forward environmentally sustainable development' [*DoE, 1995b*], and its objectives are:

- to develop new areas of consensus on difficult issues of sustainable development and where this is not possible, to clarify and reduce difference;

- to inform and involve others, building wider support for emerging consensus;

- to help identify the agenda and priorities for sustainable development;

- to provide advice and recommendations on actions to achieve sustainable development; and,

- to help evaluate progress towards objectives [*DoE, 1995b*].

Along with the environmental NGOs, members were specifically invited by the DoE from academia, the Church of England, Trade Unions, business, local government associations, the medical and farming professions, and consumers. The Secretary of State for the Environment is the government's representative and co-chairman.[4]

So far the Round Table has focused on transport, energy efficiency, and mechanisms to secure environmental improvements, concentrating on the obstacles to sustainability. It published three interim reports, the work of its sub-groups, in January of 1996 [*UK Round Table on Sustainable Development, 1996a; 1996b; 1996c*]. These have now been incorporated, with general observations into its first annual report [*1996d*]. The two reports on freight transport and environmental auditing were fairly uncontroversial, but, the other working group's recommendations and actions have attracted greater political attention.

In 1995 the working group on energy proposed that an amendment to the Gas Bill should be made placing a duty on OFGAS, the economic regulator of the privatised gas supply industry, 'to have in mind the objectives of sustainable development' [*ENDS, 1995b*]. Its view on receiving evidence from representatives of the energy industries was that the liberalisation of the energy market in 1998 will not encourage suppliers to promote energy efficiency, and unaided the market will not be able to meet the economic, environmental, and social objectives of a sustainable energy policy [*1996b*]. Despite initial support from the Secretary of State for the Environment, the government rejected the need for such an amendment, with the Department of Trade and Industry claiming that sustainable development has been taken into account in the structuring of the regulatory regime [*ENDS, 1995c*]. The Round Table had placed itself squarely in the middle of a conflict between the DoE and the Department of Trade and Industry/OFGAS that had been brewing over the funding of the Energy Savings Trust.[5] The Round Table has since withdrawn in order to fight another day [*Hill, 1996*].

This early foray into the government's macro-economic and industrial policy could be perceived as loss of face for the Round Table, and indeed there have been criticisms of its failure to influence the government's policies so far [*ENDS, 1996b*]. For example, the report *Defining a sustainable transport sector* [*UK Round Table on Sustainable Development, 1996e*], the work of one of its sub-groups, was published with very bad timing just after the government had produced its Green Paper *Transport – The Way Forward* [*HM Government, 1996c*] therefore its impact was substantially diminished, as illustrated by a governmental response that did no more than reiterate the Green Paper. In addition, at the launch of its first annual report it came under substantial pressure to show evidence of its influence but was unable to point to anything specific; a lack of inter-departmental communication and co-operation are the major obstacles facing it in this regard [*ENDS, 1996b*]. Subsequent to the OFGAS conflict, it has become apparent that to avoid failure and to harness the potential of this institutional device for achieving consensus, or at the least commonly agreed positions on many issues as basis for policy, there has to be greater support for it and its objectives amongst Ministers.

The significance of the Round Table as a mechanism for change in government policy, and its facility as a forum for debate and consultation, remains to be seen. It is, however, more transparent than the Panel, with more concrete objectives and therefore easier to monitor. So far it is making its presence felt on a wide range of issues and has made a start on networking with other initiatives, interest groups and government departments. The Round Table by its actions has proved that it does not want to be only a 'talking shop' and indeed it will address the issue of its role and experience so far in its second annual report in 1997. Although, it was only set up for two years it is not expected to be disbanded and so this report will be an opportunity to make it more effective in the future. ENDS [*1996b*] reports that likely change will occur in the following areas: *size*, as the Round Table feels that it is too large to debate issues usefully; *remit*, which is currently too like those of other government bodies; *output*, which is likely to be reduced now that it is established to create space for the consideration of more complex issues; *reporting*, moving away from reports by consensus to communicating the nature of debates within the Round Table; and lastly, how it can assess its *effectiveness* on areas of policy.

The Citizens' Initiative

This has now been renamed 'Going for Green' (GFG), and was formally launched in February 1995, with all party support. It is intended to be a citizen driven, civic minded campaign [*DoE, 1995c*], local and small-scale: 'Going for Green aims to identify and explain what sustainable development is and what we as individuals can do about it' [*1995c: 1*]. At present it appears there is little governmental support outside of the DoE, or cohesion of effort with other initiatives. Although, it is commendable that in these financially difficult times some money has been allocated to this initiative, in comparison to its objectives this is meagre. The 1996 budget was £2.2 million, the DoE will continue to fund GFG at the level of £1.5 million until 1999/2000 [*HC Debates, 1996b*]. In 1996 it became a limited company and attained charitable status in order for it to secure private sector funds, improving its chances of survival, as long as it is successful in raising the necessary funds. So far it has worked on several fronts, such as: developing a public relations campaign; a 14-point code for individuals to encourage sustainable behaviour patterns; a sustainable communities project looking at the implementation of this code; and an eco-schools project. These are all rather small scale initiatives and represent no real advances in terms of local or individual sustainability compared to its larger objectives, or the work of some NGOs and local authorities under the LA21 banner. In general, GFG can be seen as a victim of low level of political support within higher levels of government for sustainability initiatives.

A Successful Strategy?

So far there appears to be little connection between these initiatives, although the Panel and the Round Table have supported the recommendations of other government appointed bodies, such as the Royal Commission on Environmental Pollution, keeping them on the political agenda. The lack of support at the level of the Prime Minister and continuing departmental wariness means that there is little evidence so far that these innovations will facilitate institutional change in the machinery of government or in wider society. More generally, the Strategy represents another missed opportunity as it has not attempted to tackle the 'bigger' issues, such as the integration of environmental considerations into economic and social policies. The trajectory of departmental policies remains largely intact; and there is no attempt to define a strategy as there are no long-term specific goals in any area of policy. Again the process of producing the document appears its main accomplishment, indicating some commitment to sustainable development, even if only in the international arena.

In March 1995 the government quietly produced its first combined review of the White Paper and the Sustainable Development Strategy [1995a]. Uniquely this set out a number of agreed and quantifiable targets for the global atmosphere, air and water quality, landfill and biodiversity. March 1996 saw the even quieter release of the second combined review [HM Government, 1996a]. Both these reviews, as the preceding White Paper reviews were, are short on new ideas, re-stating commitments made elsewhere, particularly under the 1995 Environment Act, fudging targets set in previous reviews and policy statements, and failing to plug the holes left by the Sustainable Development Strategy. The only new announcement of the 1996 report is the proposed use of economic instruments to aid water conservation, although no details are included, and equal billing is given to voluntary agreements as a tool for achieving sustainability for the first time. This is really just a continuation of the White Paper exercise in that: 'it does not drive policy, it reiterates and probably consolidates, so that all those who are supposed to deliver are aware of what they need to do' [Hill, 1996]. As such it is a step in the right direction, or perhaps a leap in comparison to other countries, but it requires greater commitment outside the DoE for the institutional and policy innovations, and the failures of the White Paper to be built on, and for the mechanisms put in place to go beyond consolidation to progression in the implementation of sustainable development.

In June 1995 the HOLSCSD evaluated the findings of its year long investigation into the government's sustainable development strategy. It called for environmental considerations to be given a higher priority in government thinking in all policy areas, and requested a 'clear and prompt re-statement of the functions and purpose of the government's own internal integration mechanisms' [HOLSCSD, 1995: 75]. Its main criticism of the government's strategy was a lack of targets, and varying performances between departments, with the DoE making encouraging attempts in this direction, whilst in contrast the Ministry of Agriculture, Fisheries and Food and the DTp have not. The HOLSCSD also advocated that the Treasury should take a more active role in environmental policy-making and greening the tax system. In March 1995 the Chancellor of the Exchequer had stated that responsibility for the Strategy lies with the Secretary of State for the Environment, and initially the Treasury declined to give evidence to the Committee on these grounds. Its eventual written submission revealed unsurprisingly that there has been no shift in the burden of taxation thus far from labour, income and profit towards consumption [*ENDS, 1995d*].

Beyond these concerns, the Committee felt that there is a leadership role for the government in the dissemination of the message of sustainable development. This can be accomplished in partnership with other agencies and initiatives, such as LA21, but 'the speed with which sustainable development is approached depends to a significant degree on the framework ... set' by the government [*HOLSCSD, 1995: 7, 13*] and evidence so far indicates this is likely to be slow. The government's response to the report [*HM Government, 1995b*] is disappointingly defensive, glossing over or dismissing many of the HOLSCSD's key recommendations. Apart from rejecting all the criticisms of its climate change strategy, the government: side-stepped further greening of the tax system; refuted the case for hypothecation; claimed that the Treasury were already involved at the early stage of all policy development; denied that greater transparency in Parliamentary surveillance was required; and only acknowledged the need for further environmental targets in a limited way [*ENDS, 1995c*].

Indicators of Progress in the Implementation of Sustainable Development

Economic Instruments

In 1992, as indicated previously, the second review of the 1990 White Paper stated a 'new presumption in favour of economic instruments rather than regulation' and unveiled a number of initiatives that 'marked a significant advance towards more market based solutions' [*HM Government, 1992: 5*]. This was the first positive move since the 1990 White Paper announced that there were definite benefits for the protection of the environment in shifting from regulation to economic instruments in terms of flexibility and cost-effectiveness. New instruments were now proposed in the areas of:

- *Water:* consultation on charging for effluent discharges, water abstraction, and a paper on charging for water to discourage water wastage.

- *Waste:* a waste management white paper to promote the use of economic instruments to encourage recycling, and levies to increase the relative costs of landfill.

* *Air:* consultation following a report on the viability of tradable emissions permits for Sulphur Dioxide.

* *Transport:* an exploration of the case for urban congestion and road pricing.

However, it is significant that a number of areas previously identified in the 1990 White Paper were ignored, for example, the introduction of incentives for the recycling of CFCs, waste oil, batteries and tyres. The 1994 Strategy also announced a series of new initiatives on demand management regarding energy, water, minerals and transport. Despite all these statements of intent only a few instruments have been developed, the key developments so far are: incentives under various schemes to farmers to protect the countryside; recycling credits; Value-Added-Tax (VAT) on domestic fuel and power rising from zero rating to eight per cent;[6] road fuel duty set at a minimum of five per cent increase per year in real terms; the differential for unleaded petrol is now 67 per cent of leaded petrol during the last four years; the duty advantage for diesel was removed in the 1994 Budget, and increased by 1p per litre in 1995; and cost recovery charges for administrating pollution control are now standard practice.

Unfortunately, in the case of at least two of these measures there has been little affect on behaviour because of a downward pressures on energy prices. The imposition of VAT on domestic fuel has been largely swallowed up: over the period 1984–94, real prices have fallen by 20 per cent [*DoE and Government Statistical Service, 1996*], particularly since privatisation. They look set to continue to fall if OFGAS puts in place price limits that will ensure that the average household bill falls by £60 per year by 2000 [*Guardian, 1996a: 4*]. In addition, road fuel duty has increased petrol prices by 2.5p per litre, but has been offset by a 2p per litre fall in pump prices resulting from low crude oil prices and fierce competition between petrol retailers. This has meant that there is little incentive to invest in measures to improve domestic and industrial energy efficiency. There have also proven to be practical problems with tradable permits for sulphur emissions, and congestion pricing [*ENDS, 1996a; 1995e*].

Evidence given by the Treasury to HOLSCSD indicates that it is proving difficult to devise economic instruments which are 'robust and actually do what we want them to do rather than something else' [*ENDS, 1995d*]. Therefore, the bulk of measures to support sustainable development continue to be regulatory in nature. This is also partially because, as the Treasury has indicated, it sees its role as responding to DoE proposals for instruments rather than taking an active part in their development [*ENDS, 1995d*]. In addition, the Treasury remains ideologically opposed to the hypothecation of tax revenues for environmental or social equity purposes, although there is evidence that they are being forced to accept some element of this in energy initiatives and the landfill tax.

In the 1994 budget the Chancellor announced a potentially important innovation, a new tax on waste disposal to landfill. This was introduced in October 1996 at £7 per tonne of waste, and a lower band of £2 per tonne for 'inert' waste. The landfill tax is significant as it is the first move away from taxation on labour towards pollution and environmental disbenefits, and it is geared to a defined social purpose. It proposes that the revenue produced is used to offset labour costs via reductions in national insurance contributions (proposed at 0.2 per cent), so that it is a zero effect tax. The environmental rationale will be fulfilled through the creation of Environmental Trusts, to be funded by voluntary payments from landfill site operators who would receive a 90 per cent tax rebate. This allows the revenue to be directed in part to a specific environmental purpose without the Treasury having to agree to hypothecation [*HM Treasury, 1995*]. These Trusts would be in the private sector, but non-profit making, able to invest in activities approved by the government, such as land restoration, and good practice in sustainable waste management. It is estimated that they will generate up to £100 million of private sector expenditure for environmental improvement [*Green Alliance, 1995b*].

None the less, it appears that the tax will, as it presently stands not be fiscally neutral for many firms and local authorities. Therefore the DoE is under a lot of pressure to make exemptions and widen the definition of wastes that fall into the lower band, which it has recently done so [*ENDS, 1995e; 1996d*]. There also is some doubt as to the ability of the tax to raise significant revenue, an estimated £450 million in its first full year of 1997-8, but the national insurance offset will cost £500 million, and recent exemptions, or rate reductions, are likely to reduce revenues by well over 10 per cent [*ENDS, 1996d*]. The landfill tax has no specific environmental target, such as the reduction of domestic waste, indicating that the environmental rationale is not strong [*Powell and Craighill, 1996*].

To be supported by the Treasury, a tax needs first and foremost to be financially robust, and have an environmental rationale. The landfill tax has both but is a rare success story. The politics of a proposed economic instrument also need to be right, without a political window even the most technically and environmentally proficient tax is unlikely to become policy. The recent political failure of the proposed increase in VAT on domestic fuel burned the DoE's fingers and reduced confidence in the likelihood of similar fiscal measures being approved in the near future [*Hill, 1996*]. But there are also concerns over the future scope of such instruments, as industry has already responded well in the main to regulation and the idea of voluntary agreements. Also, the costs of implementing such instruments are high as there are many practical and political obstacles to be overcome, not least of which are the distributional implications. A further problem is presented because many EU Directives do not give the UK a choice of instruments. And finally, and most importantly, there needs to be support across Whitehall. However, this approach is still the preferred one of the government for meeting environmental objectives (although voluntary agreements have recently been flagged as very significant tools [*HM Government, 1996a*]) and there are a number of areas where future developments are possible: pricing water to limit abstraction in water shortage areas; pricing aggregates to raise the cost of new aggregates and to encourage the recycling and reuse of existing aggregates; commitments to international conventions mean that tax or permit approaches to limiting Sulphur Dioxide, Nitrous Oxides, and Volatile Organic Compounds may still be on the agenda; and, measures to limit total emissions on use of specific polluting substances.

Green Accounting and Sustainability Indicators

Green accounting is still external to political decision-making, and has a long way to go before it will have utility in informing these processes. There are a number constraints to the development of robust indicators, primarily: a lack of agreement upon methodology; a lack of transparency in government and expert decision-making processes; and a large number of conflicting interests. Indicators can also be problematic for governments because they can highlight poor performance, and so can have a powerful effect on political agendas. Indicators are not a purely technical issue, and the emphasis on them in recent years as the answer to discovering what sustainable development can mean for a country or locality has meant they have become increasingly political.

In the Sustainable Development Strategy the government indicated that it would be producing a preliminary set of sustainable development indicators by the end of 1995. This it did on 12 March 1996. John Gummer claimed they were a significant part of making sustainable development 'the touchstone of the UK's policies' [*Independent, 1996*]. A hundred and twenty indicators in 21 areas are set out in the report, about a third show progress away from sustainable development, whilst for many no interpretation of good or bad is attempted [*DoE and Government Statistical Service, 1996*].[7] Significantly only 12 have targets attached, something that is surely required if there is to be a move beyond information to action.

The production of these indicators was welcomed by environmental

NGOs. In particular, the statistics on transport[8] have already provoked considerable public debate about the environmental implications of increased mobility [*Guardian, 1996b; Financial Times, 1996*]. The government has, however, come under criticism for its choice of standard economic indicators and its failure to relate these to social and environmental objectives in the long-term: '[t]he assumption is still that growth in Gross Domestic Product increases standards of living, and a healthy economy is more 'able to afford environmental goods' [*Green Alliance, 1996a*]. Significantly, it was noted that 'standard of living' to be achieved by economic growth was used as society's key objective, along with environmental protection for the future, not a higher 'quality of life' which is a wider concept more in keeping with the broader radical agenda of sustainability [*Mullaney and Pinfield, 1996*]. The production of indicators appears to have been a very useful co-ordination exercise for Whitehall, if nothing else, and the interest generated highlights the potential for such an annual exercise to stimulate debate and possibly policy change.

The government announced during the same week its intention to incorporate the costs associated with damage to the environment by pollution into official economic data for the first time. August 1996 saw the publication by the Office for National Statistics of the first in an annual series of official environmental accounts. Although they only look at the three themes of air emissions by sector, environmental spending by industry, and the depletion of oil and gas reserves, there are plans to expand them into other areas in the coming years. The accounts draw in the main on existing official sources of environmental and economic data, but are innovative in some areas in the way this data is pulled together. Cautious support has been expressed [*ENDS, 1996e*] for the potential of the accounts to inform policy-making and so promote greater sustainability in the economy, by indicating the sectors who are the worst polluters and how certain measures could affect their ecological 'footprint' and contribution to economic wealth. Nevertheless, there has been criticism over the failure to attribute financial costs to environmental damage [*MacGillivray, 1996*] the benefit of which is itself controversial [*ENDS, 1996f*].

The Environment Agency

Another piece in the institutional structure of environmental policy in the UK has been created in the form of an integrated environmental agency, which came into being in April 1996. Its birth was long and protracted: five years after it was first announced, and nine years after the idea was first proposed. It is part of a move away from the established system of environmental protection in the UK, characterised as it was by fragmentation, decentralisation, pragmatism, administration, discretion and voluntarism [*Carter and Lowe, 1994*]. The Environmental Agency, as a DoE non-departmental public body, combines the regulatory functions and duties of: local waste regulation authorities set up in 1990; the National Rivers Authority, established to regulate the water environment in 1989; and Her Majesty's Inspectorate of Pollution, established in 1987 to regulate emissions of the more dangerous categories of pollutants to all mediums. As such it is one of the largest such organisations in the world. It was created to follow through with the logic of Integrated Pollution Control established in the 1990 Environment Protection Act. According to the Secretary of State for the Environment the Agency 'represent[s] an important step in the government's policies of sustainable development' and 'combine[s] economic development with the protection and conservation of the environment' [*Environmental Digest, 1994*]. This represents a substantial reorganisation of the environmental regulatory framework in the UK, and a shake-up for regulators not long established, and partly for these reasons it has come under a lot of criticism.

Initially there was no framing sustainable development duty placed on the Agency. Although now it does have a principal aim of protecting and enhancing the environment, there are still fears that this is too weak. There is no stipulation for the Agency to have regard for sustainable development in decision-making, but Ministers are required to give guidance on this issue [*DoE, 1995d*]. In this way the concept can be part of the Agency's remit covering the use of economic instruments, improved social valuation techniques for safeguarding natural areas, and for a higher level of citizen involvement in different decisions. However, beyond the semantics the focus is now on the corporate plans of the Agency, how it plans to develop its role, and how sustainable development will incorporated through guidance into that [*Burton, 1995; Hill, 1996*].

Business and the Environment

Business can never be fully self-sufficient in environmental and social terms, and still remain competitive and profitable. But degrees of reduction in the size and growth of their ecological 'footprint' are being sought by UK business. For the most part this action is spurred by increasingly tough European regulations driven by articulate and inquisitive consumer and environmental groups. However, there is evidence that a new breed of environmentally literate managers, huge technical and accounting opportunities to reduce wastage, and a strong ethical envelope in which concern for possible impacts on indigenous peoples and high profile ecosystems, mean that attention is now being paid to where goods are supplied from and what happens to products in use and disposal.

A study by an environmental consultancy Entec, in association with the

Green Alliance, an environmental lobby, found [*Green Alliance, 1996b*]:

- 70 per cent of leading UK firms take environmental issues more seriously than a year ago;

- 76 per cent of companies have, or plan to have, formal environmental management systems, such as the EC's Eco-Auditing and Management System (EMAS);

- 58 per cent of companies are pro-active in the sense that they are taking initiatives beyond compliance;

- there is a general willingness to accept tougher regulations and tax regimes to make all competitors face similar performance requirements.

Nevertheless, the vast majority of business leaders hold back from environmental investment because of costs, lack of awareness of long-term benefits and a general absence of knowledge and information. Significantly, there has been a poor response to environmental management schemes, particularly among smaller businesses [*ENDS, 1996g*]. Among business generally uptake of EMAS remains behind that of other Member States, the UK has only 20 of the 400 registered sites [*ENDS, 1996h*]. One cause, confusion over the various standards in the UK, it is hoped has now been clarified with the replacement of British standard BS7750 with international standard series ISO14000. Rates of certification are now expected to grow, particularly as evidence is emerging from certified companies that there are cost effectiveness benefits [*ENDS, 1996h*].

Although, there is movement in environmental performance through such innovations, it is primarily confined to major companies with good-housekeeping procedures, conscious of their public image. Unless the perceived penalties of a loss of competitiveness are overcome by more common regulations, and unless there is a much higher profile policy promoting good business practice, this element of the sustainability transition will always lag. A positive note has however been sounded by Greenpeace's first conference for business in September 1996, where examples of effective partnership between businesses and other stakeholders, allowing them to take advantage of the growing market for solutions to environmental problems, were heralded as the way forward [*ENDS, 1996i*].

LA21

Local government in the UK has no power of general competence (it is a creature of national government statute) and can only act under specific direction from Parliament [*Elcock, 1994*]. However, with slow progress so far at national level it is local government which is proving to be the most active and innovative in implementing sustainable development in the UK, through the creation of LA21s. As such it is important to sketch this local response and how the national agenda is the context for it in many ways. Local government in the UK has a long tradition in the field of environmental protection and the idea of sustainability has been relatively eagerly taken up so far. This is partly as a response to emerging global environmental issues, but also as a result of several domestic factors, such as: the unexpected success of the Green Party in the 1989 European Elections; lobbying by NGOs; and the desire of local authorities to re-assert and develop their role in an area when many responsibilities have been removed from local government control [*Christie, 1994; Cope and Atkinson, 1994*].

Over the last two decades, central government has placed a straightjacket of constraints on the powers, resources and abilities of local government. Power has been eroded from local government, centralised and fragmented. There has been a process of deregulation and contracting out of many local authority functions, and the rise in the number of unelected (and therefore politically unaccountable) bodies taking over the responsibility for these functions. This has resulted in a reduction in local government's autonomy and status. Simultaneously, management and administrative structures are more flexible and open to change. As a result there is considerable policy space for local government to undertake LA21, particularly the public participation aspects of it, in order to legitimise their democratic role [*Ward, 1993*].

The 1994 Strategy placed LA21 within the remit of local authorities officially, but committed no extra resources to local authorities to undertake this role. So far national policy on local sustainability has been piecemeal and, crucially, new powers, duties and requirements have not been accompanied by funding, undermining the ability of local government to carry them out. However, the 1996 review of the Strategy has an interesting presentational innovation, examples of good practice at the local level, indicating a significantly higher profile for LA21 in the UK in the light of its relatively high international profile.

Responsibility for co-ordinating the LA21 initiative lies with the Local Government Management Board (LGMB), under guidance from a steering group consisting of various stakeholders and interest groups, set up by the local government associations. The LGMB has produced an explicit, non-prescriptive framework for local authorities which sets out: important aspects of the policy-making process; policy principles; and implementation tools [*LGMB, 1993a; 1993b; Hams et al., 1994*]. The LGMB has also been active in lobbying the government for funding, to the tune of £57,554 for

1995–96, to support these activities [*HC Debates, 1996c*]. Its key challenge, however, is to establish some minimal baseline of competence, whilst allowing each local authority to establish its individual programme. The goal to date has been some form of action plan by the end of 1996 to feed into a report by the local authority associations to the CSD in June 1997.

Whilst some local authorities have pioneered LA21's development and continue to do so, others have done nothing except perform their traditional environmental protection role as required by central government. A survey of local authorities responses to LA21, commissioned by the LGMB in 1996 [*Tuxworth and Carpenter, 1996*] indicated that 91 per cent of respondent authorities[9] are committed to participating in a LA21 process, with 40 per cent committed to producing a strategy document by the end of 1996. This survey also shows that although many authorities were tackling LA21 within existing institutional arrangements and progress is slow, there is considerable evidence of new administrative mechanisms, policy integration, public participation mechanisms, partnerships with other stakeholders, the development of environmental management systems, state of the environment reporting, environmental audit, and sustainability indicators [*Tuxworth and Carpenter, 1996*].

The institutional structure of local authorities appears to be a significant factor in willingness to undertake these new initiatives, with deeper institutional change by professionals and in administrative procedures still to occur. It is all very well to add on environment forums of interested groups and citizens and policy integration committees to the machinery of local government, but a harder task is changing what already exists and the institutional cultures that support it. Research into the responses of local authorities to LA21 has shown that there are a number of factors that when present at local level are important in respect to LA21's successful take-up, and these can overcome both local and national barriers:

- *networking channels* for the dissemination of knowledge and best practice;

- *policy entrepreneurs or enthusiastic local political parties*; and,

- *partnerships* with NGOs and local business to attract resources, disseminate information, and develop shared strategies for LA21.

We can see from this section that there is evidence of institutional adaptation at the local level, but that the potential for greater progress on this front is influenced by other policy areas and the national context within which local government operates in the UK.

Conclusion

Despite the fact that the UK is prompt in discharging its documentary commitments with regard to A21, being one of only 13 countries that had submitted a national report for 1996 to the CSD by the end of January 1996, the real signs of progress or its lack can only be seen with regard to institutional change. There are institutional mechanisms and tools that are developing in many areas, but these are only the beginnings of the necessary institutional adjustment towards sustainable development. This at present appears to be falling into the pattern of material change, but producing little in the way of shifting policies and administrative cultures which are required to produce real results in the long-term. In this paper we have suggested that this is because of a number of reasons. First, there is *no clear consensus on the definition of sustainable development.* The evolution from a notion of reliable and durable economic growth, through stewardship towards civic empowerment is only barely discernible, and there is certainly little political debate driving it, and no intellectual leadership or vision of sustainable development from any of the three major political parties. Secondly, the *administrative and regulatory cultures are operating conservatively and incrementally,* departmental territorial attitudes and inertia continue to place the administrative focus for sustainable development in the DoE. Thirdly, *meddling with the tax regime, no matter how alluring, is practically difficult and politically contentious.* Fourthly, *the pattern of responses is currently very haphazard.* Taken collectively, these could produce a coherent effort to considerable effect. Greater high level political support and leadership could foster this coherence, but the environment continues to remain low on the political agenda in comparison to employment, taxation and welfare so there is little incentive towards a greater co-ordination of effort. Finally, *the role of the citizen is seen as a rhetorical focus, but a practical nightmare.* To involve citizens effectively requires changes in the patterns of power, representation, and a transparency of operations that the political parties are not willing to condone at present.

    At this point one can only look for signs of policy and process inter-linkage that could herald a more robust shift towards sustainable development. In the UK context, the following developments are worthy of note: *cross party interest* in the topic, at least at the level of a manifesto chapter; *general interest in sustainability indicators, green audits, budgetary and policy assessments*; *the landfill tax and environmental trusts* could be possible precursors to charitable public/private partnerships across a range of policy areas; *increasing interest in the notion of environmental citizenship* through entitlement and education at all levels; and the *relative success of LA21*, as an organising concept that is driving action, more so in the UK than elsewhere in Europe, as a possible primary focus for a more socially just and empowering political culture, and the beginnings of civic activism around such issues.

Sustainable development becomes more daunting and a greater force for change as we move away from the economists' definition to the wider social and political aspects of the concept. Its survival as an ever-challenging organising force relies on support from all levels of society, and this can be engendered by evidence that there are threats and that progress can be made in countering them which will benefit society in the long term and overall. There is sufficient evidence of institutional innovation occurring in the UK to be confident that there is a cautious shift towards addressing sustainable development beyond the rhetoric. Building on this capacity so that previously neglected policy areas and interests are included in a coherent transition is the current and continuing challenge.

NOTES

1. This study deals specifically with the UK's response to A21, not the national response to other environmental initiatives, even if they have a sustainability element, such as the United Nations Framework Convention on Climate Change, the UN Convention on Biodiversity, or the host of EU environmental directives. Although, we believe progress on these areas to be important and indeed movement politically and substantially is observable [e.g., *O'Riordan and Jäger, 1996*], we are interested only in those institutional adjustments that provide the context for, or are a direct result of, A21.
2. The *Blueprint* series published via Earthscan provide an accessible summary of this debate [e.g., *Pearce, Barbier and Markandya, 1989*].
3. Local Agenda 21 is the name for initiatives that are being undertaken under chapter 40 of A21 [*UNCED, 1992*], of which the main requirement is that local authorities should consult with their communities and other stakeholders to reach a consensus on the implementation of sustainable development (by 1996).
4. A rather larger role than most of the respondents to the consultation process had wanted.
5. The government created the Energy Savings Trust (EST) in 1992 as one of the main tools for promoting and encouraging energy efficiency to meet its Rio targets [*EST, 1995*]. The EST is, however, chronically underfunded. The current regulator of the Gas Industry, Clare Spottiswoode, has refused to authorise the required levy on consumers to pay for energy savings projects run by the EST, on the grounds that ensuring competition, not energy efficiency is her prime duty, in this she is supported by the Department of Trade and Industry. It is estimated that in order to meet the EST's target of a reduction of 2.5 million tonnes of carbon dioxide by the year 2000 an investment of £1.5 billion is needed [*Owen, 1995*]. The regulator of the electricity industry has authorised funding levels of £100 million for the period 1994–98, but funding from British Gas remains in dispute. In May 1995 the Government agreed to fund the EST to the tune of £25 million a year until 1998. However, this figure was reduced to £15 million for 1997, and £10 million for 1998 in the November 1995 budget statement [*ENDS, 1995f*].
6. The March Budget of 1993 announced the government's intention to put VAT (Value Added Tax), at an initial rate of eight per cent, on domestic fuel prices, rising to 17.5 per cent in the following year. However, when the government came to increase VAT in a second stage move from eight per cent to the full 17.5 per cent, it failed. Initially introduced as an environmental measure, this rationale was not sustained and the compensation package for

the 'nearly' poor was not in place. It was politically attacked on all sides and rejected by Parliament.

7. The results of deliberations by an inter-departmental working group, published by the DoE and the government Office of National Statistics, indicating a notable co-ordination effort on the part of the government and Whitehall.

8. These showed that since 1970 travel by car had almost doubled, becoming the dominant form of transport even on short trips, and that fuel use for road transport had risen by nearly 90 per cent, to account for a quarter of all energy consumption now [*DoE and Office of National Statistics, 1996*].

9. The response rate was 56 per cent (identical to that of the previous survey in 1994–95) although local government reorganisation makes it difficult to determine this figure exactly as responses came in both sides of the reorganisation, reducing the number of authorities.

REFERENCES

British Government Panel on Sustainable Development (1995), *First Report*, London: HMSO.
British Government Panel on Sustainable Development (1996), *Second Report*, London: HMSO.
Burton, T. (1995), 'The Environment Act 1995: blessing or bane?', *ECOS*, Vol.16, Nos3/4, p.6.
Carter, N. and P. Lowe (1994), 'Environmental Politics and Administrative Reform', *Political Quarterly*, pp. 263–74.
Christie, I. (1994), 'Britain's Sustainable Development Strategy: Environmental Quality and Policy Change', *Policy Studies*, Vol.15, No.3, pp.4–20.
Cope, S. and R. Atkinson (1994), 'The Structures in Governance in Britain', in S.P. Savage, R. Atkinson and L. Robins (1994), *Public Policy in Britain*, London: Macmillan.
DoE (1989), *Sustaining Our Common Future*, London: HMSO.
DoE (1991), *Policy Appraisal and the Environment: A Guide for Government Departments*, London: HMSO.
DoE (1994), *Environmental Appraisal in Government Departments*, London: HMSO.
DoE (1995a), *A Guide to Risk Assessment and Risk Management for Environmental Protection*, London: HMSO.
DoE (1995b), *News Release: UK Round Table on Sustainable Development*, 19 Dec. 1995.
DoE (1995c), *News Release: Going For Green*, 6 Feb. 1995.
DoE (1995d), *News Release*, No.618, 11 Dec. 1995.
DoE and Government Statistical Service (1996), *Indicators of Sustainable Development for the United Kingdom*, London: HMSO.
DTp (1995), *The Transport Report 1995: The Government's Expenditure Plans 1995–96 to 1997–98*, London: HMSO.
Elcock, H. (1994), *Local Government: Policy and Management in Local Authorities*, Third Edition, London: Routledge.
EST (1995), 'Memorandum to HOLSCSD', *Report from the Select Committee on Sustainable Development*, Vol.II, HL Paper 72, Session 1994–95, London: HMSO, pp.68–73.
ENDS (Environmental Data Services Ltd.) (1995a), 'Government Falls Behind in Energy Efficiency Drive', *ENDS Report* 244, p.32.
ENDS (1995b), 'Sticky start for Round Table with rebuff on energy policy', *ENDS Report* 245, p.3.
ENDS (1995c), 'Business Almost as Usual on Sustainable Development', *ENDS Report* 249, pp.28–9.
ENDS (1995d), 'Treasury Put to Test Over Sustainable Development', *ENDS Report* 242, pp.29–30.
ENDS (1995e), 'DTP Backs M-way Tolls, Stalls on Urban Road Pricing', *ENDS Report* 247, pp.13–14.
ENDS (1995f), 'Energy Efficiency, Air Quality Lose Out in "Green" Budget', *ENDS Report* 250, pp.4–6.
ENDS (1996a), 'Ministers Obfuscate Over Progress in "Greening" Whitehall', *ENDS Report* 253, pp.29–30.

ENDS (1996b), 'Government Gives Nothing to Round Table on Transport', *ENDS Report* 260, pp.35–6.

ENDS (1996c), 'Round Table Responds to Ineffectiveness Charges', *ENDS Report* 255, pp.9–10.

ENDS (1996d), 'Arguments Over the Landfill Tax Get Down to the Nitty-Gritty', *ENDS Report* 252, pp.20–23.

ENDS (1996e), 'Green Accounts Point to Integration of Economic and Environmental Policy', *ENDS Report* 259, pp.16–19.

ENDS (1996f), 'The First Shade of Green in the National Accounts', *ENDS Report* 259, p.2.

ENDS (1996g), 'DoE Widens Small Firm Grants for EMAS Registration', *ENDS Report* 260, p.33.

ENDS (1996h), 'ISO14001 Aarrive – but EMAS Uptake Stays at Low Level', *ENDS Report* 261, p.7.

ENDS (1996i), 'Strategic Alliances for Environmental Solutions – The Greenpeace Recipe for Business Success', *ENDS Report* 260, pp.19–20.

Environmental Digest (1994), 'UK Environment Agency Proposal', *Environment Digest*, No.88, October.

Financial Times (1996), 'Car Emerges as Villain in "Green" Survey', *The Financial Times*, 13 March 1996.

Green Alliance (1991), *Greening Government: The Failure of the Departmental Annual Reports to Reflect Integrated Policy Making*, London: Green Alliance.

Green Alliance (1992), *Greening Government 2: Update to the 1991 Report*, London: Green Alliance.

Green Alliance (1993), *The Parliamentary Newsletter*, w/e 4 June 1993, p.1.

Green Alliance (1995a), 'Memorandum to HOLSCSD', *Report from the Select Committee on Sustainable Development*, Vol.II, HL Paper 72, Session 1994–95, London: HMSO, pp.539–41.

Green Alliance (1995b), *Guidance to the Environmental Agency under the Environment Bill on its Objectives, Comments by the Green Alliance*, London: Green Alliance.

Green Alliance (1996a), *The Green Alliance Report*, 96/1 March, London: Green Alliance.

Green Alliance (1996b), *The Parliamentary Newsletter*, w/e 24 May 1996, p.1.

Guardian (1996a), *The Guardian*, 7 June 1996, p.4.

Guardian (1996b), 'Car-Bound Britain is Wasting Its Fuel', *The Guardian*, 13 March 1996, p.6.

Hams, T., Jacobs, M., Levett, R., Lusser, H. and D. Taylor (1994), *Greening Your Local Authority*, Harlow: Longman.

HC Debates (1996a), Vol.271, col.626–627, 16 Feb.

HC Debates (1996b), Vol.275, col.497, 26 April.

HC Debates (1996c), Vol.273, col.104–105, 5 March.

HM Government (1990), *This Common Inheritance*, Cmnd 1200, London: HMSO.

HM Government (1991), *This Common Inheritance: The First Year Report*, Cmnd 1655, London: HMSO.

HM Government (1992), *This Common Inheritance: The Second Year Report*, Cmnd 2068, London: HMSO.

HM Government (1994a), *Sustainable Development, The UK Strategy*, Cmnd 2426, London: HMSO.

HM Government (1994b), *This Common Inheritance: The Third Year Report*, Cmnd 2549, London: HMSO.

HM Government (1995a), *This Common Inheritance: UK Annual Report*, Cm 2822, London: HMSO.

HM Government (1995b), *Government Response to the Lords Select Committee Report on Sustainable Development*, Cm 3018, London: HMSO.

HM Government (1995c), *Government Response to the First Annual Report of the Government's Panel on Sustainable Development*, 29 March, London: DoE.

HM Government (1996a), *This Common Inheritance: UK Annual Report*, Cm 3188, London: HMSO.

HM Government (1996b), *Government Response to the Second Annual Report of the Government's Panel on Sustainable Development*, 30 March, London: DoE.

HM Government (1996c), *Transport – The Way Forward: The Government's Response to the Transport Debate*, Cm 3234, London: HMSO.

HM Treasury (1995), 'Memorandum and Oral Evidence to HOLSCSD', *Report from the Select Committee on Sustainable Development*, Vol.II, HL Paper 72, session 1994–95, London: HMSO, pp.669–83.

HOLSCSD (1995), *Report from the Select Committee on Sustainable Development*, Vols.I and II, HL Paper 72, session 1994–95, London: HMSO.

Hill, Julie (1996), personal communication, March 1996.

Hill, Julie and Andrew Jordan (1993), 'The Greening of Government: Lessons from the White Paper Process', *ECOS*, Vol.14, Nos.3/4, pp.3–9.

Independent (1996), 'Gummer Admits to "Green" Failure', *The Independent*, 13 March 1996.

LGMB (1993a), 'UK Local Government Declaration on Sustainable Development', in LGMB, *A Framework for Local Sustainability*, Luton: LGMB.

LGMB (1993b), *A Framework for Local Sustainability*, Luton: LGMB.

MacGillvray, Alex (1996), 'A Case of Pilot Error?', *Town and Country Planning*, Vol.65, No.10, Oct., pp.258–9.

Mullaney, Andrew and Graham Pinfield (1996), 'No Indication of Quality or Equity', *Town and Country Planning*, Vol.65, No.5, May, pp.132–3.

O'Riordan, Timothy and Jill Jäger (eds.) (1996), *Politics of Climate Change: A European Perspective*, London: Routledge.

Owen, G. (1995), *Energy Policy, the Government and the Energy Regulators: A Case Study of the Energy Savings Trust*, CSERGE Working Paper GEC 95-35, Norwich: CSERGE.

Pearce, D.W., Barbier, E. and A. Markandya (1989), *Blueprint for a Green Economy*, London: Earthscan.

Powell, Jane C. and Amelia Craighill (1996), 'The UK Landfill Tax', in T. O'Riordan (ed.), *Eco-Taxation*, London: Earthscan, Ch.15, pp.304–20.

Sachs. W (ed.) (1993), *Global Ecology. A New Arena of Political Conflict*, London: Zed Books.

Tuxworth, B. and C. Carpenter (1996), *Local Agenda 21 Survey 1996*, Luton: LGMB.

UK Round Table on Sustainable Development (1996a), *The Domestic Energy Market: 1998 and Beyond*, London: DoE.

UK Round Table on Sustainable Development (1996b), *Freight Transport*, London: DoE.

UK Round Table on Sustainable Development (1996c), *Environmental Management and Audit*, London: DoE.

UK Round Table on Sustainable Development (1996d), *First Annual Report*, London: DoE.

UK Round Table on Sustainable Development (1996e), *Defining a Sustainable Transport Sector*, London: DoE.

UNCED (1992), *Agenda 21*, http://unep.unep.no/unep/partners/un/unced/agenda21.htm

Ward, S. (1993), 'Thinking Global, Acting Local? British Local Authorities and Their Environmental Plans', *Environmental Politics*, Vol.2, No.3, pp.453–78

World Commission on Environment and Development (1987), *Our Common Future*, Oxford: Oxford University Press.

Acronyms

A21	Agenda 21
CSD	United Nations Commission on Sustainable Development
DoE	Department of the Environment
DTp	Department of Transport
EDE	Ministerial Committee on the Environment
EMAS	Eco-Audit and Management System
ENDS	Environmental Data Services Ltd.

EST	Energy Savings Trust
EU	European Union
GFG	Going for Green
HM Government	Her Majesty's Government
HOLSCSD	House of Lords Select Committee on Sustainable Development
LA21	Local Agenda 21
LGMB	Local Government Management Board
NGO	Non-Governmental Organisation
OFGAS	Office of the Gas Industry's Regulator
UNCED	United Nations Conference on Environment and Development
VAT	Value-Added Tax

Norway's Institutional Response to Sustainable Development

LIV ASTRID SVERDRUP

The Norwegian process relating to sustainable development has been marked by shifting political support. In the period leading up to Rio, a broad participatory, and state-initiated process was carried out. Since the United Nations Conference on the Environment and Development, interest in a specific national process related to sustainable development has been more limited. Today, few signs of a distinct process for sustainable development can be found. However, a wide range of efforts have been made to improve Norwegian environmental policy. The established structures and procedures at both the national and local level continue to function more or less independently of fluctuations in political interest for the issue of sustainable development. Environmental considerations have to a large extent been institutionalised into the existing political system. This is for instance the case in the planning and budget routines of the various ministries and in the various initiatives taken to promote inter-ministerial co-operation on environmental policy issues. This process has been supplemented with environment-friendly changes also in the business and industry sector and among non-governmental organisations. However, many of the changes have developed independently of the international process for sustainable development. Hence, the causal relationship between the United Nations process for sustainable development and the Norwegian response cannot easily be isolated. A broader perspective than the specific national process related to sustainable development, is therefore necessary in order to fully comprehend the Norwegian case.

The first period of change following the launching of the World Commission on Environment and Development's report [*1987*] was marked by broad enthusiasm for the concept of sustainable development in Norway and led to the production of a national follow-up report, presented to Parliament as early as 1989. Today, few signs of a distinct national process

Liv Astrid Sverdrup is a Researcher in the Programme for European Energy and Environmental Studies at the Fridtjof Nansen Institute. She would like to thank Helge Ole Bergesen, Jon Birger Skjærseth, Steinar Andresen and Oluf Langhelle for their valuable comments on earlier drafts of this contribution.

for sustainable development can be found. The concept of sustainable development has turned into a slogan so frequently used that it has lost much of its sense and power. The weakening of this distinct process does not imply, however, that there have not been institutional changes towards sustainability. The development of inter-ministerial co-operation, environmental legislation, environmental targets and data gathering, and of green budgets and taxes, are some of the central institutional changes that have been made at state level. Moreover, these developments have been supplemented by a wide range of interventions at the local level, in the business and industry sector and among non-governmental organisations (NGOs). However, political interest in, and willingness to push for a more specific and ambitious sustainable development process is missing. This lack of support stems from both the top and from the bottom. In order to understand the Norwegian institutional response to sustainable development this study explores below how it has evolved around the development of both a specific national response *process* for, and central *institutions* to enhance, sustainable development. The aim is to give an overview of the central measures initiated, a complete evaluation of the actual impacts of the various measures will not be given, but some aspects of the functioning of the various measures will be highlighted. To get a broader picture of the national response process relevant *attitudes and activities* of environmental NGOs, the business community and local governments in relation to sustainable development are also identified.

The causal relationship between the United Nations (UN) process for sustainable development and the Norwegian response that we seek to describe below cannot easily be isolated and is not always clear. Of more than 150 international environmental agreements currently in existence, Norway has signed 60 [*Skjærseth and Rosendal, 1995*]. The UN process for sustainable development and the *Agenda 21* (A21) document with its 40 chapters covered a wide range of environmental policy issue areas, that partly also are covered in other international environmental policy processes. This interlinkage of environmental issue areas and regimes makes it difficult to identify what is caused by the international process for sustainable development and what is caused by other international environmental policy processes. One should therefore be aware that what may seem as measures set out to respond to United Nations Conference on Environment and Development (UNCED) may be measures initiated to respond to other international environmental regimes. Moreover, various national efforts identified as measures introduced to respond to the recommendations of the World Commission's report and A21, may also have been part of national programmes and projects that would have been implemented independently of the international processes. The development of a Norwegian environmental policy started much earlier than 1987. Other explanations may therefore be found for the initiation of various national measures. The timing of the formation and implementation of the various measures may be a simple but useful indicator to reveal the causal relationship between the international process and the national initiatives.

Interpreting the Concept

When the World Commission on Environment and Development issued its report in April 1987 several international trans-boundary environmental problems had already entered on to the Norwegian political agenda. Acid precipitation, the discovery of the hole in the ozone layer and the Chernobyl accident led, together with national events such as the algae invasion of fresh waters in the South of the country and invasion of seals in the North, to increasing public and political attention, and a change in the public mood regarding environmental problems. Also, the increased attention directed towards environmental issues at the international level and the dual role of Gro Harlem Brundtland, as Prime Minister and leader of the World Commission, increased awareness about environmental policies generally. This created a politically receptive climate for highlighting environmental policy and more specifically the concept of sustainable development.

An important dividing line in the debate over Norway's environmental policy can be drawn between those who want to integrate environmental protection into the established political and economic system, and those who wish to rank environmental considerations above all other sectors and interests. The former view dominated the making of Norwegian nature and environmental conservation policy. The concept of combining growth and environmental protection was central to several Government White Papers in the 1960s and 1970s, in the establishment of the Ministry of the Environment (MoE) in 1972, and was supported by several key NGOs. So when the idea of sustainable development and growth within environmental limits was launched in 1987 in the World Commission's report, it had already been established as an important concept for the environmental policy community in Norway.

On the basis of the World Commission's discussion of the concept and a variety of terms which had already been a part of the national debate – such as the principles of endurance or nature's carrying capacity – the translation of the term 'sustainable' as '*bærekraftig*' (something capable of being upheld) was proposed. Both the MoE and the Prime Minister's Office played an important role in choosing a suitable formulation. Alternative terms were proposed like '*holdbar*' (durable) and '*varig*' (permanent), '*sjølbærende*' (self-supportive) and '*sjølbergende*' (subsistence). Despite these alternative concepts, the translation '*bærekraftig*' gained broad acceptance. The term '*bærekraftig*' had earlier been used for describing farms where the soil is of such character and is kept in such a manner that farming can be profitable. The term had, however, not been in popular usage and did not evoke very clear associations, opening it up to multiple interpretations.

In order to launch a debate on the report and to mobilise popular participation, the Norwegian Campaign for Environment and Development was established in April 1987, and was funded by the government. More than 100 organisations took part in the Campaign, involving co-operation between interest groups that did not normally meet or collaborate [*Aasen, 1994*]. Only a month after the launching of the World Commission's report, the Campaign arranged a national meeting attended by high-level politicians and NGOs of all kinds to discuss the concept of sustainable development. Attitudes towards the concept were very positive and the basis for a popular movement was considered good. At this initial stage the various interest groups embraced the concept as a political slogan and the term was not perceived as controversial. Yet, as discussions on developing specific measures for sustainable development progressed, the term itself became more politicised, which led to a less consensual NGO approach. The government's report *Programme for Norway's Follow-Up of the World Commission's Report on Environment and Development* [*MoE, 1989*] contained a theoretical discussion of sustainable development as a concept. Here both economic and developmental aspects of sustainable development were highlighted. The use of market forces and mechanisms were indicated to be central to any process, but it was also underlined that market mechanisms alone cannot take environmental considerations into account in a satisfactory way [*MoE, 1989: 7*]. The developmental and global aspects were also highlighted: 'sustainable development is primarily meaningful in a global context. The sum of various countries' national efforts in accordance with united international goals will therefore be decisive' [*MoE, 1989: 15*].

The government signalled its intention to follow up this global aspect through aid donations to developing nations and active participation in international environmental arenas where Norway could act as a driving force. The government's argument that 'there is still time for a gradual re-orientation towards sustainable development' [*MoE, 1989: 7*] shows an incremental rather than radical understanding of the concept. With regard to the Norwegian context the government argued that:

In many areas, Norway, has anticipated developments in environmental politics. This does not mean that requirements for future environmental policies can be lowered; on the contrary, high standards must be set for further efforts. The tasks are demanding for us as well, and major changes will be needed in the way we use energy and other resources before developments in Norway are brought within natural tolerance limits [*MoE, 1989: 6*].

In spite of this early and broad process for interpreting and integrating the concept of sustainable development, enthusiasm for the concept has declined significantly over time. Yet the term has survived as a normative intention. The Norwegian philosopher Arne Næss describes the concept's function:

> Thanks to the Brundtland report, the eco-political argumentation has risen to a higher level. It is now possible to declare that a political decision is logically incompatible with the approved Brundtland Report, that a logical contradiction is present, an inconsistency. Now that 'all' politicians pretend to be of a (moderate) shade of green, the debate may be effectivised. Who will admit to being out of step with themselves? [*1991: 37*].

The introduction of a policy for sustainable development therefore provides an opportunity to put pressure on national governments and political parties to follow-up on their international commitments concerning sustainable development [*Lafferty and Langhelle, 1995*]. Yet, the question is who is willing to make such criticisms?

The National Response Process

The Norwegian government stated early on its intention to respond to the recommendations of the World Commission's report. To support its efforts, a State Secretary Committee for Environment and Development was created, which, led by the MoE, recommended a broad public inquiry into the World Commission's report. In June 1987, a consultation process was entered into with both an internal hearing including all ministries and directorates, local and county authorities, and an external hearing including trade and labour organisations, political parties, voluntary organisations, and research communities.

It is interesting to note that the first initiative to induce various ministries to include the concept of sustainable development in parts of their policy areas came from the Ministry of Foreign Affairs. In August 1987, it established an Environment/Development section, which worked both to integrate the concept of sustainable development into Norway's foreign policy and to persuade various international organisations to incorporate the recommendations of the World Commission's report into various resolutions. An important result of the first objective was the development of a set of guidelines for Norway's foreign policy. These were made in co-operation with other relevant ministries and included decisions concerning a wide range of issue areas, such as population growth, food security, biodiversity, energy, industry, urban development, oceans, and education. The output was presented in June 1988 in the report *Norway's Contribution to International Efforts for Sustainable Development*, which also pointed out that Norway was in a good position to support and strengthen the international process.

In February 1988,[1] a Government Environmental Committee consisting of several ministers was established to discuss the political implications of the World Commission's report for the various sectors, the use of different political measures, and the initiation of research projects. The committee proposed that a White Paper should be produced to follow-up the World Commission's report. The work of the committee, led by the MoE, formed an important basis for the report. The MoE led the national process and each Ministry was asked to define targets and measures for its own sector. Initial attitudes in the different ministries were optimistic and innovative. However, as it progressed many ministries found target-setting and the selection of measures problematic. Questions of principle concerning ministerial responsibility for a national strategy on sustainable development were also raised. During the process several ministries became less willing to submit information to the MoE. The process was complex and difficult to co-ordinate for the MoE which seemed to lack the necessary authority and support from a higher political level. Several drafts therefore had to be made before *White Paper No. 46* [*MoE, 1989*] was finally presented to Parliament in April 1989.

The White Paper introduced principles and measures to achieve sustainable development. It endorsed the main findings of the World Commission's report and declared that sustainable development was to be the overriding objective of the government's future policy. This was to be achieved by cross-sectoral policies at all levels of society. The White Paper presented a range of national goals and measures to these ends.[2] Some of which were very specific, such as the quantitative carbon dioxide (CO_2), nitrogen oxides (NO_x) and sulphur dioxide (SO_2) targets, and those for the reduction in discharges of nutrient salts and toxic substances into vulnerable parts of the North Sea. The White Paper was declared the framework and action plan for Norway's follow-up to the World Commission.[3] The ensuing parliamentary debate on the report was characterised by broad consensus, the political parties attempting to outbid each other in a 'green beauty contest', which resulted in the adoption of several ambitious environmental targets. The need for proper organisation and development of effective instruments for governance and control to handle sustainable development was also discussed in the Report. It stressed that targets should be quantifiable and verifiable, and that routines for the evaluation of results, reporting and budgeting were important. The implementation of the measures was left to the relevant sectoral ministries under the MoE's co-ordination. It was also proposed that the government should prepare a status report on national and international progress to follow up the World Commission's recommendations in the next session of Parliament, but several ministries opposed the idea and no report of this kind was made.

Public information, consultation and participation have long traditions in Norway, so it was natural for the government to invite NGOs to participate in the shaping of a national policy and in the broader international process for sustainable development. The Norwegian Campaign for Environment and Development played a central role in co-ordinating Norwegian NGO participation. In May 1990, Norway hosted the regional conference 'Action for a Common Future' in Bergen for the UN Economic Commission for Europe, as a follow-up to the Report of the World Commission.[4] Here, NGOs were, for the first time, granted full delegate status. The NGOs thus participated both in the preparations and in the actual negotiations. The Ministerial declaration resulting from the Bergen conference put forward the proposal that NGOs should also participate in the preparations for UNCED. Subsequent to the Bergen Conference, and on the basis of the experience gained from it, the government established a National Committee for UNCED, also known as 'The 1992 Committee', composed of representatives from eight ministries and eight NGOs, with environmental groups as well as business and labour organisations participating. The committee took part both in the preparation of the Norwegian negotiating positions and in the drafting of the national report.

After the UNCED, the government decided to issue a comprehensive report to Parliament on the results: *White Paper No. 13* (1992–93). It was produced by a small inter-ministerial working group and gave a synopsis of the decisions taken at UNCED, and the Norwegian government's assessments of its positions on these decisions. The original A21 document was not translated into Norwegian and is still not publicly available. A central focus of the government's White Paper was Norway's international efforts to promote the ideas spelled out at UNCED and its implementation of A21. However, the White Paper claimed that Norway was already implementing sustainable development in various sectors, and it was therefore not perceived as necessary to set out a 'new' process with the same broad approach after Rio. The measures proposed were instead seen as a follow-up to the work started with the White Paper issued in 1989

[*MoE, 1989*]. The report also indicated that not all UNCED recommendations were appropriate to the stage of development in Norway:

> The action plan Agenda 21 contains a large number of recommendations and targets that the various countries are expected to strive to realise. Norway started working towards environmental targets early and is far ahead in many fields ... The theme of the conference was environment and development, and a number of the concrete recommendations from UNCED are addressed in the first instance to countries at different stages of development from Norway. Norway will have to work harder to live up to other recommendations, and work on environment and development at national, regional and global levels will continue to be a major objective of the government [*MoE, 1992a: 10*].

The government's attitude, portraying Norway as a front-runner, both concerning its early response to the World Commission and to UNCED, combined with the perception that sustainable development is primarily meaningful in a global context, may have contributed to the lessening of the pressure for a further national follow-up. After Rio the national response process changed character. The government chose to focus on the development of policies for specific environmental issues, rather than to develop a national sustainable development process any further. The government's reports to the United Nations Commission on Sustainable Development (CSD) are merely seen as communications so that the CSD's Secretariat can be informed of and synthesise the national processes. The Ministry of Foreign Affairs co-ordinates and prepares the reports with the participation of other relevant ministries. The reports are not fed into the national policy-process and are not used as instruments for monitoring the progress or integration of national policy.

After Rio, the government set up two co-ordinating bodies, with representatives from various ministries, local and regional governments, NGOs and the business and industry sector: *Committee for Sustainable Development* and *National Committee for International Environmental Questions*. In Norway's reports to the CSD these two are presented as the key national co-ordination mechanisms for the Norwegian A21 process. The Committee for Sustainable Development supervises the follow-up to A21 with a special focus on national implementation,[5] and the National Committee for International Environmental Questions[6] meets to discuss international environmental issues. However, these potential stakeholder bodies do not meet regularly and appear to have purely information gathering roles. Hence, the committees do not maintain the central co-ordinative role as claimed in the national CSD report. Yet, the lack of formal co-ordination meetings does not imply that government agencies and the various NGOs do not meet to discuss environmental policy. More informal contact and co-operation does take place with various NGOs, but often on more specific environment-related issues.

Norway's follow-up on the international process is mainly focused upon the MoE's promotion of the issue of sustainable consumption and production. As part of the preparations for CSD meetings, the Norwegian government has hosted an international symposium on 'Sustainable Consumption' in January 1994 [*MoE, 1994a*] and a follow-up round-table meeting held in February 1995, preparing a work-programme for the forthcoming CSD session. This work has also been followed up at the national level with various efforts to promote more sustainable domestic consumption and production in co-operation with NGOs and the business community. Since Rio, most environmental NGOs have not taken measures to re-establish a general debate on sustainable development, apparently preferring to work on projects related to more specific aspects of sustainable development, especially sustainable consumption. The MoE supports a wide range of NGO projects and a special emphasis is given to promoting efforts for sustainable consumption and the development of relevant NGO networks for this work, both at the local and international level. The Environmental Home Guard[7] and the Forum for Environment and Development[8] are two central NGOs engaged in this work. Also other societal groups, for instance the Church of Norway's Council for Ecumenical and International Relations, has in recent years endeavoured to promote the idea of reduced consumption and the need for a change in consumption patterns.

We may conclude that the World Commission's Report and the subsequent UN process received much attention in Norway and were driving forces for the Norwegian national process in the period leading up to UNCED. The government also put much effort into an international promotion of the World Commission's report. The period leading up to UNCED was marked by broad enthusiasm and support for the concept. The MoE carried the responsibility for co-ordinating the broad domestic response, a process that also gained wide support from a wide range of NGOs. Although the making of the first White Paper on sustainable development proved difficult due to inter-ministerial disagreements, it did provide a certain basis for a national sustainable development strategy with defined targets and specific measures for different sectors. However, neither the signalled follow-up of the first national action plan nor a systematic evaluation of the implementation of the first national action plan have so far been made.

Since Rio, interest in developing a distinct national process for sustainable development has been small, both within the government and other political parties. Nevertheless, in May 1996 the Minister of Environment signalled that a new White Paper on sustainable development will be presented by the MoE in spring 1997. This may lead to a revitalisation of the process. The White Paper is supposed to provide a status report on Norwegian policy for sustainable development and as a specification of the government's next long-term programme, to be issued in the beginning of 1997. The MoE will co-ordinate the process, which will be broad, involving various other ministries, local governments and NGOs. Together, these two reports will constitute the basis for the Norwegian participation in the CSD session in 1997. The weakened political process for sustainable development after Rio, does not, however, necessarily imply that there has not been any development of the Norwegian environmental policy in a more sustainable direction. The following sections explore some of the most important institutional developments that have occurred so far at the national level, in the business sector and among local governments.

Co-ordinating Mechanisms

Environmental administration in the 1990s is characterised by increasing co-operation and co-ordination between ministries [*Jansen and Oseland, 1996*]. In the government's 1989 follow-up report to the Parliament on the World Commission, the government underlined the need to integrate environmental considerations into all sectors in order to achieve sustainable development:

> The Government emphasises the integration of sustainable development into all societal planning and sectoral policy. The authorities of agriculture, fisheries, energy, and transport, etc. should all carry the responsibility to ensure that development and planning within these sectors are in accordance with sustainable development and that budgetary and other measures can be applied in such a manner that existing environmental problems can be reduced and new ones can be prevented [*MoE, 1989*].

Specific targets (preferably quantifiable) were to be set for all sectors. Both the implementation of measures and the control of achievements were to be the responsibility of each sector, with some reporting back to the MoE. The MoE was to co-ordinate the setting of the ministries' targets and develop systems for supervision. Yet, the process through which this co-ordination should take place as well as the authority which the MoE can exert on these processes was unclear [*Jansen and Oseland, 1996*].

To enhance inter-ministerial co-operation, the following four measures have been set out:

- new planning and budget routines concerning the State Budget;
- the establishment of a State Secretary Committee for Environmental Issues;
- the use of inter-ministerial working groups; and
- a new routine for environmental impact assessments within ministries.

For the first time in September 1988, the State Budget proposal to Parliament included an environmental profile. The purpose of the budget review was to establish a method by which all ministries were obliged to report to Parliament, via the MoE, on the environmental effects of their allocations. The routine was meant to serve as an incentive to promote sustainable development and provide greater transparency on the state's performance in each sector with regard to its environmental objectives. Since 1992, environment-related expenditure has been split into three categories: expenditure with primary environmental effects; expenditure with significant environmental effects; and expenditure with limited environmental effects. In the 1996 Budget, this routine has been further developed as all ministries present their efforts within 19 different categories. The application of a new set of categories is intended to provide a more comprehensive overview and thus form a better basis for possible evaluations of the total set of ministries' environmental activities. All ministries are also responsible for reporting on their environmental achievements.

These reports include a description of the environmental and resource problems in the ministries' respective sectors and likely trends if no new measures are put into effect. Moreover, the reports include goals for meeting these challenges and proposals for long and short-term measures to solve existing environmental and resource-management problems and to prevent problems from emerging. The measures' impacts are, if possible, quantified. The quality of the ministries' reports and budgets has steadily improved and today most ministries report on all the issues listed above [Lindseth, 1995]. The MoE and the Ministry of Finance maintain close contact with the other ministries on the preparation of these reports. As part of the reporting procedure the units of the MoE may evaluate and comment upon the ministries' budget and report proposals. The procedure provides the MoE with early and extensive information on planning in the various ministries and enables the MoE to signal at an early stage in the budget process to other ministries or to the government if the specific or overall environmental profile is unsatisfactory. However, the MoE's ability to report back on possible inconsistencies in the other ministries' budgetary reporting is still limited; it has no direct legal authority over other ministries and the co-ordinating role of the MoE still lacks power.

In 1989, the government developed a second co-ordinating measure, the establishment of a State Secretary Committee for Environmental Issues – a forum for inter-ministerial co-operation and co-ordination on environmental policy, chaired by the State Secretary for the Environment. This Committee is involved in developing methods to achieve better co-ordination of a comprehensive environmental policy, and provides a valuable function as a forum were inter-ministerial conflicts may be solved here at a lower political level before they reach Cabinet level. The Committee also discusses possible improvements in the total State budget's environmental profile each year. Discussions in the Committee have several times led to changes in budget priorities, resulting in increased funding in some parts of the budget [*Lindseth, 1995*]. Meetings are held monthly, which enables stable, operative and flexible co-operation between the ministries. Much effort has been put into the development of the Committee's work to establish a smoothly functioning, internal political process of co-ordination.

A third integrative measure taken is the formation of several more or less permanent inter-ministerial committees and working groups, representing an effort to promote better integration on cross sectoral environmental issues. The method is based on consensus building around a problem and the measures needed to solve it. However, the processes are often time-consuming and can lead to conflicts and possible stalemates. Here, the role of the MoE is often to guide and influence rather than direct the other ministries. The initiatives taken so far are seen as positive, reducing conflicts and increasing the basis for co-operation between ministries [*NOU, 1995: 147*]. However, the work partly depends upon the willingness of the ministries concerned to give priority to environmental issues over other sectoral interests. The MoE exercises no absolute control in such issues and therefore has to negotiate with other ministries over environmental targets and strategies. For instance, inter-ministerial working groups have been established to work on climate policy.

An inter-ministerial working group published a comprehensive report on climate policy in March 1991, primarily as an effort to consolidate a national consensus on the natural science basis for climate negotiations [*Sydnes, 1996*]. The group comprised high level ministerial representatives from the Prime Minister's Office, the Ministries of Environment, Foreign Affairs, Transport, Industry, Finance, Oil and Energy, and Agriculture. The work on this report was an important educational process. Also, Norway's participation in the international climate negotiations was prepared by an inter-ministerial group and the Norwegian delegation had representatives from four ministries: Environment, Foreign Affairs, Finance, and Industry and Energy. After Rio, the government signalled its intent to develop a national plan of action – as a follow-up to the Norwegian CO_2 target. The actual report was, however, much delayed partly due to a de-centralisation of the work with the report. Various ministries were asked to write separate parts in their respective fields of responsibility. The work revealed differences in points of view and caused problems with the making of a national action plan. The MoE co-ordinated the process, and all drafts were discussed in the high level group. Representatives of various ministries have stressed the advantages of an inter-ministerial process in developing a mutual appreciation of each other's positions [*Sydnes, 1996*]. However, there are still great difficulties in defining the level of ambition. Moreover, the much acclaimed learning process, has, so far produced little when it comes to practical policy co-ordination: oil and transport policies are still on different tracks, largely unaffected by the climate debate, driven by domestic interests and powerful lobbies [*Sydnes, 1996: 295*].

Of particular significance within the environmental policy area is also the work of the following three, now dissolved, investigative commissions: The Environmental Tax Commission, the Commission on Instruments of Environmental Policy, and the Green Tax Commission, consisting of both high status officials and top economists. These commissions functioned as arenas in which the various ministries sounded out responses to their policy proposals for discussion and co-ordination [*Jansen and Oseland, 1996*]. Co-ordinating efforts have also been carried out between the MoE and the Ministry of Agriculture. Here co-ordination takes place in a committee led by the general secretaries of the two ministries as well as in a contact group whose members are lower status civil servants. A further organisational development that probably will improve co-ordination is the setting up of environment sections in other ministries. For instance, such a section was set up in the Ministry of Transport and Communication.

A fourth integrative mechanism is the development of environmental assessments within the ministries. Impact assessment involves reporting on the consequences of ministries' work with public reports, regulations, proposals and reports to Parliament. Since December 1994, the routine has been extended to also include environmental consequences. All ministries are now required to consult with the MoE concerning the assessment of environmental impacts. Such assessments are undertaken by the MoE, which provides it with the possibility of directing the activities of other ministries as to environmental consequences.

Despite all these efforts at co-ordination, the experience has so far been mixed. According to the Organisation for Economic Co-operation and

Development (OECD): 'integration does not operate in practice as satisfactorily as it should ... These sectors do not always seem to work as closely with the Ministry of Environment as might have been expected in view of their role in environmental protection and degradation' [*1993: 80*]. The lack of inter-ministerial co-operation has also been confirmed in statements by the Minister of the Environment, which highlight problems with establishing common interests and targets for sustainable development within the central administration.[9] Sustained political pressure to persuade sectoral ministries to accept and apply integrative mechanisms and procedures is therefore vital. Today the MoE seems to be fatigued with 'struggling' with other ministries in its attempts to create a sector-encompassing environmental policy, and the position of the Minister of Environment within the government is relatively weak. The State Secretary Committee for Environmental Issues may partly sustain pressure for a integrated environmental policy, but also here stalemates may occur due to inter-ministerial disagreements.

As far as political leadership and support from the Prime Minister is concerned, the situation also seems to have changed. In 1987, Gro Harlem Brundtland in her dual role as Chairman of the World Commission and Norway's Prime Minister was important in pressing for an ambitious environmental policy. In recent years she has preferred to focus more on other issues, such as European Union (EU) membership, welfare, unemployment and oil and gas production. The reduced leadership role from the Prime Minister in putting environmental issues high on the political agenda may have made cross-sectoral co-operation more difficult to achieve.

Environmental Legislation

Norway's environmental policy has been significantly strengthened since the establishment of the MoE in 1972. The majority of Norway's environmental legislation was developed in the 1970s and early 1980s, with some recent amendments. The Pollution Control Act, the Nature Conservation Act, the Cultural Heritage Act, the Planning and Building Act, the Product Control Act, and the Pollution Control Act of 1981 (amended in 1983 and 1993), are all important tools in environmental policy.[10] In June 1992 an amendment to the Constitution was made to integrate the principles behind the concept of sustainable development into Norwegian legislation:

> Every person has a right to an environment that is conducive to health and to natural surroundings whose productivity and diversity are preserved. Natural resources should be used on the basis of

comprehensive long-term considerations whereby this right will be safeguarded for future generations as well. In order to safeguard their right in accordance with the foregoing paragraph, citizens are entitled to be informed of the state of the natural environment and the effects of any encroachments on nature that are planned or have commenced. The State Authorities shall issue further provisions for the implementation of these principles [*The Constitution of the Kingdom of Norway, Article 110b*].

The amendment can be seen as a confirmation of the principle of sustainable development in Norwegian policy, touching upon the individual's right to a clean environment and to knowledge about the effects of any degradation planned or underway [*Aardal, 1993*]. The principle of sustainable development has also been integrated into new legislation as one of the legislation's purposes [*Røhnebæk, 1995*]. Earlier proposals to make environmental protection part of the Constitution had been rejected, often on the grounds of unwillingness to include into the Constitution principles that lacked legal implications. Eventually, in 1992 Parliament unanimously agreed to amend the Constitution. It is interesting to note that the right-wing Progress Party was initially sceptical about the inclusion of such laws that were not legally binding for citizens in courts of law, yet, they supported the proposal, arguing that they '... did not want to be regarded as opponents to environmental protection in the political debate because they could not see that the decision would lead to any important damage' [*Aardal, 1993*]. Clearly illustrating that environmental protection had become something that no political party could afford to oppose. The first, and so far only, use of the amendment was a Supreme Court decision in May 1993 concerning the interpretation of the Pollution Control Act.[11] In May 1996 a panel of a consensus conference on biodiversity declared that Article 110b should be more visible, which would produce actual effects for legislation and administration in general and more specifically concerning biodiversity [*Aftenposten, 1996*].

Although Norway is not an EU member, its environmental legislation is heavily influenced by the EU's environmental policy because it is a signatory to the EU's European Economic Area (EEA) agreement. Therefore, it has integrated large parts of the EU's environmental legislation into national law and will continue to do so. Currently few differences between the EU's and Norway's environmental legislation can be found [*Dahl, 1994*]. The agreement may reduce Norway's national freedom of action to create its own environmental legislation, and there is limited opportunity to influence the formation of this legislation. Yet, as an EEA member, Norway may veto new EU directives. Despite opposition from left-wing and centrist political interests towards several EU directives, the Parliament has so far not vetoed any EU environmental directives.

The Setting of Targets, Reporting on Achievements

Quantitative targets are one of the most distinctive features of Norwegian environmental policy [*OECD, 1993*]. Ambitious emission targets for CO_2 and NOx and targets for land-based ocean pollution were set immediately after the World Commission's report, but today the government faces problems in actually achieving many of these. Moreover, the economic cost of adopting the targets has become a more visible factor, changing the content of many of the environmental policy debates to focus more on meeting existing targets, rather than setting new ones. Various documents present figures on targets and achievements, though no single document covers them all. The documentary process tends to be fragmented and is only to a small extent connected to the policy-process.

An important reporting mechanism within Parliament is the annual Environmental Statement by the Minister of the Environment, begun in 1987.[12] The content of the statements vary from year to year, depending upon what the Minister would like to draw attention to or away from. Since 1991, an additional section of environmental background data accompanies the statement, which has gradually become more comprehensive. However, neither the statement nor the background data section gives a complete overview of targets or trends based on a systematic use of indicators to monitor and report on status and progress. The statement is barely used as an instrument for control, but it does ensure an annual debate on the government's environmental policy in Parliament where criticism can be made. A further planning document is the government's long-term programme, issued every four years, prepared mainly by the Ministry of Finance. The two latest both contained a separate chapter on sustainable development and the environment, but again failed to provide a systematic overview and evaluation of achievements towards established targets [*MoE, 1994b; 1995*]. As from 1994, the state of the environment in the Nordic countries is to be reported annually by means of environmental indicators. The indicators used refer to different stages of the cause-effect change and are described as the Pressure-State-Response concept.[13] The work on the Nordic indicators closely follows the OECD's work on environmental indicators. Moreover, the Norwegian State Pollution Control Authority has started a pilot project to develop indicators for sustainable production and consumption.

Environmental Taxes and Green Accounting

Norway has taken the lead among OECD countries in terms of environmental taxation [*OECD, 1993: 86*]. From 1989 to 1990, the use of environmental taxes and other economic instruments has increased. On the government's initiative, a Green Tax Commission was set up in December 1989 to study economic principles, strategies and measures for use as yardsticks in evaluating the various aspects of the environment. Three years later, the Commission's work resulted in a comprehensive report and proposals for more extensive use of economic instruments to promote a more cost-effective environmental policy [*NOU, 1992: 3*]. In its latest long-term programme (1994–97), the government signalled a further increase in the use of economic instruments, yet, for 1996 no new environmental taxes are planned. Any further development of the CO_2 tax will, according to the government, due to Norway's small economy, depend upon the developments of taxation in Norway's neighbouring countries and the EU.

In June 1996 the conclusions of a second Green Tax Commission were presented. The Commission's mandate was to examine how the tax system may be used to improve the environment and at the same time increase employment. A range of measures were suggested, among these were an increase in the CO_2 and SO_2 and diesel tax, cuts in environmentally damaging public subventions, studded tyre tax and road tolling. The Commission argued that in the long term these measures would possibly lead to a two per cent reduction in employer taxation. The launching of the report was characterised by high political tensions. The representative of the Confederation of Norwegian Business and Industry leaked out the most controversial tax issues just before the finalisation of the report, claiming that an increased CO_2 tax could not be accepted by Norwegian industry.

Moreover, the three high level officials from the Ministry of Finance, the MoE, and the Ministry of Transport and Communication, changed their opinion on the issue of increasing the CO_2 tax, while the Ministry of Energy and Industry opposed the increase. Originally the three other representatives supported the Commission's general line on the need to expand the CO_2 tax. However, the three former representatives changed their view, now arguing for the need to leave the issue of CO_2 taxation to be considered by the politicians. The report caused some discussion, however, the short-term measures suggested by the Commission were not included in the Government's 1997 annual national budget. The government will first invite the Parliament to discuss the report. This will obviously lead to a further delay of any changes in the pattern of environmental taxation. The final result of the Commission's report therefore remains to be seen.

Since 1989, a popularised version of the state budget has been issued annually as a 'Green Book' containing a report on environment-related expenditure by all ministries and a short commentary on the overall green profile of the state budget. The budgeting process is, however, a rather passive collection and reporting of pro-environmental efforts and does not contain the evaluation, reporting and control function that it was intended to have [*NOU, 1995: 4*].[14] Criticism has also been made of the use of environmental expenditure as an indicator of long-term sustainability. This is not a mechanism of control and so bodies such as the Auditor-General or Parliament have not paid much attention to it.

An interesting effort to develop new methods of so-called green accounting have been set out by the Norwegian Society for the Conservation of Nature and the research Project for an Alternative Future/ProSus[15] together with the Ministries of Finance and the Environment. This Project for a Sustainable Economy established a set of indicators of sustainable development and studied the scope for and impacts of sustainable development requirements within Norway's long-term planning apparatus. The project also sought to develop co-operation between groups that have not tended to work together. It is hoped thereby to increase the understanding of each other's arguments. The project has been a valuable learning process challenging traditional thinking about the environment and economy and has been met with interest both in the MoE and Ministry of Finance. We may conclude that several relevant issues concerning green taxation and green accounting have been identified and discussed in the Norwegian context but this has so far not resulted in any major political changes in the economic system.

Greening of Business and Industry

From playing an often defensive role, mainly adapting to state regulations and directives, surveys indicate that large sectors of business and industry in Norway are willing to recognise the environmental challenge and take steps towards 'greening' [*The Nordic Business Environmental Barometer, 1995*]. The Confederation of Norwegian Business and Industry has urged its members to put environmental issues on the agenda and prepare their own environmental reports. Approximately 100 companies have hitherto done so but only very few companies give quantitative environmental information. The information given is often fragmentary and does not always provide any good basis for an evaluation of the companies' environmental status [*Deloitte and Touche, 1995*]. The government plays a major role in promoting a greening of business and industry. In March 1991 it ordered all public and private activities to implement a documented internal control system for health, safety and the environment. A further reporting instrument is the obligation on all companies listed on the stock exchange, by virtue of the Joint Stock Company Act, to include in their annual report a paragraph on the pollution caused by the company and mitigation measures [*Dahl, 1994*].

The government gives special emphasis to the promotion of more sustainable patterns of consumption, and in order to develop, pilot and promote methods of green management, the MoE in 1991 established a Green Management Programme involving business, trade unions, local authorities and environmental NGOs. In 1995, the programme was established permanently as the Norwegian Centre for Sustainable Production and Consumption, its remit to motivate and facilitate sustainable development in Norwegian business and focus on the market effects of environmental policy. There have so far been pilot projects for the sectors of: advertising, banking and finance, commercial buildings, information technology, local authorities, retailing, and tourism. Voluntary agreements has also been sought and developed with those parts of the industry sector that are exempted from the CO_2 tax. To develop an environmentally sound public procurement policy a project called 'a green state procurement policy' has been introduced to steer public purchasing, in 1993 amounting to NOK 140 billion, towards more sustainable alternatives. No regulations exist in Norway regulating environmental labelling of goods (apart from prohibitions of certain chemicals which shall be indicated pursuant to legislation). There are, however, some non-binding arrangements. Among these is the foundation 'Environmental Labelling', organised by the Nordic Council, which has introduced the 'swan-mark' in Nordic countries.

The Role of Local Governments and the Local Agenda 21 (LA21) Debate

Until recently, the issue of LA21 has not been discussed extensively in Norway. Yet, this does not imply that local environmental policy and the idea of 'thinking globally, acting locally' has not been a subject for local and central authorities. In 1987 the government launched the comprehensive Programme for Environmental Protection at the Local Level (EPLL). The programme was later developed into a reform covering all local authorities, including projects highly relevant to a LA21 process, such as: the appointment of environmental protection officers, delegation of environmental tasks from central government to local authorities, and the making of a first, and also partly a second, generation of local environment and natural resource programmes or plans. Moreover, a network of competence and experience called the Forum for Local Environmental

Protection has been developed between the environmental protection officers. NOK 700 million has been transferred from the state to local government to fund the programme. It is, however, necessary in the making of the next generation of plans to promote a broader participatory process, the inclusion of more global environmental issues and the application of a longer-term perspective.

The experience gained through EPLL and various other programmes and projects initiated, provides a broad and valuable basis for the further development of a more specific LA21 process. An Eco-municipality Programme set out in 1985 by a small number of rural municipalities was the first specific project for local sustainable development. The project provides experience concerning political participation and has also generated interesting research into issues highly relevant for the LA21 process, such as environmental education for politicians, and local environmental planning and environmental auditing. While the eco-municipality project focuses upon rural district municipalities, the MoE has initiated a project for Sustainable Cities and Towns to develop models for sustainable urban municipalities and has been quite successful as far as adaptation of global problems and a long-term approach are concerned. Environmental NGOs have also become involved in work at the local level. The independent foundation Idea Bank, together with ProSus, and the Environmental Home Guard, execute an important function in pushing for, and providing information on, the LA21 issue. Also interesting, is a more recently established co-operation on local environmental policy between the Norwegian Society for Nature Conversation and the Trade Union for Municipal Employees.

The late beginning of a specific LA21 process may partly be explained by the general perception held by the government that EPLL and the environmental plans made under it were in accordance with the development of LA21 plans. This point of view has during the past year been modified and in April 1996 the Minister of the Environment signalled the need to develop specific LA21 plans. So far the development of models and pilot cases has been heavily emphasised in many of the projects. What is vital now is to assemble the experience gained and make it available to local governments. By the end of 1996 both EPLL and the eco-municipality programme will have been completed. The launching of a more ambitious LA21 policy process with a wider participatory aspect, including the broader local society, and with a more active participation from NGOs, could be a useful continuation of the Norwegian process. To successfully realise such a process a more co-ordinated and comprehensive support from the central government will be vital.

A Future Sustainability Process

The Norwegian national response process to sustainable development started early. In the period leading up to Rio much political energy was fed into the process, which gained broad support in the government and the political opposition, and among a wide range of NGOs. After Rio, political interest for the process waned. Five factors may explain this:

* the interpretation of the concept;

* the government's perception of Norway as an environmental front-runner;

* lack of political leadership and the absence of a strong political opposition;

* the perception of fewer and less environmental threats;

* and finally, a perception within the government that it was more appropriate to focus on a wider set of specific environmental issues than to develop further a process for sustainable development.

The Norwegian interpretation of the concept of sustainable development accorded well with the already prevailing ideology of combining economic growth and environmental protection. The incremental rather than radical approach to, and understanding of, the concept probably reduced the likelihood of achieving a more fundamental reorientation. However, the term sustainable development seems to have survived as a normative principle providing an opportunity to put pressure on the national government to follow up on their commitments. Despite this, for the time being, such criticism is not very strong.

The government's programmatic statements concerning Norway's front-runner status with regard to the recommendations in A21 may have eased internal pressure for a continuation of the national follow-up process. The image of being a front-runner has, to some extent, been accepted by the public, diminishing a potential bottom-up pressure for action. The front-runner role, is, however, proving difficult to continue and realise due to high economic costs and the lack of political willingness in pursuing an ambitious environmental policy.

The political opposition to the government is weak and no party is willing to take any green leadership role at the moment. The 'green beauty contest' among the political parties has definitely come to an end. The Parliament's interest in environmental matters can be measured by the number of environmental questions posed to the Minister of the Environment in Parliament [*Skjærseth and Rosendal, 1995*]. Since

1987–88, a steady increase in the annual number of questions can be traced, peaking at 32 for 1991–92. But in 1992–93, only four questions were raised. Continued lack of interest in environmental issues is also one of the observed trends from the local elections in September 1995. The elections resulted in a turn towards a more Conservative policy at the local level. The Socialist Left Party, known for its concern for environmental policy, lost voters while the right-wing Progress Party gained increased support. Moreover, there has been a decreased interest in environmental issues in public opinion. The period between the two latest Parliamentary elections (1989–93) has seen a strong decline in the interest in the environment. In 1989, 37 per cent of the electorate emphasised environmental protection as the most important issue, while in 1993 only seven per cent gave this issue top priority [*Aardal and Valen, 1995*], indicating that support from public opinion for an ambitious environmental policy cannot be taken for granted.

A possible explanation for this reduced interest in environmental issues in general may be found in a change in environmental threats. When the World Commission presented its report, several international environmental problems posed a threat to Norway and led to broad interest and enthusiasm for the concept of sustainable development. Today Norway's environmental situation seems to have undergone a change. Acid rain continues to cause problems but political solutions are in sight, and the Norwegian government co-operates closely with Russia to reduce the risk of nuclear accidents. The lack of severe environmental threats to Norway combined with the government's self-image of being a 'front-runner' in all senses may have led to less attention being directed to environmental policy issues. The successful Olympic Winter Games at Lillehammer in 1994, the Oslo Channel in the Middle East peace process the same year, the debate and the result of the EU referendum in 1994, and Norway's economically strong position due to oil and natural gas exports – all these may have strengthened the Norwegian self-image of being a front-runner in a general sense.

The government's weak interest in developing further a distinct sustainable development policy process may, however, also be due to a perception within the government that it is more appropriate to focus on a wider set of specific environmental policy issues such as climate change, biodiversity, water pollution, waste management, and sustainable consumption, and to develop targets, policies and evaluations within each of these issue fields. Taken together, these form a whole environmental policy. A separate sustainable development process is not seen as necessary. This may partly explain why so little political energy has been fed into a specific sustainable development process after Rio.

In spite of this weakened process for sustainable development, a range of institutional mechanisms have developed at the national administrative level, which provides a guarantee for a certain standard of environmental policy. Mechanisms to develop inter-ministerial co-operation, environmental legislation, the setting of environmental targets and data gathering and the development of green budgets and taxes are some of the most important measures carried out at the state level. Taken together these form a considerable system of environmental policy protection. These existing structures and procedures, many still in their early stages, will also continue to function in a relatively stable manner independent of fluctuations in public and political interest in environmental policy. A rapid institutionalisation of environmental policy both at the political and administrative level seems to have taken place [*Reitan, 1995*]. Environmental considerations have to a large extent been co-opted into already existing legislative and political-institutional systems. The development of new systems has therefore not been seen as necessary since existing institutions have adopted the environmental policy aspects.

The developments at state level are supplemented by the development of relevant activities among environmental NGOs, within the business community and at the local government level. At the local level various environmental programmes have led to an improved local environmental policy. The experience gained from these programmes and projects initiated at the local level does, despite some shortcomings, form a wide and valuable basis for the further development of a more specific LA21 process. Increasing interest in a LA21 process may in the longer-term also spill-over into the national response. Business has also recognised the environmental challenge and taken steps towards greening, a development which is strongly supported by various government initiatives. Yet, the business and industry sector does not promote the development of a national process towards sustainable development.

As to the younger generations, increased interest in environmental education both in schools and within environmental NGOs may form the basis for a more long-term and stable environmental awareness among citizens. Nature conservation and environment has been a compulsory subject taught in the Norwegian educational system since 1971. In 1991 the Ministry of Education, Research and Church Affairs formulated a national strategy for integrating education on environment and development throughout the school system and in the national curriculum guidelines. Also environmental NGOs work to increase children's environmental awareness. One of the most successful initiatives is Blekkulf's Environmental Detectives, established in 1989, under the auspices of the Norwegian Society for the Conservation of Nature. Through radio and television programmes and books, children learn about 'Blekkulf', a cartoon octopus who needs help to clean up nature.

Today Blekkulf has 15,000 individual members as well as approximately 600 kindergartens and school classes. More recently, in December 1995 the Norwegian Research Council arranged a national hearing on sustainable development to discuss the content and role of the concept in public policy strategies. The panel recommended the continuation of the debate in a series of national hearings on more specific aspects related to sustainable development. These hearings may, if they are carried out, contribute to re-establish a broader debate on sustainable development. The outcome of the MoE's recently launched proposal for a new White Paper on sustainable development, by spring 1997, may also lead to a revitalisation of the process for sustainable development in Norway, but the final outcome of this process still remains to be seen. In the first part it was pointed out that the introduction of a policy for sustainable development provides for an opportunity to put pressure on national governments and political parties to follow up on their international commitments concerning sustainable development.

An indicator of the political willingness to push the issue for more sustainable development further may be the recent political debate on the plans to build two natural gas power plants in Norway. Here efforts have been made to link the issue of sustainable development to the debate, arguing that the government's energy policy can hardly be legitimised as a sustainable policy. Production of electricity from natural gas at these two plants will render impossible the fulfilment of Norway's CO_2 emission reduction targets. The power plants will also be exempted from CO_2 tax to ensure their profitability. The government's main argument for building the power plants has been that export of Norwegian natural gas will replace more polluted energy production, such as coal, in Finland and Denmark, and hence contribute to a reduction in the total Nordic CO_2 emissions. However, the government has so far not been successful in reaching any agreements with the relevant importing countries, on any replacements.

Researchers have pointed out that new coal power plants will, due to the application of new technology, not necessarily produce any higher CO_2 emissions than those from the planned natural gas power plants in Norway. The State Pollution Control Authority, signalled that it will not give any complete evaluation of the building, due to what they consider as an inconsistent environmental impact assessment report from the entrepreneur Naturkraft. The Conservative 'grand old man' and former prime minister, Kåre Willoch, engaged himself in the discussion, arguing together with parts of the political opposition and various environmental NGOs that the environmental arguments against the building are convincing. However, the government, including the Minister of the Environment, and a majority in Parliament, has approved the building. This signals that there are still highly competing priorities in Norwegian environmental policy-making today between energy production interests and environmental interests. So far the first cluster of interests seem to win as long as there are significant economic interests at stake. This is also the general conclusion of Jansen and Oseland [*1996: 207*]:

> In the 1990s the characteristic pattern seems to have been a steady current in favour of institutionalising environmental values in new and widening areas of public policy. This apparently general development has, however, often been broken when significant economic interests have been at stake and the Government has had to make a choice on grounds of principle between economic growth values and environmental values. On a number of such occasions the MoE has lost the battle.

Conclusion

The political process related to the Norwegian response to sustainable development has been characterised by shifting political support. During the period from 1987 to 1992 a broad participatory, state-initiated process was carried out to follow-up the World Commission's report and to prepare for UNCED, both at the national and international level. After UNCED, the interest in pursuing a distinct national process for sustainable development both within the government and in the political opposition has been limited. However, also after Rio, efforts to promote sustainable development practices continue, both at the state level and among NGOs, in the business and industry sector and at the local level. These structures and procedures continue to function relatively stable and more or less independently of fluctuations in the political interest for sustainable development. Many of the institutional developments described above started or were planned before the launching of the World Commission's report. This indicates that the Norwegian administrative and political system for environmental policy has developed independently of the international process for sustainable development. To get a total picture of the institutional developments for a more sustainable development in Norway, it is therefore vital also to look beyond the specific national response process related to the World Commission's report and UNCED.

NOTES

1. At the same time the work of the first State Secretary Committee for Environment and Development was terminated.
2. National sectors for which goals and measures were presented were energy, transport, industry, genetic resources, agriculture, fisheries, education, health and consumption patterns, local government, and development aid. International issues were climate change; depletion of the ozone layer; other long range pollution; pollution in the North Sea/Skagerrak; industrial discharges; hazardous wastes; chemicals and oil pollution control; and the natural resource base.
3. Concerning the fulfilment of the targets some ministries have put a lot of effort into it, while others have at best shown a slow internal process to implement the goals.
4. The Bergen Conference generated two documents, a ministerial declaration and an action plan. The Bergen Ministerial Declaration supported the precautionary principle and the idea that there are limitations to what nature can tolerate. These principles were fed into the UNCED process at a later stage.
5. The committee is chaired by the Prime Minister and consists of the following members: the Ministers of the Environment, Transport and Communications, Industry and Energy, representatives from the Norwegian Society for the Conservation of Nature, Norwegian Confederation of Trade Unions, Confederation of Norwegian Business and Industry, and Norwegian Association of Local and Regional Authorities.
6. Seats are held by the Office of the Prime Minister; Ministries of Foreign Affairs, Environment, Industry and Energy, Finance, Fisheries, Agriculture, Transport and Communication together with representatives from various NGOs such as the Norwegian Society for Conservation of Nature; the Confederation of Norwegian Business and Industry, the Research Council of Norway, the Norwegian Confederation of Trade Unions, the Norwegian Association of Local and Regional Authorities and the Norwegian Forum for Environment and Development.
7. The Environmental Home Guard works to achieve a general reduction in the level of consumption and to make consumption more sustainable. The organisation has currently more than 80,000 individual participants. In addition, schools, offices and 60–70 local authorities participate in the project. The Home Guard co-operates with existing local voluntary organisations and local governments to develop local networks for sustainable consumption. Since 1992, funding from the MoE has more than doubled amounting now to (Norwegian Krone (NOK) 5.4 million annually).
8. The Forum for Development and Environment (ForUM) was established subsequent to the Rio Summit, as the successor to the Norwegian Campaign for Environment and Development which was disbanded in December 1992. ForUM is an umbrella organisation and network of 55 organisations. Its main task is to follow up the process for sustainable development through national and international NGO co-operation. A special working group has been set up to look at sustainable consumption, and ForUM played a central role at both the MoE's Symposium on Sustainable Consumption and at a subsequent round-table meeting contributing to the discussions.
9. Thorbjørn Berntsen in the Parliamentary Environmental Debate, 13 May 1993 and in interview in Aftenposten, 17 April 1994.
10. In the government's White Paper on Environment and Development [*MoE, 1989*] it was pointed out that Norwegian legislation had severe shortcomings when it came to ensuring the implementation of substantive requirements. The government therefore identified several measures to counter this: (1) review laws and regulations in all sectors and propose amendments to the rules to promote sustainable development; (2) table proposals for general rules in the Planning and Building Act for impact assessment reports for measures with considerable effects on the environment, natural resources and the community at large; (3) table a new Energy Act; (4) table proposals for stronger measures to counter criminal acts affecting the environment [*MoE, 1989*].
11. Here, the Supreme Court stated that the avoidance of pollution: 'is a matter of considerable importance across a number of administrative sectors. In that respect this is part of the

universal environmental considerations that it is the aim to have incorporated into the decision-making process – see the principle now built into Article 110b of the Constitution – and that it is the duty of the environmental protection authorities to take care of' (The Norwegian Research Council, 1996) (my translation).

12. Environmental statement to Parliament by the Minister of the Environment, 27 May 1987. See MoE [*1987; 1994b; 1995*].

13. Human activities exert pressure on the environment in different ways, for instance through emissions, this is reflected in changes in the quality and quantity of natural resources (state). Society's response in order to prevent these changes or repair environmental damage is the third step of the concept.

14. An exception was found in 1989, when Gro Harlem Brundtland – then in political opposition – proposed an alternative budget to that presented in the 'Green Book'. Parliamentary support for her proposal led to an increase in the environmental budget of approximately NOK 100 million.

15. January 1996 Alternative Future changed its name to Programme for Research and Documentation for a Sustainable Society (ProSus).

REFERENCES

Aardal, Bernt (1993), *Energi og miljø, Nye stridsspørsmål i møte med gamle strukturer* (Energy and Environment: New Controversial Questions Meet Old Structures), Report 93:15, Oslo: Institutt for samfunnsforsking.

Aardal, Bernt og Henry Valen (1995), *Konflikt og opinion* (Conflict and Opinion), Oslo: NKS-forlaget.

Aasen, Berit (1994), *Strategic Review of the Norwegian Campaign for Environment and Development*, Norsk Institutt for By- og Regionsforsking/NIBR, Working Paper 1994:104, Oslo.

Aftenposten (1996), *Vil bruke grunnloven* (Wants to use the Constitution), *Aftenposten*, 24 May 1996.

Constitution of the Kingdom of Norway 1685–1993, The (1993), Oslo.

Dahl, Agnethe (1994), *EUs og Norges miljølovgivning – Likheter og forskjeller* (EU's and Norway's Environmental Legislation – Similarities and Differences) Fridtjof Nansen Institute Report 1994:5, Oslo.

Deloitte and Touche (1995), *Miljøinformasjon i norske selskapers årsrapporter* (*Environmental Information in Norwegian Companies' Annual Reports*), Oslo.

Jansen, A.I. and O. Oseland (1996), 'Norway', in P. Munk Christiansen (ed.), Governing the Environmental Politics, Policy and Organisation in the Nordic Countries, Copenhagen: Nord 1996:5, pp.181–259.

Lafferty, William and Oluf Langhelle (eds.) (1995), *Bærekraftig utvikling – Om utviklingens mål og bærekraftens betingelser* (Sustainable Development – The Development and Preconditions of Sustainability), Oslo: Ad Notam Gyldendal.

Lindseth, Anne (1995), MoE, personal communication.

Ministry of Environment (Moe) (1987), *Environmental Statement to Parliament by the Minister of the Environment*, 27 May 1987.

Ministry of Environment (1989), *Report to the Storting No. 46 (1988–1989) Environment and Development Programme for Norway's Follow-Up of the Report of the World Commission on Environment and Development*.

Ministry of Environment (1992a), *Norges nasjonalrapport til FN-konferansen om miljø og utvikling*, Brasil 1992 (Norway's National Report to UNCED Brazil 1992), Oslo.

Ministry of Environment (1992b), *White Paper No. 13 on the UN Conference on Environment and Development, Rio de Janeiro (1992–1993)*.

Ministry of Environment (1994a), *Report Symposium: Sustainable Consumption*, 19–20 Jan. 1994, Oslo.

Ministry of the Environment (1994b), *Environmental Policy Statement Minister of Environment Thorbjørn Berntsen's Policy Statement to the Storting*, 11 April 1994.

Ministry of the Environment (1995), *Environmental Policy Statement (1994) Minister of Environment Torbjørn Berntsen's Policy Statement to the Storting*, 11 May 1995.

Ministry of Foreign Affairs (1988), *Miljø og Utvikling Norges bidrag til det internasjonale arbeid for en bærekraftig utvikling* (Environment and Development, Norway's Contribution to the International Work for Sustainable Development), *Aktuelle utenrikspolitiske spørsmål* – Nr. 45, Oslo.

Ministry of Foreign Affairs (1993), *Norway's Follow-Up to the United Nations Conference on Environment and Development, National Report to the UN Commission on Sustainable Development*, Oslo.

Ministry of Foreign Affairs (1995), *National Report of Norway to the United Nation's Commission on Sustainable Development*, Oslo.

Ministry of Foreign Affairs (1996), *National Report of Norway to the United Nations' Commission on Sustainable Development*, Oslo.

Næss, Arne (1991), 'Den dypøkologiske bevegelse: aktivisme ut fra et helhetssyn' (The Deep-Ecological Movement: Activism in an Overall View), in S. Gjerdåker, L. Gule, B. Hagtvet, *Tanke og handling i miljøkampen* (*The Insurmountable Boundary: Thought and Action in the Battle for the Environment*), Chr. Michelsens Forlag/J.W. Cappelens Forlag, pp.21–43.

The Nordic Business Environmental Barometer (1995), Bedrift-søkonomens forlag, Oslo.

NOU (1992), *Mot en mer kostnadseffektiv miljøpolitikk* (Towards a More Cost-efficient Environmental Policy), Oslo, Norges Offentlige utredninger/NOU 1992:3.

NOU (1995), *Virkemidler i miljøpolitikken* (Environmental Policy Instruments), Oslo: Norges Offentlige utredninger/NOU 1995:4.

OECD (1993), *OECD Environmental Performance Review Norway*, Paris.

Reitan, Marit (1995), 'New Nordic Member States and the Impact of EU Environmental Policy: The Deviant Case of Norway', paper prepared for presentation at the workshop 'New Nordic Member States and the Impact on EU Environmental Policy', Sandbjerg, 6–8 April.

Røhnebæk, Ørnulf (1995), *Miljø og Jus Oversikt over norsk miljørett med innføring i jus og forvaltningsrett* (Environment and Law – Overview of Norwegian Environmental Law with Introduction to Law and Administration Law), Universitetsforlaget, Oslo.

Skjærseth, Jon Birger and Kristin Rosendal (1995), 'Norges miljøutenrikspolitikk' (Norway's International Environmental Policy), in Torbjørn Knutsen, Gunnar Sørbø and Svein Gjerdåker (eds.), *i Norges Utenrikspolitikk* (Norwegian Foreign Policy), Christian Michelsens Institutt/J.W. Cappelens Forlag, pp.21–43.

Sydnes, A.K. (1996), 'Norwegian Climate Policy: Environmental Idealism and Economic Realism', in T. O'Riordan and J. Jäger (ed.), *Politics of Climate Change a European Perspective*, London: Routledge, pp.268–97.

The Norwegian Research Council (1996), *Report from the Consensus Conference on the Management of Biological Diversity in Norway*, Oslo, 23 May 1996.

World Commission on Environment and Development (1987), *Our Common Future*, Oxford: Oxford University Press.

Acronyms

A21	Agenda 21
CO₂	Carbon Dioxide
CSD	United Nations Commission on Sustainable Development
EEA	European Economic Area
EPLL	Environmental Protection at the Local Level
EU	European Union
LA21	Local Agenda 21
MoE	Ministry of the Environment
NGO	Non-Governmental Organisation

NOK	Norwegian Krone
NO$_x$	Nitrogen Oxides
OECD	Organisation for Economic Co-operation and Development
SO$_2$	Sulphur Dioxide
UN	United Nations
UNCED	United Nations Conference on Environment and Development

The Sustainability Transition in Germany: Some Early Stage Experiences

CHRISTIANE BEUERMANN and BERNHARD BURDICK

The issue or concept of 'sustainable development' entered onto the public and political agenda only relatively recently, and, five years after signing Agenda 21, perceptions of it are still ambiguous. A review of organisational adjustments and of German communications to the United Nations Commission on Sustainable Development shows that the German government's level of commitment to Agenda 21 is still low. This view is supported by an assessment of developments, and the Government's poor performance so far, in three institutional indicators. However, there is evidence that some incremental steps towards a sustainability transition are being taken as in some areas of business and industry and local government attitudes are begining to change. In addition, awareness of sustainable development is being raised by the efforts of non-governmental organisations and the scientific community. Generally though, the lack of institutional reorganisation is the major obstacle to a German sustainability transition. This is an expression of the generally low priority of environmental and global development issues in the aftermath of German unification and the related economic and social problems. The traditional economic paradigm where economic growth is believed to be the pre-condition for welfare prevails and is considered by a majority of decision-makers not to be compatible with the sustainability transition.

Compared to other countries, in Germany the concept of sustainable development was established late on in public discourse. It was also relatively late in arriving both on the political agenda and in scientific discussion. Presently it seems that, although ozone depletion was the major concern of the late 1980s and global climate change subsequently, the issue of sustainable development could acquire an overriding importance in the

The authors are with the Climate Policy Division of the Wuppertal Institute for Climate, Environment and Energy, Germany. they would like to acknowledge the fruitful discussions with the project team and, in particular, comments by Dr Jill Jager from the International Institute for Applied System Analysis (IIASA) on earlier drafts of this study. Responsibility, as always, remains with the authors.

second part of the 1990s. Owing to growing concern over the levels of unemployment and the economic recession 'the future' has recently started to dominate public debate. Discussions concerning Germany's industrial base and economic future are torn between the high hopes for the idea of sustainable development by the more ecologically and socially oriented parts of society, and the lack of imagination in, or even the fear of, following a sustainable development path evident in the conservative and economically oriented sectors.

This paper aims to provide an overview of the steps that have been taken so far to introduce and further the implementation of sustainable development in Germany. In doing so, first, a short description of how the issue of 'sustainability' is perceived is provided. Subsequently, the emergence of sustainability on the political and non-governmental organisation (NGO) agenda is reviewed. Given that in 1992, Germany signed Agenda 21 (A21), compliance with the resulting reporting obligations is taken here as a first indicator of how committed the federal government is to sustainable development. In the following section, the effectiveness of the German approach towards sustainability is evaluated on the basis of three groups of indicators, derived from *Agenda 21*: firstly, the increasing involvement of different actors in society in the preparation and implementation of sustainability, as well as the approaches taken by them; secondly, the development of public awareness building and the implementation of 'green' instruments, namely green accounting and eco-taxation; and finally, the implementation of A21 at the local level. From the observations made with respect to these, major impediments to the implementation of sustainable development in Germany are extracted. Finally, some conclusions and perspectives for its further development are drawn.

German Perceptions of Sustainability

The Use of the Term 'Sustainability'

Sustainability is not a new issue in Germany. Historically, the ideas underlying the concept of sustainability have origins in forestry management practices going back to the early Middle Ages. At the turn of the 19th century, these practices resulted in the concept of '*nachhaltige Forstwirtschaft*' (lasting forestry). The basic idea was over a certain period of time the amount of wood harvested and consumed must not exceed, but, at maximum, has to equal the regrowing capacity of that period. In the early 1980s, in response to general environmental discussions, the focus of public awareness on trans-boundary air pollution, and the related issue of '*Waldsterben*' (forest die-back), the concept of 'lasting forestry' was rediscovered. Because of this deep-rooted connection to forestry, from the mid-eighties until 1990 the term sustainability was associated with the issue of tropical deforestation and, hence, climate change. Sustainable forest management was controversially discussed as an option to protect tropical forests and, generally, to protect and improve sinks of greenhouse gas emissions. Moreover, at that early stage, discussions on sustainability were still connected to both questions of development and environmental policy.

Due to the high political priority of the issue of climate change in that period, several political and scientific institutions, such as the parliament's Enquete Commission[1] 'Protecting the Earth's Atmosphere' and the Scientific Advisory Council of the federal government on Global Change (WBGU), were established [*Beuermann and Jäger, 1996*]. In particular the intense discussions between experts and politicians in the Climate Enquete Commissions ensured that in every political party, regardless of their general interest in environmental issues, knowledge and expertise on the complexities of the issue of climate change was developed and made more generally available. Furthermore, the analysis of the scientific and socio-economic causes of the anthropogenic greenhouse effect made the connection with development problems (for example, increasing population) obvious [*Deutscher Bundestag, 1989b*]. Referring to these difficulties, the social democratic opposition partly demanded that the concept of sustainable development, as formulated by the Brundtland Commission, should be the basis of the relationship between the environment and the economy. In addition, sustainable development, however defined, should be taken as the main criterion to evaluate the effectiveness of federal development policy [*Deutscher Bundestag, 1989a*].

'Sustainability' in Official Documents (1986-1994)

To generate a first impression of how the issue of sustainable development was covered in political decision-making processes, official documents of the German Bundestag (parliament) and the German Bundesrat (representing the Länder) over the period 1986–94 were reviewed. The way that the term sustainability or sustainable development was used in these documents falls into several categories:

- *as a slogan:* throughout this period, the term was used constantly for general statements without further detailed explanation, and in connection with many different issues. For example: 'sustainable waste disposal system'; and 'sustainable reduction of pollution'.

- *in connection with tropical forests:* the sustainable management of tropical forests was discussed constantly in this period.

- *in connection with climate change:* in almost all of the documents dealing with climate change one finds at least some paragraphs on the necessity of implementing measures to initiate sustainable development. But there was seldom an explanation of what that really means, so, in a way, it was also used as a slogan. Because the issue of climate change played a dominant role in the political and public discussions at the end of the eighties and in the early nineties, the public perception of the United Nations Conference on Environment and Development (UNCED) process and the concept of sustainability was often confused with the climate issue.

- *treated as an issue in its own right:* the number of documents focusing solely on sustainable development have slowly been growing over time. Sustainable development is seen by the federal government as the ultimate goal of a fairer and more socially and environmentally concerned economic system. The most important characteristic of sustainable development was defined as the implementation of the precautionary principle in national and international policies [*Deutscher Bundestag, 1988b*].

Translations and Their Use in Public Debate

An interesting feature of the German sustainability discussion is that there is no common understanding of how it should be translated. Confusion about which translation should be used is not restricted to the use of the term sustainability by different actors, inconsistencies can also be found in different translations made by the same group of actors. For example, different words are used in German translations of legal texts of the European Union demonstrating different perceptions of what is meant by sustainability [*Haigh, 1996*]. Somehow, this situation reflects the openness of discussion on sustainable development and the lack of consensus in the interpretation of sustainability, with different elements of sustainability highlighted by the terms chosen. The following list of German translations is not exclusive. Some of the translations, such as '*tragfähig*' (tolerable; acceptable) and '*durchhaltbar*' (something can be kept through or hold out) have been used occasionally but are of minor importance in the discussion process and are not explained further.

Umweltverträglich: environmentally compatible (for example: the

Preamble of the Treaty on the European Economic Area). This is a very broad term describing the goal or principle of taking into account the general compatibility of measures, and decisions with protecting the environment. It is very similar to the term '*umweltgerecht*' which means environmentally sound.

Nachhaltig: lasting; to have a strong, deep effect or to deeply impress someone (for example: Rome Treaty Art. 130u). The Federal Environment Ministry (BMU) uses this translation in official documents, for example, in the German translation of A21. Though it has a positive connotation it is disputed by the German Council of Environmental Experts (SRU), as not having a strong public environmental interpretation and a perception of being 'insistent' and 'intensive' [*Thoenes, 1994: 46*].

Dauerhaft: durable; (long-)lasting (Maastricht Treaty Art. B). This word was consistently used in the German translation of the Brundtland Report [*Brundtland and Hauff, 1987*]. However, it is disputed for its emphasis on perpetuating the status-quo, which disregards the required reorientation of long-term policy strategies; in combination with economic terms (especially growth), it is likely to be interpreted as continuous growth. In addition, it has a nationalistic connotation as 'Sustainable Germany' translated as 'Dauerhaftes Deutschland' sounds like 'Germany forever' [*Loske, 1995*].

Beständig: continual, continuous; permanent; lasting, stable (Treaty of Rome Art.2 only). Both the translation and the context make it obvious that sustainable was interpreted in the traditional economic sense as continuous economic growth, as such it is in keeping with the German tradition of the 'magic square'.[2]

Zukunftsfähig: sustaining future opportunities/actions; developing future capacity. This has a very general meaning, and did not have an environmental or economic connotation prior to the sustainable development debate but expresses a positive and progressive feeling. It was invented in 1991 [*Simonis, 1991*] and used mostly in scientific discussions [*WBGU, 1993; BUND and Misereor, 1995*]. With the publication of the study *Zukunftsfähiges Deutschland* it became a slogan of the public debate on sustainable development, and has subsequently been applied to discussions about future issues.

Dauerhaft-umweltgerecht: durable and environmentally sound. The SRU used this translation in its Environmental Report 1994: *For a sustainable development*. The SRU argued, that in contrast to others, its translation makes the concept of sustainable development evident: starting from the widening of the time perspective (*dauerhaft*), the ecological conditions are of priority significance (*umweltgerecht*) under a dynamic concept (*Entwicklung*) [*Thoenes, 1994: 46*].

The three most commonly used German translations for sustainability (*dauerhaft, nachhaltig, zukunftsfähig*) are increasingly found in almost every context, for example, the advertisement campaigns of the chemical industries. The flexible translation of the term sustainable development promotes a broader discourse on the concept and enables all groups of society to clearly express their understanding of sustainability. This kind of publicity may push the issue to the top of the political agenda. At the same time, it appears that in many cases, the term sustainable development is used for green or social labeling or as a non-committal slogan [*Thoenes, 1996*]. In that sense, there is a danger of watering down the whole idea of sustainability to a commonplace in public discussion.

Searching for Evidence: The Sustainability Transition in Germany

Establishing Sustainable Development on the Political and NGO Agendas

Governmental response to sustainable development before UNCED: During the preparation for UNCED, sustainable development was discussed constantly but very vaguely by the federal government and in parliament. Just before the conference discussions intensified with the efforts made by the social democratic opposition to focus on the content of the concept, rather than the rhetoric. It was only in early 1992 in response to a parliamentary question that the federal government presented its interpretation of sustainable development as:

> a policy which harmonises the economic and social development of a nation with the preservation of the environment and of the natural resources and with respect to the interests of future generations. This implies the consequent development or rather the further development of a precautionary environment policy and the integration of environment protection in all areas of political action in industrialised and developing countries [*Deutscher Bundestag, 1992b*]

However, this was again a vague interpretation and the measures taken into account did not go beyond those being discussed in other environmental policy contexts.

As an important first step in the discussions on sustainable development, in February 1992, the Enquete Commission: 'Protection of Man and the Environment' was established.[3] The Commission justified its recommendations in its first interim report mostly with the results of earlier international studies, such as the Club of Rome's reports of 1972 and 1992, the report of the Brundtland Commission, and with the generally accepted connection between global environmental problems and production processes and consumption patterns [*Deutscher Bundestag, 1993*].

NGO response to sustainable development before UNCED: For a long time national and European environment and development policies, and also public awareness, were characterised by selective and regional environmental problems in the developed world or analogous regional social problems in the developing world. The first NGO initiative on the theme of sustainable development was the 'One World for All' project, initiated in 1989 by more than 30 NGOs (almost exclusively development NGOs). Its aim was to raise public awareness about sustainable development, by preparing information campaigns and working through the media [*Geschäftsstelle Eine Welt für alle, 1991*]. The environmental NGOs were relatively late in responding to this issue because they were more focused on local issues. The larger NGOs (BUND, DNR and WWF[4]) claim that they began to work internally on the issue of sustainable development in 1986/87, in preparation for, and in response to, the work of the Brundtland Commission. But until 1991 there were no public campaigns on the theme of sustainable development. The main obstacles to an earlier response were [*Unmüßig, 1995*]:

• insufficient teamwork and networking between environment and development NGOs within Germany, and at the international level;

• NGOs weak positions on the 'new themes';

• and, the lack of experience in actual political and media work, especially of the environmental NGOs.

As a result of this delayed response the NGOs missed their chance to work within the National Committee, which was founded in June 1991 by the government to prepare the national position for UNCED.

In June 1991, however, more than 20 NGOs[5] and various church organisations, founded 'Clearinghouse '92'. The main objective of which was to stimulate discussion on the environment and development between different social groups. Their work was not only aimed at UNCED but at the world economic summit in July 1992 in Munich. Mainly on the initiative of BUND and DNR a national NGO Secretariat, called 'UNCED '92', was founded in August 1991 to help prepare the NGO position for UNCED. The BMU together with BUND and DNR partly funded the NGO Secretariat which ceased its operations in September 1992. During the whole preparation process there was disagreement between the NGOs, weakening their influence and partly damaging their potential participation which they had demanded.

The Federal Governments' Reporting to the United Nations Commission on Sustainable Development (CSD)

Clearly, sustainability had not reached the status of an priority issue at the level of government or NGOs in Germany prior to UNCED. Nevertheless, the government signed A21 seeing it as the first international consensus on how sustainable development could be interpreted. Bearing the insufficient response prior to UNCED in mind, and given the non-legally binding character of A21, it could be assumed that the federal government was only marginally committed to the weak obligations of A21. To test whether this is the case, German communications to the CSD on the implementation of A21 in Germany are reviewed below.

What has been reported to the CSD and who prepared the reports? In August 1994 the federal government approved the report *Environment 1994 – German Strategy for Sustainable Development [BMU, 1994a]*. This report together with the National Report (in the form of a completed questionnaire) was submitted by the German federal government in December 1994 to the third session of the CSD, held in April 1995 in New York [*BMU/BMZ, 1994*]. The 1996 CSD Report also took the form of a completed questionnaire [*BMU/BMZ, 1995*]. The reports gives basic information on the sustainable development co-ordination mechanisms in Germany, the participation of major groups in the process, as well as the implementation of policies and measures as required in specific sectoral chapters of A21. Neither reports to the CSD have been translated into German or officially published in Germany, therefore they have attracted very little public attention.

The report *Environment 1994* is almost exclusively a description of the past and present (successes of) German environmental policy, and is not a strategy for implementing sustainability in the future. In fact in its progress report on the implementation of the EU's Fifth Environment Action Plan, the European Commission [*1995*] stated that Germany has no national sustainable development strategy at all. The CSD Reports were prepared both by the BMU and the Federal Ministry of Economic Co-operation and Development (BMZ). Both reports emerged through close co-ordination between the Chancellor and all federal Ministries. The BMU and BMZ are jointly in charge of the co-ordination of the Rio follow-up, particularly the implementation of A21. This procedure is not a new development resulting from the sustainability discussion, as inter-ministerial co-ordination is usual on cross-sectoral issues.

Commitment of the federal government to A21: The federal government explicitly declares its commitment to the concept of sustainable development in its official documents for UNCED and CSD [*BMU, 1994b*]. Moreover, there is a consensus among the political parties, the confederation of German Trade Unions and numerous industrial federations in acknowledging the importance of the concept. In the government's opinion, the report *Environment 1994* contains Germany's environmental action strategy, as shaped by the decisions of UNCED and the European Union's Fifth Environmental Action Programme [*BMU/BMZ, 1994*]. In fact, the federal government holds the opinion that German environment and development policy is based on the principle of precaution, implemented in the first environment program in 1971, and is already now to a large extent identical with the aims and demands of the A21 [*BMU/BMZ, 1994; BMU, 1994a*]. Moreover, there is a belief that Germany's good example leads international efforts and has done since the early 1970s. In addition, the official conviction is that a re-orientation of German environment policy is not necessary at present. Therefore, the general commitment to A21 in terms of any re-orientation of policy and practice can be assessed as low.

The basis for the federal government's judgement that it has made a good start towards sustainability are the successes achieved by past environment policies, for example in water conservation and air quality control [*Wessel, 1995*]. However, these successes are judged to be a product of a reactive rather than a precautionary environment policy. Moreover, it is suggested that there is a general lack of implementation concerning precautionary environment policy in Germany [*Weidner, 1995*]. The SRU considers the government's confidence to be nothing more than rhetoric because only a few people or groups work on strategies to implement A21 [*Thoenes, 1996*].

The BMU's low level of interest appears to be partly linked to the departure of the former environment minister, Prof. Klaus Töpfer,[6] at the end of 1994. This led to a weakening of environmental policy, particularly in the areas of internationally oriented climate protection and sustainability policies. In the reorganisation of ministries Töpfer was moved to the Federal Ministry for Regional Planning, Building and Urban Development (BMBau), where he is again taking up the progressive environmental policy which he developed in his previous ministry and as former CSD chairman. It seems that in his new area of responsibility he will better be able to put his ideas into practice (for example, thermal insulation, solar energy use), and this has resulted in a growing interest in sustainable development in BMBau. The German Report to the United Nations Habitat II conference in Istanbul in June 1996 was characterised by a constant reflection on the implications of sustainable development for urban development [*BMBau, 1996; Töpfer, 1996*]. Other Ministries widely ignore and neglect the concept of sustainable development and A21. This illustrates that progress on sustainable development strategies initially depends on the personal engagement of innovative politicians and other actors.

The German Parliament's Enquete Commission: 'Protection of Man and the Environment', which was dissolved as planned at the end of the legislative period in 1994, was reinstated in 1995. It was given a mandate to work out goals for and approaches to the operationalisation of sustainable development by the end of the legislative period 1994–98 [*Deutscher Bundestag, 1995*]. In so doing, the Commission was given the task of developing a national (ecological) action plan.

Effectiveness: Developments Pointing the Way for the Sustainability Transition?

From the above observations it can be concluded that Germany's sustainability transition is only in its initial phase, if at all. The response and commitment of the government are some of the most important but not the only indicators of a move by society towards sustainability. In order to investigate the opportunities for, and trends in, implementing A21 in Germany, the response of different groups of actors towards A21 and their involvement in the process is described below. In a second step, the adaptation of economic and social institutions to sustainability is reviewed briefly.

Major Groups Influencing the Sustainability Transition

NGOs: Being partially funded by the federal government prior to UNCED, the NGOs almost failed to assure the continuation of that funding afterwards through administrative error. Due to power conflicts between the different NGOs an application for further funding was not filed. As a result, the NGO-secretariat was dissolved. In December 1992, however, DNR applied for and received funding becoming the sole co-ordinator of a new NGO Forum for Environment and Development [*Bleischwitz, 1995*]. This Forum brings together some 60 individual environment and development associations and NGO networks with more than 100 member associations. It operates through working groups and will probably be funded until 1997. A Steering Committee has been established for the Forum, consisting of representatives from each of the environment and development NGOs and women's and youth organisations. It defines the tasks of the Forum, and voices the positions and demands of the Forum to the government and the public. It has been suggested that the ministerial pressure to ensure effective working procedures which initiated the Steering Committee is an indication of the interest of BMU and BMZ in a qualified and co-ordinated input from the NGOs to back up their own position in inter-ministerial bargaining [*Unmüßig, 1995*].

In addition to the structures described above, BMU and BMZ funded[7] a new NGO secretariat which: distributes position papers drafted by the Forum members or its working groups; maintains contacts with organisations in developing countries; works with international organisations and networks on joint activities; and monitors the international Rio follow-up. One of its main tasks is public and press relations to inform the German public on the link between the environment and development. After initial mistrust and minor quarrels, the secretariat has worked quite well for almost four years now, and has established a network of contacts in relevant parts of the governmental machinery.

In preparation for the CSD sessions, the NGO Forum has organised different conferences, meetings, and discussions between NGO representatives and ministries to draw up positions on relevant sectoral issues. The results and working group statements and demands were published at the national and international level. Though the work of the Forum is quite successful it is still weakened by insufficient co-ordination between the environment and development NGOs and between the different working groups. Another weakness is that the Forum is mainly supported by the 'subordinate level' of the big NGOs and by numerous small NGOs that use the Forum for public relations. It is still necessary to improve awareness about the need for a follow-up to Rio at the higher management level of many big NGOs [*Unmüßig, 1995*].

Beyond simple funding, co-operation between the federal government and NGOs on the issue of sustainability takes place in two bodies, the Forum, and the National Committee for Sustainable Development (formerly National Preparatory Committee for the UNCED) [*BMU/BMZ, 1994*]. The Forum is the main point of contact with NGOs for the federal government, who funds NGO participation in the CSD through this body. Moreover, a number of the Forum's working group representatives are widely recognised for their competence and now advise BMU officials in preparing for and during CSD sessions. However, contacts between the federal government and NGO representatives during preparation for CSD sessions are judged by some to be no more than lip service as it appears to have accepted few of their demands or recommendations. For the first time in 1996, the Environment Minister, Mrs. Merkel, invited five representatives from major stakeholder groups to the CSD session [*BMU, 1996*].

As part of the national preparations for UNCED a National Committee was set up in June 1991. It comprised a total of 35 representatives from environment policy and development policy organisations, science and research, industry and commerce, trade unions, churches, agriculture, women and youth organisations, Länder and local governments, the German parliament and the political parties. This National Committee is to continue its advisory work until the Special General Assembly of the United Nations in 1997. Meetings take place two or three times a year, chaired by the Environment Minister. Until now its has mainly worked on the international follow-up to UNCED. At the meeting in February 1996 the Environment Minister suggested that they should focus more on the national implementation of sustainable development in the future. In preparation for the General Assembly in 1997, Mrs Merkel declared herself to be against concrete decisions or resolutions on single issues and proposed that the National Committee should work out a common declaration on sustainable development [*BMU, 1996*].

Business and industry: Parts of business and industry 'discovered' environmental protection quite some time ago. Ecology as a marketing strategy is used for advertising and public relations. Sustainability grows in importance, and meanwhile, in some cases, appears as a motive for enterprise policy or even as an advertising slogan. The development of new instruments (product liability and Eco-Auditing) is closely watched and questions of norms and standardisation have gained strategic importance [*Leitschuh-Fecht and Burmeister, 1994*]. The aim is that the environmental compatibility of production and products is to be clear to customers, thus becoming criteria for the decision to buy, as the experience of the 'blue environment angel' label introduced in the 1970s showed.

Though representing only a small section of business and industry, the more interesting developments or starting points with regard to a re-orientation towards sustainability are the forming of new coalitions between the interests of the environment and the economy, for example: the 'strategic alliance' between BUND and 16 firms [*Wuppertal Bulletin, 1995; BUND, 1995*]; and the common declaration of BUND and the Federation of Young Entrepreneurs8. Both coalitions mentioned above have formed in order to promote the introduction of ecological tax reform [*Leitschuh-Fecht and Burmeister, 1994; BJU/BUND, 1993; Beuermann and Jäger, 1996*]. Another example of a new NGO/business coalition is the 'European Business Council for Sustainable Energy Futures', corresponding to the 'Business Council for Sustainable Development'. It was founded in February 1996 in Brussels, mainly on the initiative of the German Development NGO *Germanwatch*. Meanwhile more than 30 German and European enterprises and numerous associations have joined this Business Council. However, the number of businesses and industries participating in these coalitions is still very small.

Beyond these concerted activities, a growing number of individual business activities have taken place. For example: big automobile producers have developed concepts for mobility services; several big car rental firms offer car-sharing; and, a producer of household goods, AEG, uses only three kinds of plastic to augment its recycling quota, and the consumption of energy and water by household machines has been reduced drastically.

All these examples are part of trends towards a growing sense of agreement between the ecological movement and, at present, small parts of the economy. However, such an agreement is rejected by the influential big and more conservative lobbies of industry and business. These ignore the establishment of new coalitions and still claim to speak 'with one voice' for the whole industrial sector. The federal government is not seen to be moderating the industy/political dialogue, as a result, a growing number of more progressive industrialists and managers are waiting vainly for clear, and above all, long-term compulsory boundary conditions such as ecological tax reform [*Leitschuh-Fecht and Burmeister, 1994*].

The scientific community: Numerous research activities on the subject of sustainability exist. All too often they deal only with minor and detailed problems, and are thus only acknowledged by experts. A systematic review of research activities on sustainable development is carried out in the advisory councils and the Enquete Commissions in order to filter and focus research results and to develop policy relevant recommendations. In the Enquete Commissions, literature reviews are accompanied by, sometimes public, hearings on specific issues. Therefore, except for the studies *Sustainable Europe* and *Sustainable Germany* (see below), these institutions have so far compiled the most comprehensive and policy relevant documentation on the operationalisation and implementation of the concept of sustainability in Germany.

When it started its work, the Enquete-Commission: 'Protection of Man and the Environment' was not explicitly working on the issue of sustainable development. Concerning itself first with the ecological effects of material flows, the Commission then extended its perspective to social and economic dimensions. At this point the topic of 'sustainable development' entered the discussion and indeed became the theme of the Commission's work. Although an agreement was reached on a theoretical and abstract level, rather than working out binding measures and aims, the Commission has contributed important work on the necessary compromise for a common interpretation of sustainable development across party lines, based on the equal representation of different parties in the Commission [*Thoenes, 1996*]. Other governmental advisory groups, like the WBGU and the SRU, have dealt with sustainable development since 1993 and published different studies on the issue. The WBGU is mainly working on indicators for sustainability, while the SRU is working on environmental quality targets and the institutional implications of sustainable development.

In April 1992 Milieudefensie (Friends of the Earth Netherlands) published the study *Nederlands Duursam* (Sustainable Netherlands) [*Buitenkamp et al., 1993*]. This study was the starting point of an intense public discussion on how to implement sustainability. As a reaction to this the European Commission commissioned Friends of the Earth Europe, together with Milieudefensie, to carry out a series of studies in all European countries. At the moment, in more than 30 European countries studies are being, or have been, carried out [*Spangenberg, 1995a; 1995b*]. Partly as a reaction to these studies the governments of Austria and the Netherlands have worked out National (Environmental) Action Plans [*Österreichische Bundesregierung, 1995; Government of the Netherlands, 1989/1993*]. Although these plans explicitly emphasise the concept of sustainable development, the title and contents of these programmes concentrate on environmental protection and do not cover aspects of social and economic development. The German case-study for the Sustainable Europe project was carried out by the Wuppertal Institute on behalf of BUND and the catholic church organisation Misereor. The study is entitled *Zukunftsfähiges Deutschland*, and was published in October 1995 and has since gained much political and public interest [*BUND and Misereor, 1995*]. The Federal Environmental Agency is also working on a study of sustainable Germany, prompted by the interest of several committed individuals. As mentioned above, different governmental advisory bodies, scientific institutes (for example, Fraunhofer Gesellschaft-Institut für Systemanalyse und Innovationsforschung) and universities, are conducting studies on the issue of sustainable development.

Social and Economic Indicators of the Sustainability Transition

Attempting to measure the effectiveness of the German sustainability transition means assessing whether the process is permanent, reliable and irreversible. In doing so it is necessary to analyse whether existing institutional arrangements based on the traditional economic growth model are evolving as part of the transition. Three social or economic indicator institutions will be reviewed: education and public awareness, ecological taxes, and green accounting.

Education and public awareness raising: The Federal Ministry for Education, Science, Research and Technology supports research projects, model experiments and conferences, often in co-operation with NGOs. In Germany the responsibility for education lies mainly at the state level in the hands of the Länder Ministries for Education. The curricula for the different school levels (including universities) are still being revised to include the cross-cutting issues of sustainable development. Teaching materials and new school books are being developed. The environment, in general, is perceived by the government to have become an integrated part of school education. Furthermore, there is some government funding of education programs, such as BMZ and the Education, Science, Research and Technology Ministry support NGOs' school and non-school projects and adult education programmes. Most activities deal with climate change, but there are also some on sustainable development.

With regard to public awareness of sustainability, it and the topic 'future' have gained increasing importance during the last two years, an illustration of which is the enormous public interest generated by the study *Zukunftsfähiges Deutschland*. At the launch of the study, there was a panel discussion with different high-ranking representatives from the sectors of politics, the economy, and the trade unions. Also the media gave the study and the issues of sustainability a very high profile. Since the publication, the authors of the study have been asked to give lectures or to participate in panel discussions, particularly in several German Länder ministries. The Enquete-Commission arranged a hearing, and in parliament the ecological party Bündnis 90/Die Grünen made a minor interjection on the influence of the study for the work of the federal government. Furthermore there were numerous talks, discussions, and scientific congresses with interested industry federations, with the DGB, the Carl-Duisberg-Society, and NGOs. More than 13,000 copies of the study have been sold since January 1996. Several follow-up research projects are planned, for example, on the themes 'globality and locality'. Moreover industry has taken part in and observes this public discussion intensively, as well as critically [*Loske, 1995*].

Eco-Taxes: In its several reports the BMU states that the sustainability transition in Germany is occurring because of an early commitment to a precautionary environmental policy. These statements are marked and influenced by the recent intensive public debate on shrinking locational disadvantages and the necessity of de-regulation. Therefore, instead of introducing new rules, taxes and decrees, policy seems to be confined to voluntary self-regulation and actions by industry and households. In the opinion of BMU officials the first steps towards ecological tax reform are well under way but this refers only to the noticeable increase in public fees for waste disposal and wastewater management [*Wessel, 1995*]. In its 1996 CSD Report the German government stated:

> Since 1992 no environmental taxes/levies/charges have been introduced in Germany. In Germany taxes and charges with an

environmental component are already levied (for example waste-water charges; petroleum excise duty differentiated by unleaded and leaded gasoline; emission-oriented motor vehicles tax). These are taxes in which the environmental aspect is one of several important aspects ... It is not possible to supply any isolated information about the proportion of revenue from these taxes and levies that is due to the environmental component [*BMU/BMZ, 1995*].

In scientific and environmental circles and small parts of the business community, taxes on the consumption of resources have been intensively discussed for years with varying momentum. Starting from discussions on the introduction of eco-taxes (most prominent were taxes on energy consumption and carbon dioxide emissions) not linked to a reduction of other taxes, the focus is now on the comprehensive re-structuring of parts of the tax system. In so doing, the social and environmental agendas have been linked [*Weizsäcker, 1992; Görres et al., 1994*], ecological tax reform can easily be interpreted and be sold as a 'labour tax reform'. This idea appeals to many across party, or other interest, lines but not to the federal government. At the moment, there is almost no political momentum for ecological tax reform as the opinion prevails that environmental protection and economic development are not compatible. Due to the severe problems Germany is faced with (for example: recession, higher public expenditure related to unification, and unemployment), priority is currently given to the traditional perception of economic growth as the motor for increasing or even maintaining welfare. There seems to be no confidence in the findings of studies on the double dividend of an ecological tax reform in terms of additional jobs in combination with environmental protection [*Greenpeace, 1994; Ostertag and Schlegelmilch, 1996*].

Green accounting: In Germany, there is no long tradition of green accounting. Discussion about it began with a research project on the costs of environmental pollution by the BMU in 1986 [*Hamilton et al., 1994*]. In 1989, the German Bundestag held expert hearings on questions related to economic growth as one of the primary goals and conditions respectively of development. Given that in the existing accounting system (which measures economic indicators), environmental costs are not internalised, this is seen to be a distorted indicator of welfare. Subsequently, the debate was extended to ecologically adjusted indicators and the sustainability of economic growth. There was a consensus on the need to develop an environmental accounting system as a supplement to the existing accounting system, a so-called satellite system.

As a result the Federal Statistical Office proposed a new system called 'Environment-Economic Comprehensive Accounting', established in 1990.

Also created was a Scientific Advisory Council consisting of economists to advise both the BMU and the Federal Statistical Office on methodological issues. However, the original impetus of that programme has disappeared as '… of March 1993, all budgets are under review as the federal government comes to terms with the re-unification in Germany' [*Hamilton et al., 1994*].

Moreover, it has been suggested that the accounting programme was not planned to support the sustainability discussion but was politically driven [*Hamilton et al., 1994*]. As the discussion of environmental accounting systems in Germany is of a theoretical nature and given the short period of both discussion and research, it is not surprising that applications are prospective. Therefore, it ' … will require many more years before a consensus on its concepts and methods can be reached' [*Serageldin and Steer, 1993*].

A quicker and more feasible method of valuing environmental impacts might be the use of labels for products, production processes or businesses. The latter method has been recently applied through the implementation of the European Commission's eco-auditing directive 1863/93 which came into force in April 1995. In the early implementation phase, the majority of German businesses did not realise the need for, and opportunities of, integrated environmental protection. When discussing the directive both the BMZ and the traditional German industrial associations argued that eco-audits would impose new additional obligations and administrative burdens on industry [*Entsorga, 1994: 152*]. This lobbying weakened the directive [*Friebel, 1994: 27*]. However, in the meantime the negative attitude changed into one of indifference or even enthusiasm. This is explained by the general acceptance of facts and the attempts to influence the implementation of the directive actively.[9] Another reason is possibly the growing relevance of 'environmental friendliness' considerations in consumer decisions. At present, the number of enterprises using this instrument is steadily growing.

Local Agenda 21(LA21)[10]: Being identified as the level closest to many of A21's stakeholders, LA21 is expected to be a decisive step in the sustainability transition. From preliminary observations it can be concluded that the implementation of A21 at the local level four years after UNCED is still a low priority issue in Germany. Exact data is not available, but it is assumed that less than 0.5 per cent of the 16121 German municipalities have initiated an LA21 process.

Given the constitutionally guaranteed municipal competencies (right of autonomy), in combination with more than 25 years of local environmental policy activity and a strong environmental awareness in the population, one would expect that LA21 would have attracted more interest and response by local actors. Comparatively successful attempts at reducing pollution, in particular at the local level, should have been good pre-conditions to broadening municipal activities. However, the margin for the development of individual local policies has been shrinking in recent years due to worsening municipal finances, an increase in compulsory tasks, and a general tendency to weaken local government. As shown from the establishment of German environmental policy in the early 1970s, there is no built-in procedure in local decision-making processes to adopt new issues automatically. Only subsequent to the emerging strong environmental consciousness of the public, or more precisely citizens, did local government demonstrate its ability to integrate new issues flexibly. Apart from in a minority of municipalities, a sufficient integration of environmental concerns into day-to-day politics has not taken place. Municipal environment policy today is still dominated by reactive measures.

There are two main obstacles to LA21 in Germany. For many local authorities LA21 is only a new term for activities they have already been doing for years. They have developed structures and procedures for local environmental policies and do not perceive there to be a need to apply a new. Others need more information on what to do when initiating and developing an LA21. Co-ordination and support has so far been provided inadequately by existing municipal associations or institutions at the federal level. The few existing LA21 processes are the result of personal commitment and enthusiasm in local authorities, or that of other interested persons, who have recognised the potential of LA21. In initiating and developing their LA21s, success depended to a large extent on new coalitions formed at different levels between:

- interested individuals in the respective municipality – forming a network to establish LA21 on the political agenda;

- interested individuals within local government across departmental borders – forming networks to promote organisational commitment to LA21 and integration across policy sectors;

- different local actor groups – to further acceptance and to establish structures for participation;

- and municipalities developing LA21s – to exchange information, via membership in 'umbrella' networks, to lobby more effectively, but also to increase and secure motivation through creative competition.

These coalitions have so far been effective as in a number of local governments, formal decisions have been made to develop and implement

LA21s. Most of these municipalities have established institutions for participation in accordance with the bottom-up nature of LA21. Furthermore, these participation structures have been shown to work by initiating an LA21 process, and focusing local public attention on the issue of LA21. As none of the municipalities have finished developing an LA21 (there are no documented strategies) so far, it is an open question how effective these coalitions will be in the LA21 implementation phase. From these observations, it is concluded that the German LA21 process is still underdeveloped, but recently there has been promising movement.

Obstacles for the Implementation of Sustainability and Agenda 21 in Germany

Having started slowly, and later, than other countries, at present, sustainable development enjoys rhetorically a wide acceptance and consensus. However the previous observations show that not many concrete steps have been taken towards implementing sustainable development. The reason is that consensus has been achieved only on an abstract level. The interpretations and motives of the different individuals and groups of actors often block or exclude each other [*Steger, 1995*]. There is a lack of political will and pressure for the operationalisation and realisation of sustainable development. The majority of the representatives of government, industry and business fear far-reaching consequences, such as the end to the paradigm of continuous economic growth. The following sections describe some obstacles and different arguments emerging from the above discussion that presently hinder implementation.

Political Obstacles

The main political obstacle to the implementation of sustainability is that the traditional political priorities have not changed. The federal government believes that German environment and development policy is quite successful, exemplary even in an international comparison. Moreover, the federal government is convinced that its environment policy is by now to a large extent identical with the aims and demands of the A21, particularly through the implementation of the principle of precaution in its environmental policy of 1971 [*Wessel, 1995*]. These successes have reduced considerably the social and political pressure for further change [*Steger, 1995*].

Consequently, UNCED and A21 were not used as an opportunity for a re-orientation of German environment or development policy, and there is no further strategy to implement A21. The concept of sustainable development is mostly ignored or interpreted in a curious manner, thus, for example, the Federal Ministry of Food, Agriculture and Forestry holds the view that agriculture in Germany has been sustainable for a long time. The SRU came to the conclusion that the concept of sustainability has not yet become a leading motive in the political practice of the federal government. It is still predominantly understood as a theme only relevant for ecological or development politics. This was demonstrated in the coalition agreements after the federal election of 1994. For the federal states it is also true that ecological questions are not sufficiently associated with economic and social questions [*Thoenes, 1996*].

Organisational Obstacles

Government commitment to A21 did not result in the adjustment of institutional or more precisely organisational infrastructure at the federal level. Neither in the government nor in the Ministries are there competent organisational units which are explicitly responsible for the co-ordination and realisation of sustainable development and of A21/LA21, except the departments that are responsible for the international environment or development policy at the CSD level. Conceptual work at the national or regional level is mostly done by individual idealistic politicians and NGOs. Except for the National Committee on Sustainability there have been no new discussion fora or round-tables established at the national level to reflect the strong participatory elements of A21.

Ideological Obstacles

The fundamental conviction that economy and ecology exclude each other is still dominant and forms a massive barrier for the implementation of sustainability. While NGOs developed numerous initiatives and concepts, the large majority of business and industries offer little more than platitudes. If they speak at all, it is about improved energy and resource efficiency, which is to be achieved by technical innovations and entrepreneurial freedom rather than by state regulations or ecological taxes. Furthermore, it is claimed that customers are not prepared to pay higher prices for ecological products. It becomes obvious from this picture that not many economic interests are concerned about social-political dimensions. At best they are concerned with the reduction of emissions, but not about the necessary change in lifestyle and the future of society [*Steger, 1995*].

The federal government's Statements are still influenced by the paradigm of stable and sustained economic growth. Environmental policy is just another factor influencing the locational advantage of the industrial base. The influence of environmental policy ends when a negative impact on economy and industry is feared. In the opinion of the government the concept of sustainability needs no fundamental change of social, political or economic paradigms. Discussion on environmental policy was almost completely edged out by the recent economic recession, the financial burden after re-unification, and fear about the shrinking locational advantages of German industries. In the last elections to the Bundestag (October 1994) environmental policy hardly played a role at all.

Instrumental Obstacles

Strategic decisions on the implementation of instruments, as recommended by the various expert councils, politicians and researchers have still not been made. In its national strategy and also in its report *Environment 1994* the federal government favours voluntary 'self-commitments' as the primary means of establishing sustainable consumption and production patterns. Appealing to industry and households is quite important but it is the responsibility of the government to establish a structural framework for the sustainable development of society. On the other hand, the government has made every effort to appeal to private households to adopt environmentally sound patterns of behaviour if only as compensation for its own political shortcomings. The above-mentioned prevailing economic growth paradigm, is one of the main obstacles to the implementation of ecological tax reform or other ecologically oriented instrumental boundary conditions at the federal level [*Forum Umwelt und Entwicklung, 1995*].

Behavioural Obstacles

The implementation of sustainability will depend to a large extent on the behaviour of individuals. Public awareness of environmental issues is generally good and there are several initiatives to expand awareness of the sustainability process. As the public perception of studies like *Sustainable Germany* shows, there is a growing interest in, and discomfort with, the traditional development models. This is reflected in the rapidly expanding public debate about 'the future'. However, there exists a considerable discrepancy between knowledge and action. According to opinion polls consciousness about environmental problems and the necessary consequences for one's own actions are often unrelated.

Conclusions and Perspectives

The previous observations show that the German response to the sustainability discussion began late when compared to other countries. At the moment, sustainability attracts growing public interest, furthered by an atmosphere of general uncertainty concerning future economic and social developments in Germany. If this public interest in the issue is a stable and continuous phenomenon it might be followed by a significant political re-orientation, becoming the fourth global environment priority at the federal level after forest die-back, ozone depletion and climate change. However, this is speculative, since sustainability has not achieved real political significance. Because of its non-legally binding character, the influence of A21, as the internationally agreed interpretation of the sustainability concept, on domestic strategic policy-making, is presently no more than rhetoric.

Because of its strong participatory elements, the interest of NGOs in A21 is strong. NGOs have from an early stage focused on it as its application would theoretically increase their influence. But as long as participation is not secured beyond funding fora for a limited time, their influence remains limited to the level also achieved with regard to other environmental issues, such as the issue of climate change. Industry's response is primarily as a power of veto over the implementation of A21 as it is still driven by traditional economic paradigms. Only a small number of businesses, which are usually also sensitive to other environmental issues, are engaged in promoting the implementation of A21. With regard to these businesses and industries, the forming of new environment and economy interest coalitions is an important step towards the sustainability transition. However, from the analysis of the existing obstacles to the implementation of A21 we conclude that the prospects for an advanced top-down sustainabilty policy are not promising at present. Increasing recent public interest in the issue, its link to other publicly discussed social issues, such as unemployment, imply that a significant impetus for future action may result from grassroots activities in a bottom-up process. At the moment, activities at the local and regional level are expected to have a stronger momentum than at the federal level.

NOTES

1. An Enquete Commission is an advisory body to the federal government. One half of the members are politicians, the other are scientists appointed by the parties represented in parliament. Enquete Commissions are established to give policy advice on complex political issues.
2. This was defined in the law on stability and growth in 1967 (Stabilitäts- und Wachstumsgesetz). According to this law, stable price levels, a high employment rate, balanced foreign trade and a 'continuous and appropriate economic growth' (stetiges und angemessenes wirtschaftliches Wachstum) are goals of German economic and fiscal policy.
3. It had the following mandate [Deutscher Bundestag. 1992a]: describe the most important problems of industrial material flows, including their historical development and work out possible strategies to solve these problems; develop scientifically reasonable criteria for the valuation of eco-balances on which a consensus might be reached among all groups of society; describe alternative scenarios for the extraction, processing and disposal of materials taking into account technical, economic, ecological and social parameters; support consensus

building processes by intensifying dialogues in the chemical and industrial political arenas; and, give recommendations for political action to the German Bundestag.
4. Bund für Umwelt- und Naturschutz Deutschland (BUND, German section for Friends of the Earth); Deutscher Naturschutzring (DNR, Umbrella of German environmental organisations); WorldWide Fund for Nature (WWF).
5. Among them were: DNR, BUND, Deutscher Gewerkschaftsbund (German Trade Union Federation); Bundeskongress Agrarkoordination; and World Economy, Ecology and Development.
6. Minister Töpfer was responsibile for the strong positions and political leadership of Germany in climate change politics in the end of the 1980s and the early 1990s.
7. Moreover, the federal government supports activities of international NGOs and NGO-networks like: the Centre for Our Common Future, the International Institute for Environment and Development, and the European Environmental Bureau. As part of its development co-operation the federal government increased the funds for assistance to international NGOs since 1993 by about DM 5 million a year.
8. Bundersverband Junger Unternehmer.
9. Apart from consideration of the traditional industry associations, above all the traditional auditors expect new economic impulses as a result of the directive because a new job-profile was created (see Förschle [*1994*]).
10. A more detailed analysis of the response of German local governments to A21 is subject to another study prepared for the European Commission DG XII of which this section has been taken [*Beuermann, 1996; Voisey et al., 1996*].

REFERENCES

Beuermann, Christiane (1996), 'Local Agenda 21 in Germany', unpublished.
Beuermann, Christiane and Jill Jäger (1996), 'Climate Change Politics in Germany: How Long Will Any Double Dividend Last?', in Timothy O'Riordan and Jill Jäger (eds.), *Politics of Climate Change*, London: Routledge, pp. 186-227.
BJU/BUND (eds.) (1993), *Gemeinsames Statement von BJU und BUND: Plädoyer für eine ökologisch orientierte soziale Marktwirtschaft.*
Bleischwitz, Raimund (1995), personal communication.
BMBau (ed.) (1996), *Siedlungsentwicklung und Siedlungspolitik. Nationalbericht Deutschland (Habitat II)*, Bonn: BMBau.
BMU (ed.) (1994a), *Environment 1994. German Strategy for Sustainable Development – Summary*, Bonn: BMU.
BMU (ed.) (1994b), *Umwelt 1994 – Politik für eine nachhaltige, umweltgerechte Entwicklung.* Bundestagsdrucksache 12/8451, Bonn: BMU.
BMU (ed.) (1996), 'Protokoll der Sitzung des nationalen Komitees für nachhaltige Entwicklung am 7. Februar 1996', unpublished.
BMU/ BMZ (eds.) (1994), 'German Report to the 3rd CSD-Session 1995', Bonn, unpublished.
BMU/BMZ (eds.) (1995), 'CSD 96 Guidelines for National Information, Part 1: Cross Sectoral Issues', Bonn, unpublished.
Buitenkamp, Maria; Henk Venner and Teo Wams (eds.) (1993), *Action Plan Sustainable Netherlands*, Amsterdam: Vereiniging Milieudefensie.
BUND (ed.) (1995), *Ökologische Steuerreform. Ein Beitrag zu einem Zukunftsfähigen Deutschland*, Bonn: BUND.
BUND and Misereor (eds.) (1995), *Zukunftsfähiges Deutschland. Ein Beitrag zu einer Global Nachhaltigen Entwicklung*, Basel, Boston, Berlin: Birkhäuser.
Brundtland, G. and V. Hauff (1987), *Unsere Gemeinsame Zukunft: Der Brundtland-Bericht der Weltkommission für Umwelt und Entwicklung*, Greven: Eggenkamp.
Deutscher Bundestag (ed.) (1988b), *Bundestags-Drucksache 11/3740, Erhaltung der Tropischen Regenwälder zum Schutz der Einheimischen Bevölkerung, des Klimas und der Genetischen Vielfalt durch Entwicklungspolitische Maßnahmen*, Bonn: Deutscher Bundestag.
Deutscher Bundestag (ed.) (1989a), *Bundestags-Drucksache 11/4863, Erfolgskontrolle in der*

Entwicklungspolitik, Bonn: Deutscher Bundestag.

Deutscher Bundestag (ed.) (1989b), *Bundestags-Drucksache 11/5175, Kritik am 7. Entwicklungs-politischen Bericht der Bundesregierung*, Bonn: Deutscher Bundestag.

Deutscher Bundestag (ed.) (1992a), *Bundestags-Drucksache 12/1951*, Bonn: Deutscher Bundestag.

Deutscher Bundestag (ed.) (1992b), *Bundestags-Drucksache 12/2286, Umwelt und Entwicklung. Politik für eine Nachhaltige Entwicklung*, Bonn: Deutscher Bundestag.

Deutscher Bundestag (ed.) (1993), *Verantwortung für die Zukunft*, Bericht der Enquete Kommission 'Schutz des Menschen und der Umwelt', Bonn: Economica.

Deutscher Bundestag (ed.) (1995), *Bundestags-Drucksache 13/1533 Antrag auf Einsetzung einer Enquete-Kommission: Schutz des Menschen und der Umwelt – Ziele und Rahmenbedingungen einer Nachhaltig Zukunftsverträglichen Entwicklung*, Bonn: Deutscher Bundestag.

Entsorga (ed.) (1994), 'Vorsorgender Denkansatz. Öko-Audits im Unternehmen gewinnen an Bedeutung', *Entsorga*, Vol.13, No.5, pp.146–56.

European Commission (1995), *Progress Report on Implementation of the European Community Programme of Policy and Action in Relation to the Environment and Sustainable Development 'Towards Sustainability'. Draft, 1 August 1995*, Brussels: European Commission.

Förschle, G. (1994), 'Umwelt-Audit als Betätigungsfeld für Wirtschaftsprüfer', *Wirtschafts-prüferkammer Mitteilungen*, Vol.33, No.1, pp.1–8.

Forum Umwelt und Entwicklung (1995), *Drei Jahre nach Rio*, Bonn: Forum Umwelt und Entwicklung.

Friebel, Matthias (1994), 'Weg von den Insabiloesungen', *Politische Ökologie*, Vol. 36, No.3/4, pp.26–29.

Geschäftsstelle Eine Welt für Alle (ed.) (1991), *Plattform*, Köln: Eine Welt für alle.

Görres, Anselm, Ehringhaus, Henner and Ernst U. v. Weizsäcker (1994), *Der Weg zur Ökologischen Steuerreform. Weniger Umweltbelastung und mehr Beschäftigung. Das Memorandum des Fördervereins Ökologische Steuerreform*, München: Olzog.

Government of the Netherlands (1989/1993), *National Environmental Policy Plan 1 (1989) and 2 (1993)*.

Greenpeace (ed.) (1994), *Ökosteuer – Königsweg oder Sackgasse?* Berlin: Greenpeace.

Haigh Nigel (1996), '"Sustainable" Development in the European Union Treaties', *International Environmental Affairs*, Vol.8, No.1, pp.87–91.

Hamilton, K., Pearce, D., Atkinson, G., Gomez-Lobo, A. and C. Young (1994), *The Policy Implications of Natural Resource and Environmental Accounting*, CSERGE Working Paper GEC 94-18, Norwich: CSERGE.

Leitschuh-Fecht, H. and K. Burmeister (1994), 'Das Leitbild sustainability muß klarer gefaßt werden – eine Bilanz der bisherigen Diskussion', *Ökologische Briefe*, No.46, 17 Nov. 1994, pp.12–16.

Loske, R. (1995), personal communication.

Österreichische Bundesregierung (ed.) (1995), *Nationaler Umwelt Plan*.

Ostertag, Katrin and Schlegelmilch, Kai (1996), *Saving the Climate – That's My Job. Mögliche Beschäftigungseffekte von Klimaschutzmaßnahmen durch die Realisierung des Toronto-Ziels einer 20-prozentigen Reduktion von CO_2-Emissionen bis zum Jahre 2005 gegenüber dem Jahre 1988. Literaturstudie: Deutschland.* Wuppertal Paper Nr. 54, 3/1996, Wuppertal: WIKUE.

Serageldin, I. and A. Steer (eds.) (1993), *Valuing the Environment. Proceedings of the First Annual International Conference on Environmentally Sustainable Development held at the World Bank, Washington D.C. September 30–October 1, 1993*, Washington, DC: World Bank.

Simonis, Udo E. (1991), 'Globale Umweltprobleme und zukunftsfähige Entwicklung', *Aus Politik und Zeitgeschichte*, Vol.41, No.10, pp.3–10.

Spangenberg, Joachim (1995a), *Towards Sustainable Europe*, Brussels: Friends of the Earth Europe.

Spangenberg, Joachim (1995b), personal communication.

Steger, U. (1995), 'Konsens ohne Worte', *Die Zeit*, Vol.50, No.37, 8. Sept.1995, p.26.
Thoenes, Hans W. (1994), *Umwelt-Gutachten 1994: Für eine Dauerhaft-Umweltgerechte Entwicklung*, Stuttgart: Metzler-Poeschel.
Thoenes, Hans W. (1996), *Umweltgutachten 1996: Zur Umsetzung einer Dauerhaft-Umweltgerechten Entwicklung*, Stuttgart: Metzler-Poeschel.
Töpfer, Klaus (1996), 'Städte sind die Zukunft der Menschheit. Ohne nachhaltige Stadtentwicklung wird es keine global nachhaltige Entwicklung geben', in BMBau (ed.), *Verstädterungsprozeß und Nachhaltigkeit*, Bonn: BMBau, pp.7–10.
Unmüßig, Barbara (1995), 'Vortrag zur Entstehung und Arbeit des Forums Umwelt & Entwicklung anläßlich des Strategieseminars des Forums Umwelt & Entwicklung am 10./11. Februar 1995 in Mülheim/Ruhr', unpublished.
Voisey, Heather, Beurermann, Christiane, Sverdrup, Liv Astrid and Timothy O'Riordan (1996), 'The Political Significance of Local Agenda 21: The Early Stages of Some European Experiences', *Local Environment*, Vol.1, No.1, pp.33–50.
WBGU (1993), *Welt im Wandel: Grundstruktur Globaler Mensch-Umwelt Beziehungen. Jahresgutachten 1993*, Bonn.
Weidner, Helmut (1995), *25 Years of Modern Environmental Policy in Germany. Treading a Well Worn Path to the Top of the International Field*, WZB report FS II 95-301, Berlin: WZB.
Weizsäcker, Ernst U. v. and Jochen Jesinghaus(1992), *Ecological Tax Reform: A Policy Proposal for Sustainable Development*, London: Zed Books.
Wessel (BMU), (1995), personal communication.
Wuppertal Bulletin (1995), 'Young Entrepreneurs and Friends of the Earth: Dialogue, not Polemics!', *Wuppertal Bulletin for an Ecological Tax Reform*, Vol.1, No.3/4, pp.24–5, Wuppertal: WIKUE.

Acronyms

A21	Agenda 21
BJU	Bundesverband Junger Unternehmer
BMBau	BundesMinisterium für Raumordnung, Bauwesen und Städtebau
BMU	BundesMinisterium für Umwelt Naturschutz und Reaktorsicherheit
BMZ	Bundesministerium für wirtschaftliche Zusammenarbeit und Entwicklung
BUKO	Bundeskongress Agrarkoordination
BUND	Bund für Umwelt und Naturschutz Deutschland
CSD	Commission on Sustainable Development
DGB	Deutscher GewerkschaftsBund
DNR	Deutscher NaturschutzRing
LA21	Local Agenda 21
SRU	SachverständigenRat für Umweltfragen
WBGU	Wissenschaftlicher Beirat der Bundesregierung für Globale Umweltfragen
UNCED	United Nations Conference on Environment and Development
WEED	World Economy, Ecology and Development
WWF	WorldWide Fund for Nature

The Evolution of Sustainable Development Strategies in Portugal

TERESA G. RIBEIRO and
VALDEMAR J. RODRIGUES

The Portuguese institutional response to sustainable development began only with the United Nations Conference on Environment and Development in 1992. Portugal is responding to the new paradigm of sustainable development but is unable so far to turn rhetoric into comprehensive action because it does not have the soical, economic or democratic capacity to do so. The major outcomes of the Rio process or dynamic have been mostly project-specific, sometimes revealing concerns with integration, but seldom providing effective policy interlinkage or societal mobilisation. The authors provide an insight into the overall institutional adjustment process, as well as at pointing out some particular responses and issues that can be categorised as touchstones, impediments or contingencies of a sustainability transition in Portugal.

The Portuguese institutional response to sustainable development has a recent history. The United Nations Conference on Environment and Development (UNCED) held in Rio de Janeiro in 1992 was definitively the starting point for the inclusion of environmental concerns into mainstream domestic politics. Portugal is a European nation with a relatively new experience of democracy, achieved only since 1974 after 48 years of a dictatorial regime. It also has an economy still trying to overcome a lack of basic infrastructure and the existence of social disparities and regional asymmetries, caused by rural exodus and the abandonment of traditional forms of agriculture. It is responding to the new paradigm of sustainable development with evidence of a basic acceptance but an inability to pursue and evaluate its own strategies regarding the sustainability transition. The major outcomes of the Rio process or dynamic have been mostly project-specific, sometimes revealing concerns with integration, but seldom

Both authors during the period of research were based in CEEETA – Centro de Estudos em Economia da Energia, dos Transportes e do Ambiente. R. Gustavo de Matos Sequeira, 28, 1°Dto, 1200 Lisbon, Portugal. However, Teresa Ribeiro is now a Commissioner in the European Environment Agency based in Copenhagen.

providing effective policy interlinkage or societal mobilisation. The challenge of the sustainability transition presumes that new actions and processes will be undertaken in Portugal, and for this to occur Agenda 21 (A21) should definitively influence or even lead national mainstream politics. Those actions and processes are manifold and include the environmental impact assessment (EIA) of policies, plans or programmes; environmental and resource accounting; ecological taxation; new approaches to environmental management in industry; and the establishment of permanent structures to define, follow-up, and evaluate the sustainability transition, such as policy co-ordination mechanisms, inter-ministerial and parliamentary committees. This study aims to provide an insight into the overall institutional adjustment process, as well as at pointing out some particular responses and issues that can be categorised as touchstones, impediments or contingencies of a sustainability transition in Portugal.

Environmental Institutional Arrangements Prior to UNCED

In Portugal, the first official action concerning environmental matters was the establishment of a National Commission for the Environment in 1971 to prepare for Portugal's participation in the United Nations Conference on the Environment held in Stockholm in 1972. The committee was initially established as part of the National Council for Scientific Research in charge of research programmes. This fostered the perception that the environment was a scientific rather than a policy or a political issue. The committee later became an autonomous body under the direct control of the Prime Minister, and was responsible for the first efforts towards public information, awareness and training programmes with regard to the environment. Another early environmental institution was the National Parks Service, established in 1974, whose objective was the creation of a framework for developing a network of natural protected areas. During the intervening years the service has assumed increased importance, and now has more than 500 people working all over the country in protected areas covering about six per cent of the national territory.

The 1974 revolution provided the conditions for the establishment of a Department for the Environment (Secretaria de Estado do Ambiente) that later became the Ministry of Quality of Life (1979–85). However, during this period nothing relevant or important was to happen. It was only in 1985 that a step forward was made with structural changes to the Ministry and the creation of a new institution: the state's Secretariat for the Environment and Natural Resources (SEARN), now part of the new Ministry of Planning and Territory Administration (MPAT). The European Year of the Environment

(1987) was a turning point concerning environmental policy and two main laws were approved: the Environmental Basic Act (EBA) and the Environmental Protection Associations Act (EPAA). These provided the legal framework for subsequent environmental action and public participation. The EBA also allowed for the restructuring of SEARN, enlarging its competencies, doubling its budget, and resulted in the first serious initiatives towards the definition of a national environmental policy. This progress can be regarded as a convergence of three major factors: Portugal was finally recovering from the economic and political chaos that had existed since 1975; the process of joining the European Community (EC) was finally completed in 1986; and SEARN was a strong political actor, willing to fight for environmental causes.

The challenge became then, the transposition of the copious EC legislative body into national regulation, and the implementation of a demanding environmental policy in a country who had undergone a political and economic rupture. In fact Portugal was adjusting to the exercise of democracy while, at the same time, trying to rebuild an economy which had been previously based on the exploitation of its colonies' natural resources and had left it with a considerably obsolete industrial base. Extensions were granted in complying with EC environmental legislation requirements in most areas, but a survey of the implementation of EC directives, undertaken in 1989, already indicated that in most areas, the country was far from meeting its commitments.

Despite the opposition of many environmentalists, which preferred a strong secretary of state for the environment in a strong ministry rather than a weak ministry of environment, in 1990 SEARN was transformed into the Ministry of Environment and Natural Resources (MENR), leaving out of its sphere crucial areas for the implementation of an effective environmental policy. An important portion of environmental competencies stayed with MPAT, which has lead sometimes to a bicephalous policy with contradicting signals and fragmentation of actions.

Until the eve of UNCED there was hardly any progress on the implementation of environmental policy, whilst at the same time considerable investments were being made in various sectors of the economy supported by EC Structural Funds. The definition of a local Agenda 21 (LA21) and the government's responses to the United Nations Commission on Sustainable Development (CSD) were the most immediate consequences of UNCED in relation to Portugal's domestic policy towards sustainable development.

The Evolution of National Strategies Towards Sustainable Development

The Environmental Basic Act (EBA, 1987)

The EBA (Law 11/87 of April 7, 1987), is often quoted internationally as one of the most interesting legal documents ever published in the field of environmental law. In the opinion of some experts [see *Reis, 1992*] the EBA has profoundly marked the judicial order in Portugal, and probably not because of its immediate effects, but because of the new possibilities that legislators have had the courage to develop, and the general principles that were established, as a result of its existence.

The term self-sustained development is introduced at the very beginning of the EBA (Art. 2, no. 2): 'The environmental policy aims to optimise and assure the continuity of natural resources utilisation, qualitatively and quantitatively, as a basic pre-requisite for self-sustained development'. This article is of special importance since, for the first time, a legal document recognised the existence of a clear association between the environment and development. The concept of sustainable development underlying the article, although not explicit, is very similar to that of the Brundtland report, suggesting that it was probably a reference point for the legislator. Other parts in the EBA refer to the principles of environmental policy adopted by the EC when the first action programme was approved, for example, Art. 4:

> The existence of an environment adequate to a population's health and welfare, and to social and cultural development of communities, presumes the adoption of measures towards ... the self-sustained social and economic development and the correct growth of urban areas, through land use planning ... and the promotion of population's participation in formulating and executing environmental and quality of life policies, as well as the establishment of continuous fluxes of information between the organs of the administration responsible for those policies and the citizens to which they are directed to.

In order to promote actions towards better environmental quality, and with special emphasis on measures for citizens and Non-Governmental Organisations' (NGOs) information and training, the EBA created a new institution which has since become the Institute of Environmental Promotion (IPAMB). The structure adopted for this institution was unique in the context of Portuguese public administration, as most of the members of the Directive Council of IPAMB are from non-governmental sectors of society.

The Environmental-Protection Associations Act (EPAA, 1987)

The EPAA (Law 10/87 of April 4, 1987) defines the rights of participation for NGOs, and what are termed Environmental Protection Associations (EPAs), in central, regional, and local administrations. EPAs are constituted in the terms of the general law, giving them judicial personality, and are non-profitable. Their objectives are: environmental protection, protection of the natural and architectural heritage, nature conservation and the promotion of quality of life. The associations are further classified into local, regional, or national, depending on the range of their actions. They must have a minimum number of members, 4000, 1000, and 200, for the national, regional, and local associations, respectively. Art. 3 declares all national EPAs, and some regional ones,[1] as associations that are generically representative. In practice this means that some political influence is attributed to EPAs, in the sense that they have specific rights, such as the status of *social partner* for all legal effects, and the right to use public television (60 minutes per year) and radio (30 minutes per month) channels to broadcast their messages and ideas (Art. 12). With respect to the role of EPAs as a social partner, they have, according to their level of action, the right to participate in the definition of environmental policy and in its major legislative outcomes.[2] Consultation rights are also consigned to EPAs (Art. 5), with regard to documents such as: regional land use plans; municipal master plans; environmental impact assessment studies; agricultural, and forest plans and projects; and the creation and management of protected areas.

Other aspects mentioned in the EPAA include the right to use administrative resources; the legitimacy of EPAs in making public the omissions, or acts perpetrated by, public or private bodies against the environment, and to act judicially when necessary (Art. 7); and the duty of co-operation between municipalities and EPAs concerning the protection and valorisation of nature and environment (Art. 8). In Art. 9 it was declared that EPAs have right to the state's support through central, regional, and local administration, for the prosecution of their objectives, and for activities that develop citizens' information and training. The IPAMB should provide, according to the EBA, the technical and/or financial support to any EPAs applying for it. This aspect will be discussed further below.

The National A21 Process

Immediately after UNCED, in August 1992, the Portuguese government created a task-force to pursue the implementation of the principles, programmes and actions arising from the Rio conference. As the result of the work undertaken by this *ad hoc* structure, a first draft version of a national A21 was presented to the Council of Ministers in January 1993. The final version of the document [*MENR, 1994*] was published after an internal debate at governmental level, and after consultation with several sectors of society.

The existence of a document setting out national guidelines for action and the interpretation of A21 within the national context, could be explained as a consequence of the commitment of Portugal to UNCED (at the time it held the EC presidency), or just as an attempt to demonstrate leadership on a pertinent issue. Besides, it was the first time that a political document on the environment had been submitted to a broad process of public discussion. In its final appraisal of the debate, the task force considered that although public participation levels were low, it was both a high profile and a useful exercise. Five major impressions emerged from the public debate: first, the urgent need for a national environmental policy plan; second, the lack of consistency between the political rhetoric and Portuguese reality; third, the need for the political commitment of all the ministries in relation to environmental questions; fourth, the need to promote the participation of civil society; and fifth, the necessity of mobilising multiple instruments for the protection of the environment.

Despite this public discussion process, its outcomes appear to have had little effect on policy. Prepared during and after UNCED, the Regional Development Plan shows no evidence of input either from the conference conclusions or from the national A21. In other words, it seems that the two processes were run in parallel by the government, with no idea of integration: on the one hand government departments were preparing the most important binding plan regarding development options until the turn of the century; and on the other hand an *ad hoc* commission was set up with the mandate of identifying the necessary action and political means required to implement the Rio conclusions at national level.

National Plans of Action for Implementing the Conventions on Climate Change and Biodiversity: Two Remarkable Cases

The action plans for implementing the conventions on climate change, biodiversity, desertification and the Declaration of the Principles on Forests, were addressed by the Portuguese Government in January 1994 [*CSD, 1994a*]. The European Union (EU) signed the convention on climate change, therefore Portugal's implementation is an EU concern. Portugal's approach to carbon dioxide (CO_2) emissions was at the time considered by many analysts as contrary to reduction, revealing a profound misreading of the principles underlying the concept of sustainable development. Because Portugal's levels of carbon and CO_2 emissions per inhabitant were (and still are) far below the EC average (1.00 and 3.67 tonnes per inhabitant in

Portugal against 2.34 and 8.58 in the rest of the EU for carbon and CO_2 respectively), the official position was that Portugal could increase emissions by 20–30 per cent by the end of the century.

With respect to sulphur dioxide (SO_2), and in order to reduce overall SO_2 emission levels, it was felt by the government that the percentage of sulphur in liquid fuels should be reduced continually without, however, endangering the profitability of the refining industry. The law currently provides for a gradual reduction in the sulphur content of fuel oil from 3.5 per cent to two per cent by the year 2000, but in accordance with the adjustment capacity of the Portuguese refining industry. It also provides for a reduction in the sulphur content of diesel to 0.05 per cent in 1996.

As far as the biodiversity convention is concerned, the document was signed in June 1992 in Rio de Janeiro, Portugal's ratification document was submitted on 22 December 1993, and the convention entered into effect on 29 December 1993. The UNCED follow-up report [*CSD, 1994a*] lists a series of projects and activities carried out by the government, activities related to protected areas (regional departments), and activities of the autonomous regions of Azores and Madeira. However, such initiatives are few and incoherent and the title of the section, national plan of action for biodiversity, is not fulfilled. In fact, it is noticeable that there is a discrepancy between the scientific knowledge achieved in areas such as bioecology, botany, entomology, ornithology, plant physiology, and the political decisions that directly affect biodiversity. A paradigmatic example of this was the political decision made on the plan for the new bridge over the River Tejo in Lisbon.

In the present, the crossing over the River Tejo in the Metropolitan Area of Lisbon is made via a single roadway bridge (Almada-Lisboa). Increasing volumes of traffic, most of which is generated in the dense urban municipalities on the river's south bank, prompted the search for alternative crossings. In 1992 the government approved the Sacavém-Montijo option for the location of the new bridge, turning down the other option at Chelas-Barreiro, which it is claimed by several experts would be less environmentally degrading and a more appropriate traffic solution. The new bridge involves building an extension of about 16 km, 5 km of which are inside the special bird protection zone of the Tejo Estuary. This is one of the ten most important wetland zones in Europe,[3] designated for protection under the Ramsar Convention and by the EU. The government is also committed to protecting it under the Bern Convention and several EU Directives. The EIA, prepared in a record time of two months, illustrates profound technical as well as legal and methodological failures, some of which are covered later. However, it is significant that the public consultation phase of the EIA in 1994 violated legal rules because it was not available to local populations, and part of it was only available after 20 days of the consultation phase had passed. In Portugal, according to EIA legislation (Decree-Law 186/90), the public consultation period is limited to 40 days. Public opinion studies have shown that the Sacavém-Montijo option is preferred by just three per cent of present bridge users, versus 81 per cent who preferred the excluded Chelas-Barreiro option [*Geota, Quercus and LPN, 1995*].

CSD Reporting

Beyond the production of a national A21 strategy other efforts are necessary to continue the process, such as the creation of a permanent institutional structure expressly concerned with sustainable development. Reports to the CSD submitted by the Portuguese government [*CSD, 1994a; CSD, 1994b*] clearly show the absence of such a structure. The two ministries involved with reporting to the CSD were, as legally defined, the Ministry of Foreign Affairs and MENR. The role of the former ministry in this process has been quite worthless, and MENR has shifted the responsibility of CSD reporting on to IPAMB, which is somewhat inexperienced with such responsibilities.

IPAMB in this role came up against substantial reporting difficulties, mainly in those areas of A21 requiring sectoral and cross-sectoral approaches. Since IPAMB had no legal mandate legitimating its actions, required information from other ministries and departments was difficult to obtain as they had no obligation to co-operate. The result is visible in the last CSD report [*CSD, 1994b*], both in the prolix character of the information presented for some areas, in the difficulty of dissociating areas and themes within the sphere of more than one ministry or department,[4] as well as ultimately in the number of non-answered questions. The lack of a national co-ordinating body with responsibility for sustainable development and the A21 follow-up explains in part the absence of sustainable development indicators and criteria for their application at the domestic level [*CSD, 1994b*].

The National Environmental Policy Plan

The National Environmental Policy Plan (NEPP) [*1995*] and the national A21 strategy are policy documents without legal force. However, the NEPP is important as it is the most recent strategic governmental document concerned with sustainable development.[5] It consists (following the format of the EU's Fifth Environmental Action Programme) of the Plan itself plus a summary characterisation of the state of the environment in Portugal in annexes. These indicate that the NEPP presumes a deep knowledge on the state of the environment, but at the same time it is transparent that reliable data is lacking and remains to be collected and properly treated. The annexes also contain indicators for environmental planning and management, adapted from the work of the OECD. In the plan itself, however, the issue of environmental information is not mentioned, neither in the strategic orientations of the environmental policy, nor in the section regarding the instruments for its implementation. Despite these omissions it does recognise as a major requirement the cross-sectoral integration of environmental objectives. The draft version of the NEPP was severely criticised for being 'wishful thinking' rather than a national plan, since it does not provide answers to questions of: when, how, and who leads the process? In fact the document could be perceived as an attempt to produce a synthesis of already existing documents, namely the Regional Development Plan, the Reports on the State of the Environment (RSEs), and the national A21 strategy, but in attempting to show coherence between them it fails, looking artificially contrived. Although significantly addressing the issue of accountability, with goals defined for different areas and sectors that are quantified and clear, the connection between these goals and the global strategies for those sectors remains sometimes very unclear.

Environmental Safeguards: The Practice of EIA in Portugal

Given the existing legal framework and the responsibilities undertaken by the government for the promotion of sustainable development, several public consultation exercises have been undertaken by the administration in the last few years, including those required by EIA legislation. As a member of the EU Portugal is forced to respect the obligatory character of the EIAs (they are an obligatory instrument for selecting the projects to be supported by the EC), and therefore since 1988, EIA studies have been undertaken and submitted to MPAT. These early EIAs displayed a general absence of coherent guidelines, had little influence on decision-making, and were typically carried out after the project's most important decisions had been made, and sometimes after the beginning of the projects themselves. After the transposition into national law of the EC directive on EIA in 1990, almost 300 EIAs were completed by until 1994. Most of them were on road infrastructure, energy, transportation, hydro and mining projects, agriculture and forest projects, and on small industrial units. However, there are some technical as well as practical gaps that cannot be disregarded when evaluating the effectiveness of the EIAs that have been performed in these recent years. Such gaps include:

• the absence of a previously defined scope or range of analysis;

• the absence of specific guidelines on the cumulative effects of projects;

- the absence of accreditation mechanisms for EIA technical teams, as well as guidelines on the composition of such teams;

- licensing and EIA procedures were not adequately integrated making it difficult to add environmental requirements to project licensing or approval processes;

- classification of the projects in several cases was not correct because the underlying philosophy disregards not only the likelihood of cumulative effects, but also the dimension or size effects, and is very project rather than site-oriented;

- it is neither a requirement nor practice to carry out EIAs on policy or planning instruments, although these might have major environmental implications;

- EIAs are presented for public discussion often after the political decision and only as a mere formality in order to ensure EC support;

- many EIAs consider no alternatives;

- there has been no political opportunity to refuse bad EIAs;

- EIAs often do not consider the differential impact of whether or not to implement the mitigation measures suggested in the studies;

- most EIAs consider only the impacts in the immediate vicinity of projects;

- many ignore existing designations with regard to land use planning where the projects are to be located;

- the majority of EIA public consultations that have been carried out presented practical deficiencies: public access to documents; the length and timing of the consultation period; and the lack of resources available in IPAMB to set-up this process;

- public sessions are considered facultative, but the law omits to state who is the competent body on deciding about whether or not to make a public session. Only about five per cent of the projects have been submitted to public sessions for their discussion;

- the follow-up commission must prepare a report on the public consultation process in the five days after consultation, however these opinions and/or suggestions are often ignored instead of being listened to or subject to refutation.

Institutional Responses to Sustainable Development

MENR

Following the Rio Conference, and based on the targets established by the EU's Fifth Environmental Action Programme, MENR underwent a process of reorganisation, apparently to adjust itself to the implementation of sustainable development strategies: ' ... it is considered an imperative adjustment of the institutional structure, reflecting the recent, nevertheless significant, evolution of the concepts of action of the state within the environmental field, now centred on the main objective of promoting a sustainable development' (Regulation 187/93).

At this time it was also emphasised that the main task of the Ministry is 'to participate in the promotion of a sustainable development that respects the environment as its fundamental support' [*ibid.*]. Sustainable development requires all actors and all sectors to become involved, but a leader is required in order to guide the process, and this seems to be lacking. The concepts of shared or joint responsibility, policy integration, and so forth, allowed MENR to identify several areas where other bodies could be responsible, and subsequently it abandoned its leading role, instead of using those concepts to force a more coherent environmental policy [*Ribeiro et al., 1996*]. In fact, MENR has been a very weak ministry. The most salient indicator of this is perhaps the Decree-Law 186/90 on the process of EIA. Amongst the many technical failures of this law, the position of the ministry on a given project submitted to EIA is neither binding nor essential for a project's prosecution.

In terms of decision capacity and influence on political decisions, MENR has fewer powers today than in 1987. Although some specific competencies have been transferred from other ministries to MENR,[6] often it is not consulted, or invited to produce only non-binding opinions in areas such as: land use planning, forest management, agriculture, transport, and energy. With respect to MENR's actual competencies, there are two basic components which are clearly unbalanced: responsibility for sanitary and hydraulic works, which occupies most of MENR's budget; and environmental management, which is almost beyond the ministry's capacity and scope. This affects MENR's ability to take a strong lead on sustainability and represents a substantial institutional barrier to further progress at national level.

Local Governments: Sustainability and Locality

In Portugal the discussion on the possible division of the country into administrative regions has been on the political agenda since soon after the 1974 revolution. No decision was taken for about 20 years, and it is only recently that new socialist government has focused its electoral speech around the idea of the division of the country into regions. Currently, regional planning is part of central administration competencies, through their various regional departments, while local planning is within the scope of local authorities (municipalities). In practice, one may say that there are only two operative levels in terms of development options: the central and the local one. Central departments generally have decentralised structures which have been created more for operational reasons, more efficient application of central policies, than to account for regional disparities and the co-ordination of the various sectoral approaches, which should be performed by a real regional structure. The result is a scattered body of competencies and planning instruments that create conflict whose resolution requires the creation of *ad hoc* structures where the various departments of the different ministries co-operate.

Local administrations have a wide range of competencies on strategic issues, namely those regarding public investments in areas such as rural and urban infrastructure, environmental resources and services, energy, education, culture and sports. However, there seems to be a discrepancy between the number of competencies and the monetary resources that are allocated for their administration by central government. The interface in terms of environment and development options between central and local administrations often occurs in a bottom-up fashion.[7] This approach is generally functional when central and local governments have coinciding priorities and points of view. Scarcity of resources has been the reason for the establishment of co-operation protocols between local and central administration in fields such as water supply, wastewater collection and treatment, and waste management, and these have been supported by EU Structural Funds. However, for the successful implementation of a sustainable development model at local level, municipalities should be more involved and informed on and about the issues that are being discussed at higher political levels and impact on local administration. The successful incorporation of concepts such as sustainable development and environmental management at local level may depend strongly on changing national policies.

Portuguese municipalities invest much more on infrastructure than on environmental protection and preservation. The investments made on infrastructure, although in most cases essential for local development, can be questionable in terms of their relative importance and/or effectiveness. For instance, amongst the various wastewater treatment plants built or commissioned by the municipalities the most visible result has been the payments to the contractors. In 1991, 14 per cent of the existing plants were inoperative, 31 per cent were poorly operated, and others were poorly sited.

The development of LA21 initiatives or programmes, in part as a consequence of the above mentioned constraints, have never been either observed or evoked by the local Portuguese policy-makers as relevant issues in their official speeches or electoral programmes.

Environmental NGOs

Portugal was one of the nations included in a survey of citizens' environmental awareness [*Dunlap, 1994; Dunlap and Mertig, 1995*]. The results showed that about 25 per cent of the Portuguese say that the environment is one of the most serious problems in the country; over 30 per cent believe in public participation to protect the environment and in the major role played by the NGOs; 85 per cent of respondents believe that the health of the next generation will be substantially affected by the degradation of the environment; and about 60 per cent say they are willing to pay higher prices to protect it. However, in Portugal, and more generally, people think of environmental problems as other people's problems, as having an external cause not related to their own activities [*Schmidt, 1993*]. NGOs could be important sources of information for the public if they had the technical capacity and the necessary staff to conduct independent studies on issues concerning sustainable development and environmental quality. However, despite recent developments involving the major environmental NGOs in Portugal, most of them have neither permanent technical staff nor technical facilities such as (accredited) environmental labs, and survive with scarce or, at least, uncertain financial support. In 1995 about 140 environmental NGOs were registered with IPAMB. Figure 1 gives some indicative numbers on the dimension and associative dynamics of the three most active national NGOs: League for the Protection of Nature (LPN), National Association for Nature Conversation (QUERCUS), and the Group for Studies on Land Use Planning and the Environment (GEOTA).

The ratios of permanent staff to the number of affiliates are on average lower than 0.3 per cent for the three associations. This indicator of the association's professional activity is obviously very low, and confirms the assertion of the predominantly amateur nature of Portuguese EPAs.

The support delivered by the IPAMB is project specific,[8] and the EPAs have submitted funding requests every year since 1988. In 1995, for instance, 178 projects were presented to the IPAMB, 74 of which were approved (about 41 per cent). The 74 projects approved applied for a budget of 100,584,000 PTE (about 0.5 MEcu[9]), but the support provided by IPAMB was only 40 per cent of this (40,002,000 PTE).

Besides IPAMB, which has been the dominant institution providing regular funding to the NGOs, municipalities and to a lesser extent industry and other economic sectors are now starting to understand the importance

FIGURE 1

Indicator	LPN	QUERCUS	GEOTA
Number of Members (N):	6000	8000	900
Number of active members (AM):	n.a.	n.a.	40
Permanent staff (PS):	5	16	3
Ratio PS/N (per cent):	0.08	0.20	0.33
Ratio AM/N (per cent):	n.a.	n.a.	4.44
Basic maintenance costs per year			
(thousands of PTE):	900 *	5000	5000

* = the central administrative nucleus, located in Lisbon only. n.a. = not available.

Source: Data supplied by the NGOs in question, 1995.

FIGURE 2
FINANCIAL SUPPORT DELIVERED BY THE CENTRAL
ADMINISTRATION TO THE EPAs SINCE 1988
(1995 constant prices)

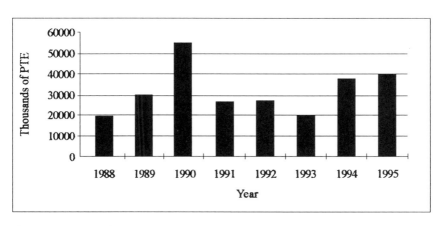

Source: IPAMB [*1996*].

of establishing protocols with NGOs in specific areas. As such new opportunities of funding are now being explored by NGOs.

Industry

In November 1994, a global agreement on the environment and sustainable development [*AGMADS, 1994*] was signed between the Government, the Confederation of Portuguese Industry, and the Confederation of Portuguese Land Farmers. The agreement involved MENR and other ministries and establishes the major guidelines for institutional co-operation towards the adjustment of various industrial sectors in line with current environmental legislation. The leit-motif of the agreement was basically the recognition that environmental legislation was being transposed at a rate clearly not balanced by the capacity of Portuguese industry to accommodate these requirements. In other words, companies in general felt that something should be done to allow for a more progressive adjustment, to delay legal enforcement, and thus to avoid the possible consequences in the meantime. This general agreement should form the basis for more specific agreements, involving particular sectors of industry in Portugal.[10] The first sectoral voluntary agreement was signed in February 1995, between the government authorities and the national federation of swine-breeders associations.

The lesson to learn from the process leading up to these voluntary agreements can be synthesised in a few points. First, companies and the industrial sector in general are more open to participation when they perceive some sectoral protection in the negotiation (or adjustment) processes. Secondly, the lack of integration between the various government departments on environmental issues causes distrust in environmental policy, and can remove potential targets from the adjustment process. Thirdly, this process has showed that, at present, most of the industries in Portugal have problems other than environmental ones, and thus awareness about the environment still tends to be seen as a secondary question. In most Portuguese industries environmental management is still a misunderstood concept. The accomplishment of legislation, which seems to be the engine of these voluntary agreements, is part of a wider process that is now being learned for the first time by many of the economic leaders of the Portuguese society.

The Message of Agenda 21 – Information and Public Participation for Decision-Making

Since public involvement in the decision-making process is a key issue for the implementation of sustainable development strategies, information represents a critical factor in their prosecution. This statement implies that information exists, that it is accessible, and that it is in a form that can be used by the general public. The message of A21 in this respect can be illustrated as Figure 3, where the oriented lines represent possible flows of information.

FIGURE 3
THE INFORMATION TRIANGLE:
POLITICAL DEICISON, PUBLIC PARTICIPATION, INFORMATION,
SHOWING POSSIBLE RUPTURES IN INFORMATION FLOWS

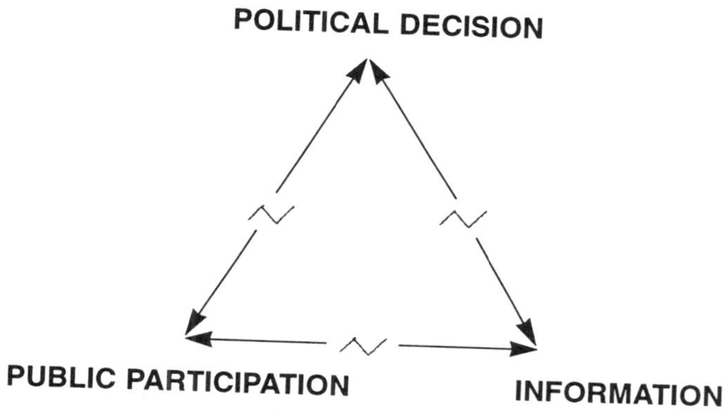

POLITICAL DECISION

PUBLIC PARTICIPATION   **INFORMATION**

Political decision-making and public participation on development issues should ideally be determined by the available information concerning each component of sustainable development, which means considering the social, environmental, institutional, and economic contexts of development [*Gouzee et al., 1995*]. It follows that whenever the existing information is scarce or insufficient, decision-making should be delayed while new elements are collected. This principle of political choice when uncertainty is great can also be termed the *precautionary principle*. On the other hand, public participation can be much more effective provided that information is good and available, with the same quality and quantity, for both the decision-makers and the public. It has been observed in Portugal that sometimes the most relevant aspects underlying development options are not clear to the average citizen or the NGOs. Whether deliberately or not, the option for the construction of the new bridge over the Tejo river in Lisbon is a paradigmatic example of this.

According to the message of A21, and in the context of a strategy towards sustainable development, it is also important to notice that none of the triangle's vertices on Figure 3 makes sense in the absence of the remaining two. Thus, for instance, the existence of a great amount of detailed information makes no sense when nobody uses it, or when decisions are made arbitrarily with no reference to public opinion. Yet, also it does not make any sense to have an inquiry into the public's opinion when the information available to the public on a given subject is not equivalent (quantitatively and/or qualitatively) to that available to the decision-maker.

Citizen's access to information is prescribed in the Constitution of the Portuguese Republic.[11] Also, the Code of the Administrative Procedure (1991) regulates in general relationships between citizens and state, focusing on questions of citizen's access to information, namely the terms by which information should be made accessible in public participation procedures. The EBA which constitutes the framework of national environmental policy, invokes the principle of public participation, establishing the requirement for the participation of the various social groups in the implementation of environmental and land use planning policies at local, regional and central levels. Simultaneously, the EPAA defines the rights of such associations, and specifically entitles them to participate and be involved in defining environmental policy and in the general outlining of legislation.

Environmental Information in Portugal

Information on the environment in Portugal is still practically a state monopoly. Hence, the informational triangle of Figure 3 is in fact incomplete (there is no bottom-up flow, that is, information from public to the decision-makers). Yet, information is scattered over a great number of governmental departments, is insufficient in some important areas, and often consists of raw or improperly manipulated data. In consequence, its potential contribution to decision-making processes, as well as to the enlightenment of public opinion, is often very small or even negligible. Since 1987, the Portuguese government has annually published an Report on the State of the Environment which is a legal obligation of the EBA (Art. 49), according to which: 'the Government assumes the obligation to present to the Parliament, together with the Major Options of the Plan, a report on the state of the environment and land planning in Portugal in the year prior to that of the Plan'. Nevertheless, these reports have never been discussed in plenary sessions of the parliament.

Analysis of the Reports between 1987 and 1993 shows that although the subjects presented are essentially the same, the sequence and nomenclature by which they are presented varies, probably due to some confusion about the objectives of the report. It is also sometimes noticeable that the data is repeated, because of the frequency of publication. General considerations without the support of objective data, neither spatially referenced nor quantified, have also been abundant. Despite being governmental reports, the Reports of the State of the Environment have focused only those sectors that are the direct responsibility of the MENR. Hence, the document's perspective does not allow an evaluation of the government's whole performance towards the goals defined by the environmental policy.

The problems, or inadequacies, of the first reports were the impetus for a new project: a White Book on the state of the environment in Portugal. It was intended that this would include contributions from experts outside MENR (mainly universities), in different areas of expertise. The White Book was finished in 1991, and includes contributions from departments of central government, municipalities, universities, and NGOs. Practical results in terms of changing environmental policy are not visible at this time.

EC Funding Opportunities and Sustainable Development

The existence of EC funding is itself a stimulus for the poorer European economies that, in the absence of such support, would not have the capacity to put into practice their most adventurous projects. On the other hand, and because of the current EC funding system, there is the possibility that funds become themselves the cause of doubtful investments, in the sense that projects may emerge as eligible motivated by the necessity of draining the funds available rather than their individual merit. The timetables imposed by the EC to apply for funding can turn the execution of EIAs or other strategic studies into an opportunity cost. Thus, under certain circumstances, the celerity with which such studies are performed, usually to the detriment of their quality, can be justified by accomplishing them in a given time schedule. Also as funds can become unavailable if no projects are presented in a given period larger projects that take up more of the available funds tend to be favoured instead of small and numerous investments. In spite of the beginning of the second round of considerable investments on the environment and other sectors through the Community Support Framework (1994–99), no new mechanisms or methodologies seem to have been introduced for monitoring and evaluating the application of EC funds, apart from those already legally required. The latter process includes a representative of the MENR in several of the existing structures to follow up on the funds application, and to leave the assessment of environmental effects to the legal disposition on EIA.

Accommodating the Challenge of Sustainability Within the Portuguese Democratic System

Despite all the convergence achieved in economic, social and other fields, there are differences amongst the Member States that cannot be ignored when analysing their institutional adjustments to sustainable development strategies. One of the major differences relies upon the political structures of each Member State, and namely upon the structure and organisation of the various democratic systems. In the EU, democratic systems present marked differences and peculiarities [*Laundy, 1989; Liebert and Cotta, 1990; PE, 1992*]. The Portuguese political system can be characterised by its very party-dependent nature. Citizens must vote for a party list and thus cannot express their preferences for a given candidate both in legislative and local elections. The lack of relationship between electors and the candidates, members of parliament, and leaders, makes the elected deputies and candidates completely dependent upon the support of their party. This can lead to the subjugation of the democratic system to what we refer to as a *party logic*. This seems to be a major handicap of the Portuguese political system.

The most voted for party in the legislative elections has the opportunity to constitute government, alone or in association with other parties (depending on the percentage of votes obtained). The prime minister is nominated by the president of the republic with regard to the electoral results, and this usually coincides with the general secretariat of the most voted party. The prime minister chooses the other members of the government, and thus the ministerial composition and structure often comes as a surprise to the citizen. Another aspect that we would like to include herein regards the nature of power that democracy confers to a party after elections. Since it is essentially political power that is transferred after elections, the elected politicians often must deal with interests previously established within their departments. Since these interests are indirectly protected by law,[12] implementing a new policy may be a quite hard task to accomplish during the limited period of a mandate. The sustainability transition may also require a transition of technical power, since sustainable development involves new concepts and technical procedures not formerly known or experienced by the technicians that are still in charge in many governmental and para-governmental offices. Under these circumstances, even a strong political will can be sometimes hindered by the administrative machinery.

Conclusions

The concept of sustainable development is still unassimilated, which means that the different institutions either base their judgements and viewpoints upon their own interpretations of sustainable development, through a more or less elaborated hermeneutic process, or simply have introduced the term into their current speech, without any concern for its measurability.

In the national context we cannot think about the existence of a real environmental conscience. This fact is related to the weak implantation of post-materialist values in Portugal, constrained by the relative immaturity of the existing democracy and by the still recent political and economic stability. On the other hand, there is a noticeable emergence of environmental awareness from almost every sector of Portuguese society. A sustainability transition in Portugal is hindered by several obstacles, namely the country's development stage, with regard to basic infrastructure, regional homogeneity, and global efficiency in the use of resources and technology; the inertia and/or inability of the different institutions, who are in general poorly prepared to face the new challenges of sustainable development; the absence of an institutional co-operation model based more on interdependence than hierarchic relationships; the degree of democratic maturity; and the organisation and functioning of the political system.

A brief look into specific aspects or sectors shows little innovation or change. Besides the voluntary agreements between a few sectors of industry or their associations and the ministry of environment, the legal diplomas produced by the two tutelary ministries (environment and industry) concerning environmental auditing, and the transposition into national law of several EC directives and regulations, although most of them without further regulations assuring the feasibility of their general principles; there is no innovation in key areas such as green accounting, ecological taxation, structure planning, and environmental analysis of regional development projects and programmes. The role of NGOs has been reinforced, but since public support for these organisations is still scarce and deficient, it certainly looks like this is due to the NGOs own efforts, presumably aided by the effect of global environment trends. On the other hand, no permanent structures have been set up yet in order to define, follow-up and evaluate the sustainability transition in Portugal, such as policy co-ordination mechanisms, inter-ministerial committees, and parliamentary committees.

NOTES

1. Those compared by IPAMB to national EPAs.
2. NGOs have a seat in the following organisations: Social and Economic Council, Directive Council of IPAMB, Consultative Council for the Attribution of Eco-labels, General or Consultative Councils for Protected Areas, National Water Council, River Catchment Councils, and General Councils for Air Management. Yet, their participation is also set down by some specific diplomas, such as the EIA legislation and the diploma on Serious Industrial Risks.
3. Classification assigned by the Directive 79/409/CEE, transposed into Portuguese law through the Decree-Law no. 280/94 of 5 Nov. 1994.
4. This is explicit in the report (CSD, 1994b: 57), when is stated that 'Chapters 11 through 14

(of the A21) must be regarded as sectors of this chapter (Chapter 10)'.

5. The document was approved in the Council of Ministers by the former social-democrat government. Until now the new socialist government (elected in Oct. 1995) has ignored the document, and any mention of an intention to bind the actual environmental policy to it has not been made yet.

6. Those concerning coastal zone management, through the Nature Conservation Institute, and climate, through the National Institute of Meteorology and Geophysics.

7. An example is the imposition by the central administration of the existence of an approved Municipal Master Plan as a requirement for the municipalities to apply for Community funds.

8. The areas covered by the projects have been mainly nature conservation, environmental education, and cultural and natural heritage.

9. 1 ECU = 200 PTE; 1 MEcu = 1,000,000 Ecu.

10. Actually, 10 voluntary agreements were established by Nov. 1996.

11. Articles 20, 37, 66, and 268 of the Constitution were regulated by the recent Law 65/93 (22 Aug. 1993), as a consequence of the transposition into the Portuguese legislation of the EC Directive 90/313/CEE (on citizen's access to environmental information).

12. Public administration and public institutions in general still provide the most stable technical careers in Portugal in terms of rights and possibilities of progression. Public administration (central and local) had 654,494 employees in 1994 [*Barreto and Preto, 1996*], which represents about 15 per cent of the country's total active population.

REFERENCES

AGMADS (1994), *Acordo global em matéria de ambiente e desenvolvimento sustentável celebrado entre os Ministérios do Ambiente e Recursos Naturais, da Indústria e Energia, da Agricultura e as Confederaç'es dos Agricultores de Portugal e da Indústria Portuguesa*, Nov. 1994.

Barreto, A. and C.V. Preto (1996), *A situação social em Portugal 1960–1995*, ICS/Universidade de Lisboa (ed.), 510 pp.

CSD (1994a), *Follow-up Report (Portugal)*, submitted to the Sustainable Development Commission, Jan. 1994, 101 pp.

CSD (1994b), *Implementation of Agenda 21 in Portugal* (UNCED follow-up), Dec.1994.

Dunlap, R.E. (1994), 'International Attitudes Towards Environment and Development', in H.O. Bergesen and G. Parmann (eds.), *Green Globe Yearbook 1994*, Oxford: Oxford University Press, pp.115–26

Dunlap, R.E. and A.G. Mertig (1995), 'Global Environmental Concern: A Challenge to the Post-Materialism Thesis', in P. Ester and W. Schluchter (eds.), *Social Dimensions of Contemporary Environmental Issues: International Perspectives*, Tilburg: Tilburg University Press.

Geota, Quercus and LPN (eds.) (1995), *Erros históricos do ambiente, Volume 1: nova travessia do Tejo em Lisboa*, Lisbon: Geota, Quercus and LPN.

Gouzee, N., Mazijn, B. and S. Billharz (1995), *Indicators of Sustainable Development for Decision-Making*, Report of the Workshop of Ghent (Belgium), 9–11 Jan. 1995, submitted to the CSD, Federal Planning Office of Belgium.

IPAMB (1996), *Boletim INformar do Instituto de Promoção Ambiental* (vários números), Lisbon.

Kuik, O. and H. Verbruggen (eds.) (1991), *In Search of Indicators of Sustainable Development*, Dordrecht: Kluwer Academic Publishers.

Laundy, Ph. (1989), *Parliaments in the Modern World*, Hants: Dartmouth.

Liebert, U. and M. Cotta (1990), *Parliament and Democratic Consolidations in Southern Europe: Greece, Italy, Portugal, Spain and Turkey*, London/New York: Pinter Publishers.

MENR (1994), *Síntese Estratégica: Aspectos mais relevantes para o seguimento em Portugal das conclus'es da CNUAD*, April, Lisbon: MENR.

NEPP (1995), *Plano nacional de política de ambiente*, Lisbon: Ministério do Ambiente e Recursos Naturais.

PE (1992), *Os sistemas eleitorais para os parlamentos nacionais nos países da comunidade europeia*, Parlamento Europeu, Direcção-Geral de Estudos, Colecção de Estudos e Documentação, Série Política, W-16.

Reis, J.P. (1992), *Lei de Bases do Ambiente, anotada e comentada e legislação complementar sobre ambiente*, Coimbra: Almedina.

Ribeiro, T., Rodrigues, V. and T. O'Riordan (1996), 'Ajustamentos institucionais às estratégias de desenvolvimento sustentável: o caso português', in C. Borrego, C. Coelho, L Arroja, C. Boia and E. Figueiredo (eds.), *Proceed. of the 5ª Conferência Nacional sobre a Qualidade do Ambiente*, Vol.I, pp.43–56.

Schmidt, L. (1993), *O verde preto no branco*, Lisboa: Gradiva.

Acronyms

A21	Agenda 21
CO_2	Carbon Dioxide
CSD	United Nations Commission on Sustainable Development
EBA	Environmental Basic Act (Lei de Bases do Ambiente)
EC	European Community
EIA	Environmental Impact Assessment (Estudo de Impacte Ambiental)
EPA	Environmental Protection Association (Associações de Defesa do Ambiente)
EPAA	Environmental Protection Associations Act (Lei de Bases das Associações de Defesa do Ambiente)
EU	European Union
GEOTA	Grupo de Estudos de Ordenamento do Território e Ambiente (Group for Studies on Land Use Planning and the Environment)
IPAMB	Instituto de Promoção Ambiental (Institue for Environmental Promotion)
LA21	Local Agenda 21
LPN	Liga para a Protecção da Natureza (League for the Protection of Nature)
MENR	Ministry of Environment and Natural Resources (Ministério do Ambiente e dos Recursos Naturais)
MPAT	Ministry of Planning and Territory Adminstration (Ministério do Planeamento e da Administração do Território)
NGO	Non-Governmental Organisation
NEPP	National Environmental Policy Plan (Plano Nacional de Política do Ambiente)
OECD	Organisation of Economic Co-operation and Development
PTE	Portuguese Escudos
QUERCUS	Associação Nacional para a Conservação da Natureza (National Association for Nature Conservation)

SEARN   Secretaria de Estado do Ambiente e dos Recursos Naturais (Secretariat for the Environment and Natural Resources)

SO_2 Sulphur Dioxide

UNCED   United Nations Conference on Environment and Development

Greece's Institutional Response to Sustainable Development

PANOS FOUSEKIS and JOSEPH N. LEKAKIS

Evidence indicates that despite some notable efforts, Greece's response to the challenge of sustainable development has been limited, the impediments being strategic, structural, and procedural. Institutional fragmentation, the drive for economic convergence with the northern countries of Europe, and the absence of a strong environmental movement in Greece, all attest to this reality. The emphasis of the research presented here is on the commitment of Greece to designing and implementing sustainable development strategies, in response to the resolutions of the 1992 Rio Conference, as well as relevant European Union initiatives. This commitment is assessed by looking at well accepted prerequisites to these strategies, including policy co-ordination, targets of accountability, green accounting, awareness raising, and the integration of environmental objectives into sectoral plans.

The World Commission on Environment and Development in 1987 coined the term 'sustainable development' to signify a new era of international economic growth within environmental limits. At the Rio Convention in 1992, the signatory parties agreed to draw-up strategies on how they would implement sustainable development at national levels, laying out commitments and targets as well as the means for achieving them. In the context of the European Union (EU), the Maastricht Treaty of 1993 introduced sustainable development into the Union's objectives and amended Article 2 of the Treaty of Rome by removing the words 'continuous economic expansion' and replacing them with 'sustainable and non-inflationary growth respecting the environment'. In addition, the Maastricht Treaty made it imperative to integrate environmental considerations into the definition and implementation of other Community Policies.

Dr Joseph Lekakis is a faculty member in the School of Social Sciences, Department of Economics, University of Crete, Rethimno. Dr Panos Fousekis is a researcher at the National Agricultural Research Foundation in Greece. They would like to thank Professor Tim O'Riordan for his guidance, the European Commission, DG XII, for financial support, and the Hellenic Ministry of the Environment for providing access to relevant data. The usual disclaimers apply.

The objective of this study is to assess the commitment of Greece to designing and implementing sustainable development strategies in response to the Rio resolutions and the new Community approach to the relationship between environment and development. This assessment will be based on the identification and evaluation of the apparatus established to support the sustainable development process both at the national level and in different sectors of the society.

The study is structured as follows. The first section analyses the public and political structure of the sustainability transition. The analysis draws on a number of interpretations and views of sustainable development which have appeared at times in official documents, scientific works and popular journals, with the objective of determining whether these interpretations and views have influenced public perceptions and policy-making. The subsequent section provides a historical overview of the national response to the United Nations' Committee on Sustainable Development (CSD). The core of the paper follows, this examines the apparatus surrounding the national Agenda 21 (A21) and the role of Non-Governmental Organisations (NGOs) in the strategy.[1] In particular, it assesses the effectiveness of the existing institutional arrangements and looks for signs of institutional innovations. The last section is devoted to the impediments to sustainable development at the national level. Three general types of blockages are considered, namely, the strategic, the structural, and the procedural, summarising the findings of the study.

The Public and Political Culture of the Sustainability Transition

Translating Sustainable Development into Greek

Both social and natural sciences have extensively borrowed from the Greek vocabulary to christen concepts which are missing in other languages. '*Economics*' and '*ecology*', which typically represent the spectrum of these sciences are truly composite Greek words. Despite the fact that the Greek language has been a goldmine of scientific terminology, a unique translation of sustainable development in Greek does not exist. While no absolute classifications can be made, the ecologist's label of sustainable development is *Aieforiki Anaptyksi*, from *aie* (always) and *faero* (bring, carry, produce). Sociologists, policy makers and politicians appear to prefer the most popular label *Viosimi Anaptyksi*, meaning viable, or capable of living. An alternative label *Ypostiriksimi Anaptyksi*, meaning supportable has been employed as well. The notion, however, of sustainable development has only recently become a part of the scientific and political jargon in Greece.

Pyrovetsi [*1994*] uses the word *Aieforiki*. According to her, societies should set the following priorities: firstly, to preserve life support processes and biodiversity; secondly, to minimise the exhaustion of stock resources; and thirdly, to function within the productive capacities of ecosystems. Pyrovetsi calls for a 'common responsibility' which necessitates a wide and active participation of governments, economic agents, and the public as citizens and consumers. Each citizen ought to adopt an ethic of 'sustainable living', reconsider his/her values and alter his/her behaviour. Thus, while advocating development which does not interfere with the productive capacity of ecosystems, Pyrovetsi calls for a change in personal values to reverse the present trend of environmental degradation.

Laskaris [*1993*] employs the label *Viosimi Anaptyksi*. For him, sustainable development occurs locally where societies are capable of integrating it into local conditions in the way they know best. Because local societies are economically, administratively, and educationally dependant on the centre, sustainable development pre-supposes institutional freedom. The vehicle to gaining it is environmental education. Thus, Laskaris's view is also value oriented, although he appears to understand the significance of political and economic factors.

Using *Aieforiki, Ypostiriksimi,* and *Viosimi,* Kousis [*1991; 1993;* and *1994*] adopts a political economy theorisation of sustainable development as a case of environmental conflict. Capitalist producers, assisted by the state, manage to transform ecosystems into *exchange values* (profits), while consumers are interested in ecosystem *use values* (for example: recreation, aesthetics, public health). For Kousis, there are two sides to the sustainability issue, the social and ecological. When these two are compatible, then the process of sustainable development can be strengthened. Sakiotis [*1993: 20–22*] adopts a political economy point of view as well. According to him, however, the main principles which ought to underlie a sustainable model of ecological management in Greece are: a balance between domestic consumption and production to ensure a dynamic equilibrium of the national economy; a decentralisation of resources, population, economic activities, and the promotion of forms of economic organisation characterised by locality and diversity; the use of environmentally friendly methods of production and sources of energy; and finally, upgrading the Greek citizen to become an active cell in national political life. For Sakiotis, the ultimate objective of a model of sustainable development must be the elimination of the 'new poverty', the establishment of social justice, and the improvement in the quality of life. The main factor in this process cannot be central government or the political parties but societal mobilisation.

From the above discussion it follows that not only are there different domestic labels for sustainable development but also a host of views regarding its interpretation and the means of achieving it. These views range from being value-oriented, emphasising citizen/consumer responsibility and the role of environmental education, to more radical ones emphasising diversity, self-reliance, democracy and fairness. The majority of views, however, appear to recognise that local societies are bound to play a very important role in the pathway of transition.

For this presentation of domestic labels and views to be complete it also has to mention that some influential figures of the Greek ecological movement appear to reject the concept of sustainable development altogether. In the words of Modinos [*1995: 19*]:

> the cunningly constructed notion of sustainable development, with the emphasis it places on the peaceful resolution of the ultimate conflict of our era (development versus environment] has played an instrumental role in assimilating the quest for political change into the market mechanisms ... Sustainable development can only bring about small scale changes through a negotiation process, which in spite of its '*solemnity*' will soon reach the limits of its own reasoning... The concept of sustainable development, in that sense, may be thought of as the most ambiguous plan of conflict resolution throughout history.

Official Labels and Views

The labels *Viosimi* and *Aieforiki* have found their way into official discourse only in the last four to five years. In official documents both *Viosimi* and *Aieforiki* have been used. For example, the Greek Editions of the Maastricht Treaty, of the Treaty of the European Economic Area, and of the National Report to CSD, adopt the word *Viosimi*, while the European Commission [*1993*] uses the label *Aieforiki*. The three alternative domestic labels for sustainable development, however, have hardly found their way into vernacular discourse. The average Greek citizen, has never heard of *Viosimi*, *Aieforiki*, or *Ypostiriksimi Anaptyksi*, let alone the concepts they embody, their goals or the implications of a sustainable development strategy. This is not only because the concept is rather new but mainly because no organised effort has been undertaken to inform the public about these issues.

The Greek Prime Minister made no reference to sustainable development in his inauguration speech to the parliament on 23 October 1993. The only politician who refers, more or less systematically, to sustainable development is the Minister for the Environment, Physical Planning, and Public Works. In addressing the parliament on 25 October

1993, he defined the objectives of the government, in general, and his Ministry in particular as:

• the 'marriage' between ecology and *Aieforiki (Viosimi) Anaptyksi*;

• the preservation of balance, harmony, and diversity in the natural environment;

• the fight against pollution, and improvement in the quality of life;

• international co-operation on environmental problems; and

• close co-operation between the government and ecological NGOs.

He went further to propose referendums on national and local environmental questions, and the establishment of an autonomous collective body which '. . . will organise and articulate the society's environmental concerns against the State's monologue'. Although, these proposals are very novel, subsequent discussion will show that good intentions (if any) are not enough. In fact, Greece has, so far, made very few and only fragmentary steps towards meeting the obligations stemming from the Rio Conference in 1992.

The National Reports to the United Nations Conference on Environment and Development (UNCED) and the CSD

The National Report of Greece to UNCED in 1992 was assigned to a preparatory committee which consisted exclusively of representatives from several ministries and other governmental agencies.[2] The preparation process was co-ordinated by the Ministry of Foreign Affairs, and the Ministry for the Environment, Physical Planning and Public Works (YPEHODE). The final draft was approved by the two co-ordinating authorities and the Ministry of National Economy. Public participation in the document's preparation was meagre. The Procedural Note to the National Report mentions that some ecological NGOs contributed through their ministries or through written views and publications. In essence, however, the preparation of the National Report to UNCED was a purely bureaucratic process. Therefore, it is not surprising that public reaction to it was non-existent.

The National Report to UNCED was written following the relevant guidelines of the PRECOX. It contains some general information about the economic situation, the state of the environment, and the difficulties in planning and implementing environmental policies in Greece. It emphasises that the pursuit of sustainable development is a real challenge for Greece because the country has not yet achieved the economic prosperity of other

EU member states. The report makes an explicit appeal for financial assistance by stating that: 'it is useless to require less developed countries to protect and rehabilitate the environment without providing them with concrete means for improvement in their economic and social conditions' [*1992: 127–8*]. Thus, the document provides a clear indication that economic growth remains the country's main priority and that Greece is determined to defend its position internationally even though it has signed A21.

Since Rio, Greece has submitted two Reports to the CSD, one in 1994 and one in 1995. Both were prepared by YPEHODE (in the Department of International Activities and EU Affairs), with the assistance of the sectoral departments of several other ministries. The 1994 Report focused on both cross-sectoral and sectoral issues, but is characterised by a tendency to overstate progress towards meeting the objectives of A21; vagueness; and incoherence. The 1995 Report also focused on cross-sectoral (for example, national co-ordination of the A21 follow-up, and combating poverty) and sectoral issues (such as: land management, reforestation, sustainable agriculture and rural development, biodiversity). Compared to the 1994 Report, the latest Report is much more informative. This is because the two documents have different formats, the 1995 National Report is based on a very detailed questionnaire produced by the CSD Secretariat. Thus, there was little room for vagueness, incoherence and exaggeration. Therefore, the latest report provides a very clear picture of how far the country has moved in following up A21.

The National Strategies for Sustainable Development

Although a signatory of the Rio Convention, Greece has not yet produced any national plan on sustainable development. The Office of International and EU Affairs within YPEHODE asserts that the country's national strategy is the EU's Fifth Action Plan on the Environment.[3] Despite the lack of a distinct national plan, one may still assess the commitment to sustainable development by examining whether there has been visible progress in establishing the mechanisms required for a sustainable development strategy, domestic or imported. These mechanisms include: policy co-ordination, targets, the integration of environmental considerations into sector plans, structures of accountability, 'green accounting', information and public participation, and awareness raising.

Policy Co-ordination

A key national co-ordination mechanism to implement A21 has not been established yet. Until now this role has been performed by YPEHODE, and it is worth noting that it has undergone no reorganisation to meet the requirements of its new role. The ability of the YPEHODE to co-ordinate environmental policies, in general, and sustainable development strategies in particular, has been the focus of several studies [*Vlassopoulou, 1991; Lekakis, 1995; Pridham et al., 1995*]. On the scientific front conclusions appear to be very similar. Sectoral fragmentation and the absence of effective inter-ministerial co-ordination are serious obstacles to implementing sustainable development strategies in Greece.[4] This is further complicated by the dual role of YPEHODE. Vlassopoulou [*1991*] has shown that the merging of the housing and public works ministries in 1986 which give birth to YPEHODE has resulted in the subordination of environmental issues to developmental concerns.

The need for a distinct and strong co-ordinating mechanism for the environment appears to be gaining recognition also on the political front. Presenting its programme on the quality of life, the leading opposition party has recently promised the establishment of a separate ministry and a national council of environmental affairs to be chaired by the Prime Minister. Also, the latest National Report on *The State of The Environment*, which is about to be submitted to parliament, contains several innovative proposals, such as: conflict resolution among governmental departments through clarifying and redefining the agencies responsible for the environment; the establishment of an autonomous body to inspect the environmental performance of sectoral departments; and the establishment of a new ministry for physical planning and the environment to initiate environmental policies which will be followed by the sectoral departments. Whether any of these promises will come to fruition remains to be seen. The accumulated experience is not very encouraging, since past attempts to break the vicious cycle of compartmentalisation and implementation deficits (for example, Law 1650/86) have not been successful.

Targets and Accountability

The only targets which have been set up, so far, are related to the CO_2 and CFC emissions. In April 1994, parliament ratified the Climate Change Convention and the country undertook to stabilise CO_2 emissions at 1990 levels by the year 2000. The follow-up plan was produced by YPEHODE and the Ministry of Industry, Energy, and Technology, and it estimated that by the year 2000, if left unchecked, CO_2 emissions would increase by 27 per cent. Despite international obligations, the Government decided that it would be more realistic to aim to achieve a level of emissions 15 per cent higher than in 1990 because of the limited time-frame, the lack of resources, the administrative weaknesses, and the inflexibility of the country's productive system. The response of Greece to the Amended Montreal Protocol has, however, been more satisfactory. Although EU Regulations

594/91 and 3252/92 allowed for production of CFCs at 15 per cent of the 1986 level, the government reached an agreement with SING (the main producer of CFCs in Greece) to reduce the quota to seven per cent. Since January 1996 SING's production of these substances has been zero.

Given the absence of targets, in general, it is not surprising that structures of accountability have been only partially developed. According to Law 1650/86 the government must bring to parliament an annual report on the *State of The Environment*. The first report was submitted in 1992 for 'acknowledgement'. The second report was published in November 1995 but it has not been submitted to parliament yet. This latest report is a well written document which largely recognises the concerns that there are substantial institutional obstacles to pursuing sustainable development in Greece, as well as subscribing to the specific proposals for change which have been long put forward by environmentalists. Overall, the document appears to have the potential to open up the discussion on sustainable development and the means to achieve it. Whether this will actually take place depends on how rigorously the leadership of YPEHODE pursues the objective stated in the report's introduction, that is, to make Greece the ecological and cultural envy of Europe.

Incorporating Environmental Considerations into Sectoral Plans

The main instrument to counter environmental degradation from economic activities has been Environmental Impact Assessment studies (EIAs), introduced by Law 1650/86 in compliance with EU Directive 85/377. However, the content and the process of approving an EIA was determined only 4 years later in Joint Ministerial Decision 69269/5387/90. As if the delay was not enough, many problems have already been identified with regard to its practical application in Greece [*Bousbouras, 1992; Tsantilis, 1994; Papayiannakis, 1994*], the most significant of which are:

- failure to perform comparative analysis of alternative solutions;

- failure to consider the cumulative effects of mega-projects. This was the case with two highly controversial projects, namely, the construction of the new international airport in Athens at Spata, and the diversion of the River Aheloos. With regard to the later project, the Superior Administrative Court ruled in the Autumn of 1994 that the plan constituted a violation of environmental legislation;

- some projects have been implemented on the basis of pre-approval where the EIA is a formality carried out afterwards; and

- some EIAs are carried out at a local level by personnel lacking the necessary skills.

No regular inspection of compliance with environmental terms exists. Inspections take place when the authorities have information or a suspicion that a particular industrial plant is polluting the environment. Sometimes an advance warning precedes inspection. To address these issues the government is planning to create a body of inspectors which will be responsible for ensuring industrial compliance with environmental terms.

Green Accounting and Pollution Control Instruments

Green accounting: Decision-making for sustainable development requires the establishment a 'green' accounting system capable of quantifying the interactions between environmental commodities and the economy [*Pearce and Turner, 1990*]. Under the current national accounting system in Greece the environment does not constitute a separate category. Value added due to 'environmental services' is recorded as the product of 'other activities'. At the same time, the system does not account for 'environmental disservices'. From the latest National Report to the CSD it appears that Greece has no immediate plans to establish a green accounting system. In any case, such a step would be premature since green accounting systems are information intensive relative to conventional systems and the country has a big gap to bridge in this respect. In the context of the EU's Fifth Environmental Action Plan, however, Greece has embarked on the creation of the infrastructure required to monitor the state of the environment and improve the availability of information. The most important measures within this endeavour are: the completion of the national networks to monitor air and water quality; the extension of the national network of environmental information so that it covers all 13 regions of the country; and the drawing up of the national cadastral.

Pollution control instruments: Generally speaking, pollution control instruments can be classified into command and control and market-based instruments. According to economic theory, market-based instruments are preferable to command and control because they are more cost effective [*Baumol and Oates, 1989*]. Greek governments appear to have no strategic approach with regard to any of these instruments, for the simple reason that environmental protection has not been the focus but the by-product of even those national policies which have been termed environmental ones. However, some command and control instruments have been introduced to cope with environmental crises. Investment grants for anti-pollution projects were employed in the 1980s to promote economic growth by strengthening aggregate demand. The only green tax instituted in Greece, so far, has been a five drachmas tax per unit of petrol sold in the Metropolitan Athens Area since 1992. A conflict, however, was soon played out in the press between the Ministry of Finance and YPEHODE as the former had withheld the revenues to fill 'black holes' in the budget. It was not until October 1994 that these tax revenues were finally transferred to YPEHODE to finance environmental projects.

Greek governments appear to consider green taxation as a threat to the manufacturing sector, an attitude evident in the reaction to the proposed EU carbon tax. Greece, in April 1994, requested an exemption from introducing such a tax from the EU Council of Ministers [*Efthimiopoulos, 1994*]. There exists a procedure to assess the potential usefulness of market-based instruments for pollution abatement in the country. Given that both economic theory and practical experience, at least in developed countries, has demonstrated the advantages of these instruments, this particular measure can be seen as nothing less than a pretext to avoid introducing green taxes in the near future.

Information and Public Participation

The right of the public to information and to participate in environmental issues has its roots in Article 24 of the Constitution: 'protection of the natural and cultural environment is the right and the obligation of every Greek citizen'. With regard to information, Law 1650/86 stipulates that citizens or their representatives can be acquainted with the content of EIAs and with the plans of central authorities to declare areas or resources as protected ones. Free access to environmental information is also dictated by EU Directive 90/313, to which member states had to comply by 31 December 1992. Greece has not implemented this Directive, in spite of threats by the Commission that the country will be arraigned by the European Court [*Papayiannakis, 1994; 1995*]. Although some institutional arrangements for access to information are in place, those who seek information often encounter the refusal of authorities to provide it. Papayiannakis [*1995*] cites the EIA carried out on the port of Kalamata as an example where access was denied on the grounds that an EIA is the intellectual property of the people who conducted it. No formal arrangement for public participation exists. Of course informal consultation always takes place, especially with those whose opinion is considered to matter, for example, consulting the business community prior to taking any action seems to be a part of the environmental authorities' routines.

Awareness Raising

Increased public awareness of environmental issues has been pursued by a variety of means including campaigns, the introduction of environmental courses into the curricula of the primary and secondary schools, and the establishment of Centres for Environmental Education. Law 1892/90 provides for the establishment of such Centres in order to raise the awareness of the youth sector, to organise seminars for adult training, and to support local environmental education programmes. The first Centre has been operating in the prefecture of Achaia since 1993. It is expected that 20 more will be established in the country by the year 2000. Public awareness campaigns focus on specific issues such as recycling, protection of wetlands and coastal areas, prevention of forest fires, and the rational use of energy. Although no markers have been developed yet, it is generally accepted that public awareness is low [*National Report to UNCED, 1992: 17*].

Since environmental education in state schools is relatively new (it was recently introduced in Law 1892/90), it is difficult to evaluate its influence over students' attitudes towards the environment. Some weaknesses, however, are becoming increasingly apparent. According to the Directorate of Environmental Education only five to six per cent of schools are currently offering courses and student participation is low (10–15 students per school, on average). In addition, teachers are not willing to get involved because of the lack of sufficient financial incentives. Environmental courses are offered at the latter periods of the school day and this does not encourage students to participate. Also, because the Greek bibliography is rather poor, translations of foreign books are used for the courses. As a result, students have difficulty relating the content of the courses to their personal experience [*Kalaitzidis, 1994*].

The Role of the Non-Governmental Sector

The Role of the Business Sector

Initiatives by industry: with respect to sustainable development environmental degradation by the industrial sector is a critical issue. Greek governments have, however, traditionally viewed environmental protection as a threat to the country's economic growth. This attitude has hardly encouraged businesses to adopt pollution abatement measures.

The behaviour of Greek industrialists until the early 1990s is illustrated by the following results from a survey of 170 big businesses:[5]

• 65 businesses (38.3 per cent) had adopted some type of environmental standards;

• 70 businesses (41.2 per cent) believed that there was no need to take any measures because they considered their activities harmless to the environment;

• 14 businesses (8.3 per cent) admitted that they had not established any standards.

From those businesses which already had an environmental programme in place only 49.2 per cent had made concrete plans to improve their environmental performance in the near future. With regard to motivating factors in the adoption of environmental standards, 50.8 per cent cited the need to comply with Community, national or international rules, 26.2 per cent to increase their competitiveness, 13.8 per cent to reduce production costs, and 21.5 per cent to improve the firm's public image. The evidence that only relatively few firms have been actively involved in environmental protection is corroborated by other research, for example, Theohary [*1995: 21–2*] finds that it is mainly the branches of multi-national companies that possess a coherent policy *vis-á-vis* the environment.

In November 1991, the Association of Greek Industrialists declared 1992 as 'the industrial sector's year for the environment', in an attempt to raise environmental awareness in the business community. As part of this initiative it undertook several measures: a series of meetings and seminars on the subject; membership of the (international) Union of Businesses for Sustainable Development; the establishment of the Hellenic Etairia for Recycling to pursue, along with government agencies and other NGOs, a national strategy on product recycling; and currently, the Association of Greek Industrialists operates a centre for information and advice on environmental issues and awards prizes to businesses with excellent environmental record. Another significant innovation, this time prompted by EU and international concern over ozone depletion, was the adoption of a voluntary protection scheme named the 'Responsible Care Plan' by the members of the Association of Greek Chemical Manufacturers (announced in May 1995) which is internationally acknowledged as the most complete currently in operation.

In conclusion, positive change appears to be occurring in the Greek industrial sector. The process, however, is likely to be very slow. Both the mentality of the Government (environmental protection results in unemployment) and the mentality of businessmen (the state rather than the private sector should care about the environment) are impediments to making the transition towards sustainable development.

Eco-labelling and Eco-management and Audit Schemes (EMAS): Eco-labelling and EMAS are new institutions designed to encourage the adoption of voluntary schemes by industry. Greece harmonised with EU Regulation 92/880 by Joint Ministerial Decision 93/86644/2482, this provides for the establishment of a Supreme Board for Awarding Ecological Labels within the YPEHODE. The Board includes representatives from several ministries, the Association of Greek Industrialists, Trade Unions, an ecological organisation and a consumers' association. Despite the publicity given to Eco-labelling, however, business interest remains low. This may be attributed to the fact that the criteria for obtaining the labels are considered by the business community to be too high.[6] Harmonisation with Regulation 93/1836, concerned with EMAS, has not yet taken place. This is because of the ambiguity of the Regulation itself (for example, it is not explicit regarding the formal qualifications of the Accredited Environmental Verifiers), and to the low level of co-ordination among the involved ministries. However, it appears that there is a lot of interest from Greek businesses, especially the larger ones, therefore the Association of Industrialists in Northern Greece is currently running two EMAS pilot projects to see if this can be harnessed.[7]

The Role of Trade Unions

Environmental degradation in urban areas and the ensuing deterioration of the quality of life for a large part of the working class, was bound to attract the attention of trade unions. In the last five years the protection of the environment has become an issue within the framework of industrial relations, alongside the 'traditional' issues of wages and health and safety. Furthermore, the concept of sustainable development has been finding its way into the jargon of prominent workers' organisations, such as the Athens Centre for Workers and the General Confederation of Greek Workers.

There are practical manifestations of the trade unions' interest in the environment: the publication by the Athens Centre for Workers of the newsletter *Drasi* (Action) to raise workers' awareness; the organisation of seminars and meetings on the environment, industrial relations, and sustainable development; and Article 11 of the Annual National Contract 1994–95 which provides for the establishment of a joint committee by General Confederation of Greek Workers and SEB to investigate industrial pollution and to propose concrete abatement measures for the greater Athens area. Addressing a meeting on Industrial Relations and the Environment, in November 1994, the president of the Athens Centre for Workers, however, recognised that there are obstacles to adoption of sustainable development as a part of the trade unions' agenda. These obstacles are both subjective and objective. The former include the low level of awareness and the belief of several workers' organisations that striving for this new goal will weaken the efforts towards the 'basic' goal of raising workers' standards of living. The objective obstacle is the general economic climate and the strong sense of insecurity about the future among Greek workers.

The Role of Local Authorities

Competencies of local authorities over environmental matters: according to the Greek Constitution of 1975 the management of local affairs belongs to local authorities or preferably locally elected governments, of which there are two types: the First Degree (OTA) and the Second Degree (NA). The former refers to communities and municipalities, while the latter refers to prefectures (counties). No formal relation between the two types exists, NAs do not supervise OTAs in their prefecture nor do they interfere with their decisions.

OTAs are an old institution which have gradually been vested with considerable power over local environmental matters, such as: the construction of water supply and waste management projects, recreation sites, grazing land management, and physical planning. Central government is obliged to consult OTAs prior to taking any action related to local physical planning and the environment. In the case of disagreement, however, central government may circumvent OTAs' objections by adducing special reasons. However, the financial ability and administrative capacity of OTAs are not, typically, commensurate with their competence over environmental affairs. Their financial strength is limited by the lack of statutory powers to raise revenue, thus they are financially dependent on central government. The lack of administrative capacity is also related to financial limitations as well as to the size of OTAs. Currently, there are more than 6000 communities and municipalities in Greece, and OTAs where population sizes of 500, 200 or even 50 is the norm rather than the exception. In the past financial incentives have been given by the state to encourage communities to merge, with limited success. A possible answer to these problems was the establishment (in September, 1995) of Regional Councils which consist of representatives of OTAs with common geographical, economic and cultural characteristics. The Regional Councils are responsible for drawing up development plans, for implementing projects with intra-community implications, and for providing technical support to their members.

In contrast, NAs are new institutions established by Law 2218/94. Accordingly, NAs undertake all powers which used to belong to the state's prefectural offices, except for those related to National Defence, Justice, Finance, and Foreign Affairs. Transition from a very centralised state to a decentralised one, however, is not easy. There is remains a lot of friction between central government and the NAs over finances and competencies. Nevertheless, the establishment of NAs is considered by many to be the most important institutional innovation in Greece in the last century. With regard to sustainable development, potential benefits from these Second Degree locally elected governments include greater accountability for local leaders to local people, and greater involvement of local people in the decision-making process. Under the previous system, prefectural governments were appointed by the central government as a reward for loyalty and service to the party in power. There is also better co-ordination of local offices and efficient management of local affairs as a result of this innovation. Previously, sectoral fragmentation and conflict at the central level over spheres of authority used to be transferred to the local level resulting in inertia, confusion and inefficiency.

Local democracy and capacity building at local level, however, are necessary but not sufficient conditions for sustainabilty. A potentially negative impact of decentralisation is the greater vulnerability of locally elected governments to local interests which may result in neglect or even abuse of the environment. Locally elected governments, therefore, have to balance the need for local legitimacy in their decision-making and the need for broader strategies (national or international) of environmental management.

Initiatives supporting a Local Agenda 21 (LA21): Chapter 28 of A21 asks local authorities to increase their co-operation, to exchange information, and to set-up a process of consultation with their communities in order to achieve consensus over a LA21. The Central Union of Local Governments in Greece in its capacity as an information agency and advisor to OTAs has been particularly active in this area. In the Autumn of 1994, it organised a conference on European environmental policy and the role of local authorities. During the conference, experiences of several countries (Holland, UK, Italy, Denmark, and Finland) were presented. In the beginning of 1995 it also drew-up a pilot project for implementing LA21 in two municipalities of the greater Athens Area, namely, Amarousion and Halandri. Partners in these projects are the Local Government Management Board-UK, the European Sustainable Cities and Towns Campaign, the International Council of Local Environmental Initiatives-Germany, and the Azienda Servizi Municipalizzati in Italy. Among the aims of the projects are: experience sharing and co-operation among local authorities in Europe on matters concerning the environment and sustainable development; awareness raising in other municipalities through extensive dissemination of the results; and strengthening partnerships among all the actors in the respective communities.

The Role of Ecological NGOs

The first ecological NGOs appeared in Greece in the early 1980s in response to the country's environmental problems and the influence of similar movements abroad. In October 1989, 46 ecological and 'alternative' organisations established a green political party called Ecologists-Alternatives, which managed to earn a seat in parliament. However, its lack of political organisation and experience, its inability to articulate a social-ecological alternative, and strife between the different factions, led to the loss of its parliamentary representation in the 1993 elections. Although the attempt to establish a 'green party' failed, Greek ecological NGOs continue to co-ordinate their activities, especially at the local level. Co-ordination at the national level is more difficult since different NGOs have different interests, however there is often international co-operation. Co-operation between the ecological NGOs and the state is limited since the former have not been considered by the state to be 'equal partners'. Occasionally, some ecological NGOs are invited to participate in committees or events because of EU or international obligations (for example, preparing the National Report to Rio, and establishing a board for awarding Eco-labels). At the national level, however, no formal arrangement has been made to allow for the participation of ecological NGOs in the national sustainable development strategy.

A particular type of ecological NGO are grass roots organisations. Tilly [1994] defines community/locally based grass root movements as *ad hoc* social movements which are temporary, specialised and relatively successful at mobilising communities against a specific threat. Kousis [1997] discusses the causes as well as the bureaucratic organisation and the power centralisation of three such environmental mobilisations in rural Greece, namely, those in Milos, Kalamas, and Astakos. In all cases local people were mobilised out of a concern for community health, and for local environmental and economic resources. Also, in all cases the local distrust of official documentation and technical reports was reflected in demands for participation in the decision-making process on environment and development matters in their region.

The Greek state has often given in to public demands for a cleaner environment. In the more industrialised nations producers are more or less inclined to adopt environmental controls and pass the costs on to the consumer, while in the less industrialised ones the state assumes the larger share of environmental investment costs. The semi-peripheral state, however, appears closer to the core state in its will to legitimise its citizenry. The presence of a strong Greek civil society during the last two decades has been pressuring the state to maintain social harmony by satisfying public demands for a cleaner environment [*Kousis, 1994: 133*]. The large variety of grass roots environmental mobilisations in terms of duration and issues makes it difficult to conclude on the fate of these NGOs.

Impediments

In the light of the above discussion, Greece has shown a rather low degree of commitment to design and implement sustainable development strategies. Despite the politicians' rhetoric and the good intentions of the country's environmental authorities, the Greek experience is still far from a sustainable development strategy, for it typically fits the picture painted by the literature on sectoral fragmentation and implementation deficits. The impediments to sustainable development at the national level can be classified as: strategic, structural and procedural.

Strategic

Sustainable development has not been a national priority. Both the Report to UNCED (prepared under the conservative government) as well as programme of the new socialist government (presented to parliament in October 1993) can testify to the fact that rapid economic growth, as a means of converging with the northern EU member states, is the ultimate national policy objective. Official documents such as the National Reports to CSD and the Reports to parliament tend to highlight the establishment of new institutions (such as, EIA, EMAS, and Eco-labelling) and the creation of networks for monitoring environmental quality, as indisputable evidence of the country's commitment to sustainable development. However, one should bear in mind that the new institutions were created under both the stick (the European Court) and the carrot (money) of the EU. In addition, Greece is notorious for the gap between formality and reality. A better indicator of the country's commitment to sustainable development is the Regional Development Plan for the period 1994–99. This plan places great emphasis on road construction (an increase in road density of 143 per cent), and the implementation of mega-projects such as the new international airport in Athens and the diversion of the River Acheloos, which are expected to incur huge and irreversible environmental damage. As such it is strongly opposed by national and international NGOs, by local authorities and even by several Greek politicians.

Structural

It is generally accepted that the holistic nature of sustainable development does not match with the fragmented and sectorised institutions established to deal with them. In Greece, there are about 50 agencies involved in the planning and implementation of environmental programmes and more than 150 pieces of legislation. Law 1650/86 has been an attempt to codify all the existing legislation and to assign the basic power of the public sector *vis á vis* the environment to a single agency, namely, the Executive Environmental Agency (EFOP). This law, however, has not achieved its objective because its implementation required a vast number of legislative acts (12 Presidential Degrees, four Acts of the Ministerial council, and 45 Joint Ministerial Decisions), and most have not been issued yet. It is interesting to note that for six of the years since 1986, power was held by the same party (socialist) which sponsored Law 1650/86. This is a clear indication that structural impediments are closely related to strategic ones, in the sense that the former stem from the low priority and lack of political will to implement sustainable development strategies. Structural blockages have been further aggravated by the lack of administrative capacity, and financial resources to implement environmental protection projects, especially at the regional/local level.

Procedural

This category of impediments is related to the level of environmental consciousness and the degree of public participation into the decision-making process. The National report to UNCED recognises that 'environmental awareness is not highly developed in Greece'. A manifestation of this low level of environmental consciousness is the lack of a domestic green movement similar to those in Western European and other developed countries. Political scientists and sociologists attribute the present state of environmental awareness to a purely articulated civil society in the country. Statism and populism together with a highly atomistic mentality and consumerism discourage collective action over broader social goals such as sustainable development [*Kousis, 1994; Pridham et al., 1995; Demertzis, 1995*]. Public participation in the decision-making process may take different forms. One way is to make formal arrangements for the participation of NGOs. Another is the organisation of public meetings and referendums on local and general environmental issues.

Finally, public participation may take the form of a greater involvement for parliament in environmental matters. As explained above, no formal arrangements have been made for the participation of NGOs. There are three reasons for this: first, the public sector in Greece is not accustomed to using external, independent advice; secondly, the attitude of most NGOs (both ecological and trade unions) has been that of denunciation rather than co-operation; and finally, in the absence of formal arrangements, governments may select for consultation only those NGOs which do not challenge their policies.

Participation in the form of public meetings or referendums has no tradition in Greece. During its first term in power (early 1980s) the socialist party encouraged public meetings over local issues. However, the process was soon discredited as it was realised by those involved that their decisions had a negligible impact on the policies of central government. The conservative governments have been, in general, reluctant to introduce institutions of direct democracy. The parliament's involvement in environmental issues is very limited. In the last two years YPEHODE was called upon only once in parliament to elaborate on its environmental policy. Harmonisation with EU directives has been taking place through joint ministerial decisions; as a result, parliament has been left out of this process. Parliament's Rules and Procedures provide for the establishment of special committees to investigate issues of national importance, their proposals, however, are rarely implemented. No special committee on the environment has been set up thus far.

Conclusions

The response of Greece to the challenge of sustainable development has been limited, partial and fragmented. Inertia at the national level is manifested in the absence of a domestically formulated A21 and of domestically initiated policy measures. O'Riordan and Jordan [1996] identified four stages of institutional adaptation to sustainable development, namely: acknowledgement by cosmetic compliance; adoption of new perspectives by social learning; formal realignment of position and influence; and second order stability around new norms. The Greek experience suggests that the country has barely entered the first of these stages.

The economic and political climate in the country, together with administrative weaknesses (compartmentalisation and sectoral fragmentation), are major blockages to a sustainable development process. The drive for convergence with the wealthier EU member states has overridden any other priority. In the last ten years the capacity of governments has been, almost exclusively, judged on the grounds of how quickly they 'absorb' Community money for the purpose of economic growth. Integration of environmental considerations into sectoral policies is desirable only to the extent that it does not result in 'lower' absorption rates. The political culture of the citizenry, having its roots in many years of 'controlled democracy' alternated with dictatorships regimes, together with economic insecurity about the future, do not favour collective action on a broader agenda such as sustainable development.

Given the country's economic problems and the lack of a strong social movement for sustainable development the question becomes: what can possibly trigger the sustainability transition in Greece? Smith [1993] identified eight possible general stimuli including change in external relations, emergence of new problems, introduction of new technologies and cultural shift. In the case of Greece, changes in external relations and in particular developments within the EU can play an important role in the short-run. In contrast with other international organisations the EU possesses the means to enforce institutional innovations. Also the reorganisation of Directorate General XI [*Wilkinson, 1995*] can serve as a model for national co-ordination mechanisms. In the long-run, the emergence of new problems, such as: economic interests being threatened by environmental degradation (for example, the tourism industry); water shortages; floods due to deforestation; and the introduction of new technologies, may stimulate the sustainability transition. Cultural shift, however, is not likely to be an influence on the process in the near future.

NOTES

1. Our focus is on their initiatives and not on the environmental problems they may be responsible for.
2. Ministries: Foreign Affairs, National Economy, Environment, Physical Planning and Public Works, Agriculture, Industry, Energy, Technology and Trade, National Education and Religious Affairs, Culture, Merchant Marine, Transport and Communications, Health, Welfare and Social Security. Agencies: General Secretariat of Equality, General Secretariat of Youth, National Tourism Organisation, National Meteorological Service.
3. Personal communication with Ms. Kritikou, YPEHODE, Athens.
4. Details on the lack of co-ordination between the ministries can be found in Vlassopoulou [*1991*], Lekakis [*1995*] and Pridham *et al.* [*1995*].
5. Published in the newspaper 'To Vima' on 8 Oct. 1992.
6. Personal communication with Mrs Katsou, YPEHODE, Athens.
7. Personal communication with Mrs Ioannidou, YPEHODE, Athens.

REFERENCES

Baumol, W. and W. Oates (1989), *The Theory of Environmental Policy*, Cambridge: Cambridge University Press.
Bousbouras, D. (1992), 'The Institution of Environmental Impact Assessment in Greece', *Nea Oikologia*, June (in Greek), pp.22–3.
Commission of the European Union (1993), *Application forms for the RTD Program, Environment* 1992–94.
Demertzis, N. (1995), 'Greece: Greens at the Periphery', in D. Richardson and C. Rootes (eds.) *The Development of Green Parties in Europe*, London: Routledge, pp.193–207.
Efthimiopoulos, H. (1994), 'The Energy Tax: Potential and Deadlock of a Policy', *Nea Oikologia*, Sept. (in Greek), pp.16–20.
Kalaitzidis, D. (1994), 'Upgrading Environmental Education in Greece', *Nea Oikologia*, Sept. (in Greek), pp.38–9.
Kousis, M. (1991), 'Development, Environment and Social Mobilisation: A Micro Level Analysis', *The Greek Review of Social Research*, Vol.80, pp.96–109.
Kousis, M. (1993), 'Collective Resistance and Sustainable Development in Rural Greece: The Case of Geothermal Energy on the Island of Milos', *Sociologia Ruralis*, Vol.33, No.1, pp.3–34
Kousis, M. (1994), 'Environment and the State in the EU Periphery: The Case of Greece', *Regional Politics and Policy*, Vol.4, No.1, pp.118–35.
Kousis, M. (1997), 'Grassroots Environmental Movements in Rural Greece: Effectiveness Success and the Quest for Sustainable Development,' forthcoming in S. Baker, M. Kousis, D. Richardson, and S. Young (eds.), *The Politics of Sustainable Development*, London Routledge.
Ktenas, S. (1992), 'Place the Burden on the Environment Rather on Production Costs', *To Vima*

(Tribune), 8 Oct. 1992 (in Greek).

Laskaris, C. (1993), 'Environmental Crisis: A World Social and Educational Problem', in *Environmental Crisis: Theory Methodology and Special Perspectives,* Athens: Synchroni Epoche (in Greek), pp.17–52.

Lekakis, J. (1991), 'Employment Effects of Environmental Policies in Greece', *Environment and Planning A,* Vol.23, pp.1627–37.

Lekakis, J. (1995), 'Environmental Management in Greece and the Challenge of Sustainable Development', *The Environmentalist,* Vol.15, pp.16–26.

Modinos, M. (1995), 'Conflict Resolution', *Nea Oikologia,* May (in Greek), p.19.

National Report of Greece (1992), *UN Conference on Environment and Development,* Brazil, June 1992, Athens: YPEHODE.

O'Riordan, T. and A. Jordan (1996), 'Social Institutions and Climate Change', in T. Riordan and J. Jäger (eds.), *Politics of Climate Change: A European Perspective,* London: Routledge, pp.65–105

Papayiannakis, M. (1994), 'Evro-Oikologika', *Nea Oikologia,* March (in Greek), pp.6–17.

Papayianakis, M. (1995), 'Evro-Oikologika', *Nea Oikologia,* Jan. (in Greek), p.20.

Pearce, D. and R. Turner (1990), *Economics of National Resources and the Environment,* Baltimore, MD: Johns Hopkins University Press.

Pridham, G., Verney, S. and D. Konstandakopulos (1995), 'Environmental Policy in Greece: Evolution, Structures and Process', *Environmental Politics,* pp.244–70.

Pyrovetsi, M. (1994), 'Our Future? Sustainability', in *Modern World Problems and the Responsibility of the Scientist,* Salonika: Aristotelian University and Institute for Education and Peace (in Greek), pp.103–112.

Sakiotis, J. (1993), 'Greek Economy. Ten Principles for a Sustainable Model of Economic Management', *Nea Oikologia,* April (in Greek), pp.20–22.

Smith, M. (1993), *Pressure, Power and Policy: State Autonomy and Policy Networks in Britain and the United States,* London: Harvester Wheatsheaf.

Theohary, C. (1995), 'Industrial Relations and Environment in Greece', in *Environment and Labour in Greece,* Athens: EKA (in Greek).

Tsantilis, D. (1994), 'Dreams and Miracles in Environmental Performance', *Nea Oikologia,* December (in Greek), pp.20–22.

Tilly (1994), 'Social Movements as Historically Specific Clusters of Political Performances', *Berkeley Journal of Sociology,* Vol.38, pp.1–30.

Vlassopoulou, C. (1991), 'La Politique de L'Environment: Le Cas de la Pollution Atmospherique a Athens', thesis, University of Picardie (in France).

YPEHODE (1992), *Annual Report on the State of the Environment,* submitted to the Parliament, Nov., Athens (in Greek).

YPEHODE (1994), *National Report to the CSD,* Oct., Athens, Greece.

YPEHODE (1995a), *National Report to the CSD,* April, Athens, Greece.

YPEHODE (1995b), *Greece, Ecological and Cultural Stock. Data, Actions, Programmes for the Protection of the Environment,* Athens, July (in Greek).

Wilkinson, D. (1995), 'Approaches to Integrating the Environment into Other Sectoral Policies: An Interim Evaluation of Experience in the European Commission and Parliament', Institute of European Environmental Policy, London, April (draft).

Acronyms

A21	Agenda 21
CSD	United Nations Commission for Sustainable Development
EIA	Environmental Impact Assessment
EMAS	Eco-Auditing and Management System
EU	European Union

LA21	Local Agenda 21
NA	Second Degree locally elected government
NGO	Non-Governmental Organisation
OTA	First Degree locally elected government
UNCED	United Nations Conference on the Environment and Development
YPEHODE	Ministry for the Environment, Physical Planning and Public Works

Towards Sustainability in the European Union? Steps within the European Commission Towards Integrating the Environment into Other European Union Policy Sectors

DAVID WILKINSON

The principal vehicle employed by the European Union to implement Agenda 21 is the Fifth Environmental Action Programme, *Towards Sustainability*, which was published by the European Commission in March 1992. A key theme running through the Action programme is the need to *integrate* the needs of the environment into the development and implementation of other policies, particularly in five key sectors – agriculture, energy, industry, transport and tourism. Integration is seen as a fundamental pre-requisite for sustainable development. The Fifth Environmental Action Programme, however, is not binding on the European Union's Member States, nor in practice on individual directorates-general within the European Commission itself. A number of progress reports on the Fifth Environmental Action Programme produced by the Commission's Environment Directorate-General (DG XI) and the European Environment Agency have noted the limited impact so far of the programme and the need for greater political commitment to its objectives.

This study does not seek to describe substantive examples of integration that have occurred in the various European Union policy sectors since the publication of the Fifth Environmental Action Programme. Rather, the study is focused specifically on the procedural steps that have been taken by DG XI within the Commission to influence the development of European Union legislative and policy proposals in sectors outside its own immediate responsibilities. In its dealings with other directorates-general, DG XI has been obliged to rely on persuasion rather than power, a 'bottom up' as opposed to a 'top-down' approach to integration. So far this has had limited effect and DG XI has begun to seek means to enhance its power in relation to the rest of the Commission in order to accelerate the process of integration.

David Wilkinson is a Senior Fellow at the Institute for European Environmental Policy, London.

Sustainable Development, Integration and the Fifth Environmental Action Programme (5EAP)

'Sustainable Development' in the Treaties

It is not surprising that the original Treaty of Rome, signed in 1957, should have made no reference either to sustainable development or even to environmental protection. In Article 2, the Treaty set as the task for the Community the promotion of: 'a harmonious development of economic activities, a continuous and balanced expansion, an increase in stability, an accelerated raising of the standard of living, and closer relations between the States belonging to it'. This was to be achieved by establishing a common market and progressively approximating the economic policies of the member states. Given that this wording was drafted in the mid 1950s the call for 'continuous expansion' is not surprising, nor is the lack of any recognition that there might be environmental limits to growth.

When, 30 years later in 1987, the Single European Act came into force, it did not use the phrase 'sustainable development', but it did for the first time provide a formal, legal underpinning for the Community's already developing environmental policy. It also laid down the important principle of 'integration' (of the environment into other policies), which is generally regarded as a principal means for moving towards sustainable development. Article 130r(2) established the principle that: 'environmental protection requirements shall be a component of the Community's other policies'.

In 1993 the Maastricht Treaty on European Union (EU) introduced into the statement of the objectives of the Union the word 'sustainable' (not 'sustainable development', nor even the more limited concept of 'sustainability'). Article B of the Treaty sets as one of the objectives of the EU:

> to promote economic and social progress which is balanced and sustainable, in particular through the creation of an area without internal frontiers, through the strengthening of economic and social cohesion and through the establishment of economic and monetary union, ultimately including a single currency in accordance with the provisions of the Treaty.

At the time there was legitimate scepticism that 'economic and social progress which is balanced and sustainable' can be achieved through the creation of an internal market, monetary union, and eventually a single currency. What occurred during the 1990 Inter-Governmental Conference (IGC) was that the word 'sustainable' was added almost as an afterthought to the pre-existing political objective of political and monetary union (which was the main purpose of the Treaty of Maastricht) without otherwise much disturbing those objectives [*Wilkinson, 1993*].

In addition, the Maastricht Treaty also amended Article 2 of the Treaty of Rome by replacing the objective of 'continuous expansion' with that of 'sustainable and non-inflationary growth respecting the environment'. Although many environmentalists have pointed out the intellectual incoherence of the notion of 'sustainable growth', nevertheless it represented an advance that subsequently could be built upon. Maastricht also strengthened the 'integration' principle in Article 130r(2) by now making it imperative: '[e]nvironmental protection requirements must be integrated into the definition and implementation of other Community policies'. The practical effect of such legal formulations may on the face of it appear to be limited, but they have been used by the Environment Directorate-General (DG XI) and the European Parliament separately as justification for introducing new, formal mechanisms and procedures aimed at ensuring that the environment is taken into account across all EU policy sectors.

'Integration'

Approaches to integration:[1] Strategies for integrating environmental concerns into sectoral policies with major environmental implications may take a variety of forms along what may be termed an *integration continuum.* Along this continuum the activities of sectoral departments are subject to increasing degrees of constraint in order that environmental objectives may be secured. The continuum extends from 'strong', or 'top-down' integration at one end, to 'soft' or 'bottom-up' approaches at the other. 'Top-down' integration depends upon the possession and exercise, normally by an environment ministry, of formal power in relation to other departments. By contrast, a 'bottom-up' approach is more incremental and piecemeal and, crucially, leaves sectoral departments greater freedom to determine the extent to which they modify their policy or programme objectives for environmental reasons.

• *Top-down integration* typically involves the establishment of binding frameworks which constrain the actions of sectoral departments. Mechanisms for enacting this approach include the development by the Government as a whole, perhaps led by an environment ministry, of sectoral Action Plans with quantified targets and timetables for reaching them. This is the approach adopted in the Netherlands in successive Environment Plans. Top-down integration requires effective review and reporting mechanisms to monitor progress in achieving targets. So in addition to playing a leading part in setting these priorities, the environment ministry or authority plays a crucial, 'horizontal' role reviewing and regulating the environmental performance of other departments, somewhat similar to that of a finance ministry in setting the overall level of public expenditure and its allocation between different departments. Top-down approaches to integration might involve the following key steps:

The development of 'rolling' National
Sustainability and Biodiversity Plans
↓

The development of Sectoral Action Plans
↓

Annual reporting by Departments on their performance
in relation to Sectoral Action Plans
↓

Regular review of Annual Environmental Reports by
Parliament/public

• A *bottom-up approach* to integration reflects the application of influence rather than formal power. Environment ministries or agencies are not able to impose constraints on the actions of other departments, which remain free to develop policies and programmes in the light of their own sectoral priorities. The integration of environmental considerations into sectoral policies comes instead from a process, often very gradual, of cultural change in which sectoral departments themselves come to take greater account of environmental considerations. The role of environment ministries or agencies in this process is to *influence* and *guide* rather than direct. In this task they may be helped by parliamentary and public opinion. The key features of the bottom-up approach are not binding Action Plans but *procedures* designed to make sectoral departments more aware of the environmental consequences of their actions. They require a process of continuous negotiation between environment and sectoral ministries, through, for example, the extensive use of inter-departmental committees or working groups, or the appointment of 'green' officials within sectoral departments.

• *Intermediate steps.* Between the two extremes of the continuum, sectoral departments may face increasing degrees of constraint through being required to apply one or more formal 'integrative' mechanisms. These may include some forms of strategic environmental assessment and appraisal (SEA[2]), or the application of environmental auditing and reporting mechanisms. The degree of constraint that these mechanisms represent will depend crucially on such factors as who undertakes the assessment or audit, and who takes the final decision on whether a policy should proceed and in what form.

The choice of integration strategy: The approach to integration adopted at EU or Member State level will depend on the degree of formal power or authority at the disposal of the environment ministry, directorate or agency. Among EU member states, most environment ministries have only recently been established. The oldest of them have been in existence as separate ministries for less than 25 years, and some (as in Italy and Spain) for less than ten. Generally they have not been sufficiently powerful in relation to other ministries to enable them to impose a 'top-down' approach to integration, even if they wished to. Similarly, within the European Commission, the political weight of DG XI is limited in comparison with, for example, DG VI (Agriculture) or DG III (Industry), both longer established and with far greater financial and staff resources. It is inevitable that powerful sectoral ministries will continue to insist on developing policies and programmes in the light of their own non-environmental priorities. In practice, therefore, environment ministries, agencies and non-governmental organisations (NGOs) seeking to advance integration need to focus *simultaneously* on several points along the integration continuum. Binding Action Plans may represent the most direct and potentially effective route to integration, but political realities need to be acknowledged and the development of softer, 'bottom-up' approaches encouraged as well.

Integration and EU environment policy: The subject of environmental integration was first given prominence in the European Community's (EC) Fourth Environmental Action Programme of 1987.[3] Section 2.3 states:

> It will accordingly be a central part of the Commission's efforts during the period of the Fourth Environmental Action Programme to make major progress towards the practical realisation of this objective – initially at the level of the Community's own policies and actions; secondly at the level of the policies implemented by Member States; but as soon as possible in a more generalised way so that all economic and social developments throughout the Community, whether undertaken by public or private bodies or of a mixed character, would have environmental requirements built fully into their planning and execution.

Initially, emphasis was to be placed on the Community's own policies and, to this end, the Commission was to 'develop internal procedures and practices to ensure that this integration of environmental factors takes place routinely in relation to all other policy areas'. Action to give effect to this promise was not forthcoming until after the publication in 1992 of the 5EAP,[4] and the strengthening of the integration requirement in the Maastricht Treaty.

The 5EAP

The European Commission adopted the 5EAP on 18 March 1992, three months before the United Nations Conference on Environment and Development (UNCED) and the adoption of Agenda 21 (A21). Nevertheless, the 5EAP was prepared in parallel with the principal Rio agreements so that it shares many of the strategic objectives and principles of A21. The 5EAP marked an important change of direction for the Community's environmental policy. Previous environmental action programmes had taken the form of lists of proposed legislation often selected in response to events, whereas the 5EAP attempted to address the fundamental causes of environmental degradation as a means of creating a more sustainable economy and society. In contrast to A21, its focus was exclusively environmental and it did not address the social dimensions of sustainable development such as poverty, gender or demographics.[5] In a Council Resolution of 1 February 1993 approving the 'general approach of the programme,' EU Environment Ministers noted that the 5EAP 'constitutes an appropriate *point of departure* for the implementation of Agenda 21 by the European Community and its Member States' (our italics).[6] Subsequent A21 Implementation Reports from the Community to the United Nations Commission on Sustainable Development have similarly emphasised that the 5EAP 'has been chosen as the Community's main vehicle for implementing Agenda 21 and the other agreements made at UNCED'.[7]

The 5EAP set the strategy for the EU's environmental policy until the year 2000. It was focused on ten major environmental problems or themes, and five economic sectors which make a significant contribution both to their creation, and by the same token, their solution. These were industry, agriculture, energy, transport and tourism. For each of the themes and target sectors, the programme presented tables setting out policy objectives, the instruments and timetables for achieving them, and the key actors from whom action is required, including the EU, member states, local authorities and industry.

Fundamental to the Programme was the principle that the environment must be integrated from the beginning into all the policies and actions of industry, government and consumers, especially in the target sectors. Other important features included a recognition that changes in society's patterns of behaviour must be achieved in a spirit of shared responsibility among all key actors, including central and local government, public and private enterprise, and the general public (as both individual citizens and consumers). It also emphasised that the range of policy instruments applied to the solution of environmental problems should be broadened beyond traditional 'command and control' legislation, to include economic instruments, voluntary agreements, and better information and education to enable the public to make more informed choices.

As a Council Resolution, the Council of Ministers' response to the 5EAP was non-binding. Moreover, EU Environment Ministers were careful to establish that the proposed actions, targets and timetables in the 5EAP did not immediately impose legal obligations upon the Member States. It was only the *general approach and strategy of the programme* that were approved. They also emphasised that in accordance with the principle of subsidiarity, 'some of the actions in the programme fall to be implemented at levels other than that of the Community'. Where appropriate, the Commission was invited to come forward with proposals to give effect to the programme, which would be considered by the Community's institutions in the normal way (and by implication could be rejected in the Council).

Less clear, however, was whether the Commission itself was obliged to develop proposals in those areas identified in the programme as requiring a lead from the Community. The view of the Commission's DG XI was that since the Commission as a whole had adopted the draft 5EAP, all DGs were bound to come forward with appropriate proposals. Other Commission officials were less convinced, however. A review in mid-1995 of how far the Commission had 'delivered' on its obligations to act by that date revealed that in respect of over one quarter of its commitments, the Commission had failed to act.[8] In contrast to A21, the 5EAP contained no suggestion that Member States should present regular reports to the Commission on their implementation of the programme. Only the UK produced such a report.[9] An Annex to the Commission's Progress Report on the 5EAP[10] seeks to present in tabular form how far the Member States had taken steps to implement the programme, but observes that 'information on some countries is limited because of too late input (*sic*) or no input by these countries'.

The European Commission's 'Integration' Procedures

The Commission's Approach to Integration

The Commission's approach to integration has necessarily been an example of the 'bottom up' approach. DG XI has no formal power over other DGs, and the 5EAP is binding neither on the Member States, nor the Commission itself (but see below, p.171). Environment Commissioner Ritt Bjerregaard has observed: 'I am a bit like someone in charge of a car-park where none of the issues which are parked there under the name of the environment are really ones I could call my own. In reality they are in fact issues which really need to be resolved elsewhere by some of my other Commission colleagues .... ' [11]

The Commission's integration arrangements were set out in an internal (and unpublished) Communication *Integration by the Commission of the Environment into other Policies*.[12] This was drawn up by DG XI and DG IX (Personnel and Administration) in discussion with the Commission's Secretariat General, and endorsed by Commissioners at the end of May 1993. The proposed arrangements were the subject of very little discussion, however, and most Commissioners seem not to have properly absorbed their full implications. In summary, the new machinery comprised five principal elements:

• A new *Integration Unit* was to be established in DG XI, reporting directly to the Director-General;

• Each of the Commission's Directorates-General was to designate an *Integration Correspondent* – a 'green' official whose task would be to ensure that policies took proper account of the environment;

• All policy proposals with significant environmental effects were to be subject to an environmental appraisal (a form of *SEA*). Those selected for this procedure would be indicated by a 'green star' in the Commission's legislative programme published at the beginning of each year;

• Each DG was to undertake *an annual evaluation of its environmental performance*. Such evaluations were to be published in the Commission's annual *General Report on the Activities of the European Union*;

• A *Code of Conduct* was to be drawn up for the Commission itself, covering such green housekeeping issues as purchasing policy; waste minimisation; energy conservation etc.

In September 1994, these requirements were elaborated and incorporated into the seventh revision of the Commission's internal *Manual of Operational Procedures*.[13]

Implementation of the Commission's Integration Machinery

DG XI Integration Unit: A Unit for Political Co-ordination and Integration was established in DG XI in 1993 with five officials charged with monitoring the implementation of the 5EAP, both within DG XI itself, and throughout the Commission. More specifically, it was to be the point of contact with integration correspondents in other DGs. The Unit has made available to correspondents information on developments in environmental policy, and, to the extent that it can, advice on such matters as the techniques of environmental appraisal. It has commissioned more structured training sessions on such techniques, and other skills related to environmental integration. In consultation with the Commission's Secretariat-General, it was responsible for proposing those items in the Commission's Work programmes for 1994 and 1995 that might be subject to an environmental appraisal (although it is the responsible DGs that ultimately decide if such appraisals should be undertaken).

Environment Integration Correspondents.[14] The Commission's internal Communication stressed that:

> In each Directorate-General a senior official closely linked to the central policy making operation of the DG will be made responsible for ensuring that policy proposals and legislative proposals developed in that Directorate-General take account of the environment and of the requirement to contribute towards sustainable patterns of development.

By mid-1994, integration correspondents had been designated by all DGs. Most correspondents were senior officials (Head of Unit or above), but in practice many of the duties of the post have been delegated to subordinates. The appointment of integration correspondents was undertaken by each DG acting independently of DG XI. In several DGs the designation was given as a matter of course to officials with pre-existing environmental responsibilities. DGs III (Industry), VI (Agriculture), and XVII (Energy) each had one or more units dealing with environmental affairs, and have continued to develop their own environment-related policies. For example, Unit A/2 in DG XVII (Analyses and Forecasts) played a leading role in an inter-service group on the Community's carbon dioxide reduction strategy, which comprises representatives of nine DGs. In DG VI, there were no less than five separate sections dealing with environmental concerns. Inevitably, such units have each had their own agendas and ways of working.

For its part, DG XI has issued no formal guidance setting out in precise terms what the role of an integration correspondent should be. There is a range of possible models, including the following:

- Spy – informing DG XI of developments in other Commission services;

- Postman – passing on information from DG XI on environmental developments and legislation;

- Policeman – vetoing 'ungreen' policy proposals;

- Technician – advising on whether and how to do, for example, strategic environmental assessments;

- Facilitator – negotiating between DG XI and the correspondent's own DG; and

- Ambassador – seeking to modify DG XI's policies to accord with those of the correspondent's own DG.

In practice, each integration correspondent has been able to interpret the role in his or her own way. Few, if any, can be regarded as DG XI 'spies' or 'policemen'. Indeed, at one of the very few meetings of all the correspondents summoned by DG XI, a significant proportion failed to attend. In those DGs with an established environmental role or unit, integration is regarded as a two-way process in which the sectoral department has as much right to influence DG XI as *vice versa*. The case of DG III may be cited as an example. An environment unit B4 ('Industrial Problems related to Environmental Legislation') had been established in April 1993, some months before the Commission's internal Communication. As early as November 1992, DG III had already produced its own Communication 'Industrial Competitiveness and Protection of the Environment' (SEC (92) 1986). DG III's environment unit set itself three principal objectives:

- to inform officials with sectoral responsibilities within DG III of relevant environmental developments within the Council of Ministers, the Organisation for Economic Co-operation and Development, and other fora. This is done through meetings of an internal environmental network of some 30 DG III officials who meet monthly; the production of a Newsletter; and the use of electronic-mail.

- to act as an *element moderateur* by making DG XI aware of industrial realities in the development of the EU's environmental policy.

- to advance the 'greening' of industry by the direct encouragement of voluntary agreements, life cycle analysis, and the diffusion of clean technologies.

Officials in DG III's environment unit have privately expressed the view that responsibility for developing aspects of environmental policy and legislation could be transferred from DG XI to DG III. DG III traditionally has had far greater contact with industry than DG XI, which is regarded as under-resourced and suffering from excessive staff turnover.[15]

Environmental appraisals of Commission proposals: The Commission's internal Communication required environmental appraisals to be undertaken of any Commission proposal with significant effects on the environment. These have been identified with an asterisk (a 'green star') in the Commission's annual legislative programme, following consultation between DG XI and the responsible DG. The ultimate responsibility for undertaking the work, however, rests with the responsible DG. Annex 6 of the *Manual of Operational Procedures* now lists a step-by-step procedure for undertaking environmental appraisals. A review of the environmental impact of relevant proposals was also to be included in Commission Communications to the Council (COM documents). However, there is no evidence that any such environmental appraisals have been undertaken. No references to such appraisals have been included in any Commission Communications issued since the new procedures came into effect. The attempt by DG XI to apply environmental appraisal on such a scale was over-ambitious. The appropriate methodology is underdeveloped, and is still being investigated in research commissioned by DG XI. In respect of its proposals for Trans-European Road Networks, DG VII (Transport) has also commissioned research on practice elsewhere. Against this background, it was optimistic of DG XI to attach 'green stars' to so many of the legislative proposals in the Commission's 1994 and 1995 legislative programmes.

Annual evaluations of environmental performance: Each DG was to draw up annually an evaluation of its environmental performance, which was to be published in the Commission's annual *General Report of the Activities of the European Union.* Unpublished evaluations were submitted to DG XI covering the period 1993–94, which formed the basis of an internal DG XI Information Note to the rest of the Commission.[16] Not all DGs, however, submitted complete information. DG XI notes that: 'numerous DGs have taken initiatives and developed measures in the environment sector, but to what extent and how the environment has been taken into account, on a systematic basis, as other types of measures and policies are devised, is rarely indicated'.[17] Some information on environmental performance was included in the *Interim Report on the implementation of the Fifth Environmental Action Programme.* However, despite the requirement in the June 1993 Internal Communication, very little information is contained in the Commission's *General Report on the Activities of the European Union* for 1994 and 1995.[18]

Internal environmental management system for the Commission: An internal consultation paper was drawn up by DG IX on the environmental impact of the Commission's own activities, but has not been published.

Only in early 1996 were consultants invited by DG XI to draw up an internal environmental management system for the Commission.

Impact of the Commission's Integration Measures

The impact of the Commission's June 1993 internal communication on practice in other DGs has been modest. Not all elements of the new integration procedures have been implemented, and where they have, their impact has been limited. Where substantive progress towards integration has occurred in the five key policy sectors identified in the 5EAP, this has been as much the consequence of exogenous factors as of the June 1993 measures. For example, what progress there has been on the 'greening' of the common agricultural policy is a reflection of a coincidence of interests between the farming community and environmentalists, while in the energy sector attempts to reduce energy demand simultaneously serve a number of different policy objectives – the classic 'win-win' situation – and are therefore more readily acceptable to DG XVII.

DG XI's disappointment with the new internal integration procedures was reflected in the 1995 Progress Report on the 5EAP:

> The measures so far have had limited impact … progress has varied according to sectors, but the message of the Fifth Programme has not been sufficiently integrated in operational terms within the Commission. The process depends on persuasion and influence and will take time. In the longer term, change is likely to take place through increased education, training and changes of attitude. It will require continued adequate resources and sustained commitment.[19]

This last sentence highlights the profound importance of the pursuit of integration for the future direction and culture of DG XI itself. Even a bottom-up approach to integration requires the application of considerable staff resources, new forms of expertise and political commitment in the department responsible for driving an integration initiative. Substantial investment is required by an environment ministry or department to: develop expertise in policy sectors outside the traditionally 'environmental'; train staff outside the environment department in such environmental techniques as SEA and environmental auditing; and develop new management skills associated with team building, influencing, and negotiation.

The willingness of officials to make this investment may be weakened by what may be perceived as the uncertain outcome of successful integration. This may be that responsibility for environmental protection shifts away from the environment department towards sectoral ministries, so that measures, for example, to prevent or minimise agricultural or industrial pollution become the exclusive responsibility of the agriculture and industry departments, with the role of environment departments limited to advice and training. Successful integration entails a fundamental redefinition of the role of the environment departments, and some loss of control over environmental policy. The dilemma this poses is that the focus for advancing integration across the activities of government may consequently become less distinct. It was for this reason that one of the earliest initiatives of the DG XI Integration Unit was to address these issues in 'reflection' meetings with all DG XI staff. Subsequently, the process of developing a new corporate mission for DG XI which acknowledges its new integration responsibilities has been given priority by its Director-General, Marius Endhoven. Work on this is continuing.

Turning the Screw: Moves Towards a Top-Down Approach

As discussed above, DG XI has had no formal authority of its own to direct other DGs to 'green' their policies, hence its reliance on a bottom-up approach to integration. This is necessarily a long-term and uncertain process which fits uneasily with the targets and timetables set out in the 5EAP. In these circumstances, it is not surprising that DG XI has sought to move along the integration continuum towards a more top-down approach. It has tacitly sought to increase its power in relation to other DGs by: forming an alliance with the European Parliament; applying for the first time provisions in the Maastricht Treaty which enhance the legal status of General Action Programmes on the Environment; and, seeking at the 1996 IGC to reinforce the Treaty commitment in Article 130r(2) to advance environmental integration.

The European Parliament and the Power of the Purse

The powers of the European Parliament in relation to the EU's annual budget are considerable, and in the past it has not been afraid to use, or threaten to use, them to extract concessions from the Commission or the Council in other policy sectors. Prior to the Parliament's examination of the draft 1996 budget, informal discussions were held between DG XI and the Parliament's Environment Committee on the possibility of using Parliament's budgetary powers to further the process of integration. An opportunity to take this forward arose after the 1994 elections to the European Parliament, when Laurens Jan Brinkhorst, former Director-General of DG XI, was elected a Member of the European Parliament (MEP) and appointed to the Committee on Budgets. He helped to influence the views of Mr James Ellis MEP, the Budget Committee's rapporteur on the draft 1996 budget, on the need for 'greening' EU spending, and was himself appointed the Budget Committee's rapporteur for the 1997 budget. Together with the Environment Committee's rapporteur on the draft budget – Karl-Heinz Florenz MEP (a Christian Democrat) – a close triangular relationship was established between the Parliament's separate Committees on Budgets and the Environment, and a few key officials from DG XI.

A long-term process was begun of seeking to insert environmental conditions in key budget lines. According to Florenz, '[a]s far as your rapporteur is concerned, 1996 will be the year of the greening of the budget'. His proposed amendments to the draft budget were explicitly designed 'to make up for the inadequacy which still exists in the Commission's internal procedures concerning the environment'.[20] Parliament's Resolution of 5 April 1995 on the guidelines for the 1996 budget included the following statement: '[The European Parliament] requests that the Commission, through the application of the principle of sustainable development, include environmental protection in Community policies, so that the impact on the environment of Community actions be taken into account before any appropriations are granted.'[21]

For the 1996 budget, the Environment Committee's proposed amendments focused principally on the appropriations for the Structural and Cohesion Funds – at 29 billion ECU, over one-third of the 1996 Community budget, and a category of 'non-compulsory' expenditure over which Parliament has the final say. As a result of an effective campaign in the late 1980s by environmental NGOs highlighting the environmental damage caused by large infrastructure projects supported by Community finance, the revision of the Structural Fund Regulations in 1993 incorporated a number of new requirements relating to environmental appraisals and the participation of 'environmental authorities' in decisions on the application of the funds [*Wilkinson, 1994*]. The failure properly to implement these safeguards on the ground in the member states, and the sometimes casual attitude to their enforcement shown by DG XVI, continued to feed the NGO campaign and the concern of sympathetic MEPs.

Accordingly, the Environment Committee's key amendment to the EU's 1996 draft budget threatened to freeze 50 per cent of the funds for the Structural and Cohesion Funds in reserve unless the Commission (that is, DG XVI) produced, by a deadline of 15 November 1995, an environmental 'Code of Conduct' governing the future use of the funds. According to the Committee, the Code of Conduct was to: require an environmental appraisal to be undertaken and published of every programme and project to be financed by the Structural and Cohesion Funds; require the continuous monitoring and evaluation of the environmental impacts of structural and cohesion expenditure; and, require regular reports on the above to the Parliament and the Council. The Committee's Opinion concluded: '[t]he

Committee on the Environment must therefore do everything in its power to ensure that the first stage of this "greening" of the budget is a complete success: only then will genuine integration with other Community policies be possible in the future'.[22] These proposals were accepted by the Committee on Budgets (although the deadline for the Code of Conduct was put back to 8 December), and subsequently endorsed by the Parliament as a whole on 26 October 1995.

The effect on DG XVI was dramatic. At the end of November the Commission issued a Communication, jointly authored by the Regional Policy and Environment Commissioners, entitled *Cohesion Policy and the Environment*.[23] It included a declaration from Regional Affairs Commissioner Monika Wulf-Mathies that: 'The environment itself is a major factor for regional development, and I personally regard cohesion policy as a significant opportunity to operationalise sustainable development.' The Communication set out a ten-point plan for tightening environmental requirements in the current use of the structural funds, within the current Structural Fund Regulations. The Communication promised: more money for environmental pilot projects, and preferential differentiation of the Community's rate of assistance for environmentally-friendly programmes; better project selection criteria, monitoring and evaluation of the environmental impact of Structural Fund activities; a clearer role for 'environmental authorities' on Structural Fund monitoring committees; tougher action by the Commission on Member States failing to apply the environmental; and, safeguards set out in the Structural Fund Regulations. The Communication promised to incorporate these strengthened procedures into the new Structural and Cohesion Fund Regulations due to be revised in 1999.

In addition, on the precise deadline set by the Parliament (8 December 1995), a Letter of Intent was dispatched from the Commission to both Florenz and Detlev Samland (Chair of the Parliament's Committee on Budgets). The letter was signed by the Regional Affairs Commissioner and the Budget Commissioner (Erkki Liikenen) and was written with the express agreement of President Santer. The letter made the following key commitments:

- the environmental role of Structural Fund Monitoring Committees was to be strengthened;

- all proposed Structural and Cohesion Fund projects larger than 50 million ECU would undergo an environmental appraisal to establish that there were no detrimental environmental effects, or that any such effects would be 'adequately compensated';

- resources within the Commission would be made available to review such environmental assessments;

- an annual list of large projects funded by the Structural and Cohesion Funds for which an environmental assessment had been undertaken would be published in the *Official Journal*;

- the European Parliament would be sent details of these environmental assessments on request.[24]

Despite some ambiguous and tortuous wording, the Committee on Budgets was satisfied with this response, calling it 'a serious effort to strengthen the environmental dimension of budget implementation'.[25] As a result, the threat to place Structural Fund spending in reserve was lifted. However, in the 1996 budget as finally agreed with the Council, alongside budget lines dealing with each of the Structural Funds and Cohesion Fund, there is a reference to the 'integration' requirement in Article 130r(2), and the statement that:

> appropriations for the Structural Funds cannot be implemented unless the measures financed by these Funds comply with the provisions of the Treaties and acts pursuant thereto, in particular those concerning environmental protection, as stipulated in Article 7 of Regulation (EEC) No 2052/88. They should be accompanied by an environmental impact commentary according to the principles of the Commission's letter of understanding of 8 December.[26]

The exact legal status of this statement remains to be tested, but at the very least it represented a political commitment by the European Parliament to use its powers to block Structural Fund spending if the Commission's commitments are unfulfilled. However, during the Parliament's consideration of the following year's budget, Florenz expressed some satisfaction with the response of DG XVI. In his report for the Environment Committee on the draft 1997 budget, he also noted that the next set of targets jointly agreed by the Environment and Budget Committees for 'greening' were the EU's agriculture, energy and development co-operation policies. In the case of agriculture, Florenz called upon DG VI to establish a code of good practice for the sustainable use of fertilisers and plant protection products. For his part, Brinkhorst called upon DG XI to establish a Unit for assessing the environmental impact of expenditure in the targeted sectors, and for advancing the use of green technology.[27]

The Co-decision Procedure and the Review of the 5EAP

In addition to associating itself with the European Parliament's use of its budgetary powers, DG XI has also attempted to increase its influence in relation to other DGs by using powers in the Maastricht Treaty which give a new legal status to environmental action programmes. As discussed above, when it was considered by the Council of Ministers in February 1993, the 5EAP was considered to be binding neither on the Commission nor the Member States, since the Council approved only the 'general approach and strategy of the programme' and not its detailed targets and timetables. Moreover, this approval was given in the form of a non-binding Resolution. However, nine months following the Council's Resolution, on 1 November 1993, the Maastricht Treaty came into effect. For the first time, it gave in Article 130s(3) a new legal status to 'general action programmes' on the environment. These were henceforward to be established under the co-decision procedure with the European Parliament, the outcome of which must be a legal instrument. Moreover, under this procedure, MEPs are given considerable powers of amendment [*Wilkinson, 1993*].

The 5EAP contained a provision for an interim review of the programme to be undertaken by the end of 1995. The European Environment Agency and the Commission both issued reports reviewing progress, and both concluded that there should be accelerated progress towards meeting the targets set in the 5EAP.[28, 29] Although the review applied to an action programme adopted before the Maastricht Treaty came into effect, DG XI nevertheless sought to use the provisions of Article 130r(3) by proposing a draft Decision incorporating what it described as an 'action plan to ensure the more efficient implementation of the approach set out in the Programme'. In an accompanying Communication, Environment Commissioner Mrs Bjerregaard observed that the Commission's internal measures adopted in June 1993 to integrate the environment across the work of the Commission:

> have still to be fully internalised by the services of the Commission in operational terms. In order to ensure the success of the priorities contained in the enclosed proposal, it will be necessary to pay increased attention to the implementation of integration measures. The College should commit itself to integration and ensure that this message is passed on to its services for action.[30]

Most of the priorities set out in the draft Decision had already been identified in the 5EAP, or in subsequent Commission Communications. In a number of cases, however, the proposed measures were either new or more sharply defined. This was the case in respect of a number of measures in the agriculture, transport, and tourism sectors, and in relation to noise, the Structural Funds, the range of policy instruments, and in respect of implementation and enforcement. The draft Decision was discussed extensively by DG XI with the relevant DGs. Their agreement to the draft was presumably facilitated by the fact that the language is imprecise (for example: 'will further develop', 'investigate possibilities', 'special attention will be given to', 'consider means how to improve'), and that, unlike the 5EAP itself, there are no quantitative targets or timetables.

Predictably, the European Parliament's Environment Committee was dismissive of the Commission's proposed Decision, describing it as 'a step backwards in relation to the original Fifth Environmental Action Programme'.[31] In its report to the Parliament, the Committee put forward over 100 amendments, and observed that only fear of further delays prevented the rejection of the Commission's proposals in their entirety. The Committee's report pointed out that the continuing deterioration in the state of the environment described in European Environment Agency's 1995 *Environment in the European Union* required 'binding Community actions underpinned by fixed time frames' to ensure that priorities are actually put into practice. Among the measures proposed by the Committee were:

- reform of the Common Agriculture Policy's set-aside arrangements to re-create permanent natural zones;

- setting targets and timetables for reducing the use of pesticides in agriculture. These should be tabled by the Commission before the end of 1997;

- a sustainable forest policy, also to be developed before the end of 1997;

- measures to attain a 20 per cent reduction of EU carbon dioxide emissions by 2005, 30 per cent by 2010, and 50 per cent by 2030 compared with 1990 levels;

- tougher measures, to be proposed by the Commission before the end of 1997, to ensure the proper implementation and enforcement of Community environmental legislation; and

- 50 per cent of EU funds currently spent in central and eastern Europe should be redirected from the promotion of fossil fuels and nuclear energy towards energy efficiency and support for renewables.

By the end of October 1996, the Committee's report had not been debated by the Parliament as a whole, nor had the Council of Ministers had more than a preliminary discussion of the 5EAP review. Negotiations between the Community institutions were expected to be protracted, not least because the exact legal status of an action plan (or programme) established by a Decision of the European Parliament and Council is unclear. EU Decisions are binding on those to whom they are addressed, and the proposed Decision throughout refers to actions to be taken by 'the

Community'. Some member states, including the UK, have been anxious to argue that this has no immediate implications for member states, and that the proposed measures in the Action Plan may only be implemented by separate detailed proposals, which will be subject to separate negotiation and agreement.[32] However, the Decision (once adopted) will certainly be binding on all Commission DGs, so that they will be bound to propose specific legislation relating to the measures listed in the Decision. DG XI's leverage within the Commission has therefore been enhanced.

'Greening' the Treaty

References in the Maastricht Treaty to 'sustainable growth respecting the environment', and to the 'integration' imperative provided DG XI with a legal underpinning for the 5EAP, and opened the way for references to 'sustainable development' to be included in some subsequent items of legislation.[33] The IGC, launched in Turin in March 1996, has provided a further opportunity for DG XI to seek to reinforce the Community's commitment to sustainable development. The Commission's Opinion on the IGC proposes reinforcing 'the provisions of the Treaty directed at sustainable development and a healthy environment'.[34] These proposals were included in the Commission's Opinion only at the last moment, at the insistence of Mrs Bjerregaard. The support of Austria, Sweden, Finland and some other member states has insured that the EU's environment policy forms part of the IGC agenda.

The Commission's Opinion proposes that 'the environment should be specifically incorporated into the other policies of the Union', implying a further reinforcement of the integration imperative in Article 130r(2). The Opinion does not say *which* policies, or whether references to integration should be peppered throughout the Treaty in articles dealing with agriculture, transport, economic and social cohesion and so on. One possibility is that a single, new Article 3(c) establishing the integration principle might be included in the Treaty, with a horizontal function similar to the 'subsidiarity' requirement in Article 3(b). According to the Irish Minister for the Environment, Mr Brendan Howlin, there is support for this option among a majority of member states, as there is for revising the tortuous wording of Article 2 and replacing it with an explicit reference to 'sustainable development' as a fundamental objective of the Union.[35] Both of these amendments can be expected to reinforce the hand of DG XI in its dealings with the rest of the Commission.

NOTES

1. The classic discussion of integration within organisations is Lawrence and Lorsch [*1969*].
2. SEA is the *ex-ante* assessment of proposed sectoral policies, plans and programmes.
3. EEC Fourth Environmental Action Programme 1987–92, *Official Journal*, C328, 7 Dec. 1987.
4. Commission of the European Communities, *Towards Sustainability: A European Community Programme of Policy and Action in Relation to the Environment and Sustainable Development*, COM (92) 23, 27 March 1992.
5. Commission of the European Communities, *Progress Report from the Commission on the Implementation of the European Community Programme of Policy and Action in Relation to the Environment and Sustainable Development Towards Sustainability*, COM (95) 624, 10 Jan. 1996.
6. Council Resolution on a Community programme of policy and action in relation to the environment and sustainable development, *Official Journal*, C 138, 17 May 1995.
7. Commission of the European Communities, *Report from the European Community to the Commission on Sustainable Development on Progress Towards Implementation of Agenda 21. The Third Session*, April 1995, p.2.
8. Unpublished review by IEEP, London.
9. Department of the Environment (1994) *EC Fifth Environmental Action Programme Towards Sustainability: Government Action in the UK*, Dec. 1994.
10. Op. cit., Annex 2.
11. Speech by Mrs Bjerregaard to ERM/Green Alliance Forum, London, 2 Nov. 1995.
12. Commission of the European Communities, Internal Communication *Integration by the Commission of the Environment into Other Policies*, SEC (93) 785/5, 28 May 1993.
13. Commission of the European Communities, *Manual of Operational Procedures*, 7th Edition, Sept.1994
14. Information obtained from interviews with Commission officials.
15. Personal communication with author.
16. Internal Commission Information Note, *Implementation by the Commission of the Measures of 2 June 1993 on the Integration of the Environment into Its Other Policies* (Dec. 1994).
17. Op. cit.
18. Commission of the European Communities, *General Report on the Activities of the European Union*, 1994, 1995.
19. Commission of the European Communities, *Progress Report on Implementation of the European Community Programme of Policy and Action in Relation to the Environment and Sustainable Development 'Towards Sustainability'*, COM (95) 624, 10 Jan. 1996, p.104.
20. European Parliament, *Report from the Committee on Budgets on the Draft General Budget of the European Communities for the Financial Year 1996* (A4-0235/95/Part D).
21. *Official Journal*, C109, 1 May 1995, p.46.
22. European Parliament, *Report from the Committee on Budgets on the Draft General Budget of the European Communities for the Financial Year 1996* (A4-0235/95/Part D).
23. Commission of the European Communities, *Cohesion Policy and the Environment* COM (95)509 22 Nov. 1995.
24. Unpublished.
25. European Parliament, *Report from the Committee on Budgets on the 1996 Draft Budget, as Modified by the Council* (A4-0305/95, 11 Dec. 1995).
26. Final adoption of the general budget of the European Union for the financial year 1996, *Official Journal*, L22, 29 Jan. 1996, sub-section B2, pp.689–794.
27. European Parliament, *Report of the Committee on Budgets on the Draft General Budget of the European Union for the 1997 Financial Year* (A4-0310-11/96 Oct. 1996).
28. European Environment Agency, *Environment in the European Union 1995 – Report for the Review of the Fifth Environmental Action Programme*, Office for Official Publications of the European Communities, Luxembourg, 1995.
29. Commission of the European Communities, *Progress Report on Implementation of the European Community Programme of Policy and Action in Relation to the Environment and*

Sustainable Development 'Towards Sustainability, COM (95) 624, 10 Jan. 1996.
30. Commission of the European Communities, *Proposal for a European Parliament and Council Decision on the review of the European Community Programme of Policy and Action in Relation to the Environment and Sustainable Development, Towards Sustainability*, – COM (95) 647, 29 Feb. 1996, OJ C 140, 11 May 1996.
31. European Parliament, Committee on Environment, Public Health and Consumer Protection, *Report on the Proposal for a European Parliament and Council Decision on the Review of the European Community Programme of Policy and Action in Relation to the Environment and Sustainable Development Towards Sustainability*, A4-0300/96, Rapporteur Mrs Lone Dybkjaer.
32. Department of the Environment, *Explanatory Memorandum*, 5641/96 on COM (95) 647, 7 May 1996.
33. See for example Council Regulation 2083/93 on the Regional Development Fund, Article 1f, OJ, L193, 31 July 1993.
34. Commission of the European Communities, *Reinforcing Political Union and Preparing for Enlargement* (n.d.)
35. Speech to conference on the Inter-Governmental Conference organised by BUND, Berlin, 4 Oct. 1996.

REFERENCES

Lawrence, P. and J. Lorsch (1969), *Organisations and Environment: Managing Differentiation and Integration*, Boston, MA: Division of Research, Graduate School of Business Administration, Harvard University.
Wilkinson, D. (1993), 'Maastricht and the Environment: The Implications for the EC's Environment Policy of the Treaty on European Union', *Journal of Environmental Law*, Vol.4, No.2, pp.221–39
Wilkinson, D. (1994), 'Using the European Union's Structural and Cohesion funds for the Protection of the Environment', *Review of European Community and International Environmental Law*, Vol.3, Issue 2/3, pp.119–26.

Acronyms

5EAP	Fifth Environmental Action Programme
A21	Agenda 21
DG	Directorate-General
EC	European Community
ECU	European Currency Unit
EU	European Union
IGC	Inter-Governmental Conference
MEP	Member of the European Parliament
NGO	Non-Governmental Organisation
SEA	Strategic Environmental Assessment
UNCED	United Nations Conference on Environment and Development

Beyond the Early Stages of the Sustainability Transition

TIM O'RIORDAN and HEATHER VOISEY

Sustainable development has been characterised in this series of essays to which this short piece is the conclusion, as an odyssey into desirable wealth creation, stewardship of ecosystems and people, community empowerment and revelation through visions sharing a common purpose. The key is to co-ordinate institutional innovation so that all these strategies can be built upon. To do this will require much more effective political leadership than is presently the case, even more mobilisation at the Local Agenda 21 level, a lot of action by business, and real progress on the eco-taxation, indicators and auditing fronts. It is all going to be hard pounding.

The contributions to this collection have all concluded that sustainable development has created some sort of institutional initiative that would not have taken place in the form of 'business as usual'. Some of these changes have been spurred on by the outcome of Brussels negotiations in environmental directives and post-Rio commitments. So we take nothing away from this important 'business as usual' dimension in contemporary environmental politics. The monitoring of environmental change is promoted by those legal requirements, as well as by the insistence on sound data gathering regularly being made by the European Environmental Agency. These two compliance procedures have given political weight to ministries long in the shadows of public works, planning, finance and industry. They have opened up the way for more comprehensive and public environmental assessments of plans and policies, as well as projects.

Admittedly the pattern of elite bias and traditions of limited consultation and even more scarce information, make most of this fairly symbolic. But the modest flexing of European Parliamentary muscles, as reported on by David Wilkinson, shows that the old ways of insider politics on big public works programmes can no longer remain beyond scrutiny. More to the point, these data and compliance requirements have widened the administrative responsibilities of the environmental protection ministries and agencies throughout the Member States, but most especially in the cohesion states. The upgrading of environmental laws and the allocation of resources to ensure that these laws are better enforced are significant developments, even though they have nothing directly to do with the specific institutional adjustments consequent on Agenda 21.

In the introductory contribution, Figures 1 and 2 outlined the possible stages of institutional innovation in the transition to sustainable development. We pointed out that each of the boxes in Figure 2 had its place in that evolution. Society does not move forward by forced consensus; more by negotiated discourse. Each position has its purpose and its legitimacy for different interests. What we are witnessing is an interesting, but uncertain, mix of markets, regulations and participatory democracy in the early stages of the sustainability transition. None of these as yet is designed to support, or reinforce any of the others. Markets are beginning to emerge in the form of green taxes, and even some real eco-taxes where the revenue is specifically directed out of the Treasuries towards sustainability orientated projects. The UK landfill tax is a fine example of this, but new moves along similar lines are being seriously contemplated in Norway, Sweden and The Netherlands [*O'Riordan, 1996*]. These are seriously addressing a rush of changes, regulations and an embryonic form of empowerment. They should be encouraged and copied. The rise of sustainability indicators, notably in the European Environment Agency and in some pilot countries, such as the UK, will help enormously to push these ideas along.

The Next Steps

What is missing is any serious political leadership. The departure of Mrs Bruntland from the Norwegian political stage has left a visionary political void that will be hard to fill. Admittedly Mrs Bruntland took less interest in sustainability matters in latter years. But she was the only political leader to carry the vision of the concept along the lines outlined in Figure 1 in the introductory contribution. Nowadays the European political leaders are obsessed with integration, monetary union and the travails of dealing with extremist political opinion to the right and left of them, to have much spare attention for sustainable development. None of the finance markets mention this notion except in its distorted sense of low inflation, falling unemployment and stable exchange rates. Until there is some sort of sustainability summit, kick started by the review of progress since Rio by the United Nations' Commission on Sustainable Development in 1997, but more likely in 2002 when the 'decade since Rio' milestone resonates around the chancelleries, we cannot envisage the kind of concentrated effort that sets out. Nor can we foresee much movement along the 'indicators' listed towards the end of that chapter: language, policy integration, inter-departmental communication, sustainability indicators, green budget accounting, business and sustainability, and Local Agenda 21 (LA21).

A real problem here lies in the permanent electoral cycle for the European 15 Member States, and the half dozen or so aspiring entrants. At any given moment one or more is passing through an election, where sustainability is the last morsel on the plate to offer to an expectant electorate. The sustainability transition, as outlined in Figure 2, does not lend itself to soundbites and to easy answers. It is simply not the stuff of electoral politics. That remains its Achilles heel. Soundbites and inter-party squabbling reduce the chance of getting serious long-term strategic issues into any meaningful political programme.

There are also other impediments. Policy integration is actually extremely difficult to do well, even when well-intentioned, unless there are common guidelines for effective co-operation. Since the bureaucratic cultures of administrative departments genuinely and often legitimately differ, this sort of accommodation will frankly take a lot of effort. In any case both sustainability indicators and green accounts will take a long time to mature before they can be used effectively as policy tools. Patterns of neo-elitism in most western political cultures, with a bias towards commerce and finance in its purpose, also make it difficult to shift the centres of power. Empowerment and revelation are not attractive propositions to 'old democratic' politicians who thrive on the status quo. Self evidently sustainable development is a truly radical agenda.

The zones of hope lie in eco-taxation, business response and LA21. Eco-taxation is a possibility primarily because it offers a source of 'sin' revenue that is politically palatable in an age where taxation is necessary to keep a country afloat economically speaking, to pay for ever increasing health, education and social security programmes, and to provide the 'civic' revenue for the public and private initiatives that must surely emerge in an age of prolonged unemployment, continuous retraining, and community support for the alienated and the vulnerable [O'Riordan, 1996].

In our view eco-taxation will emerge by stealth, creeping through the finance ministries as programmes on alternative transport, waste minimisation and more sustainable agriculture need long-term investment, labour training, and guaranteed funding. Some initiatives will also be spurred by developments in green budgeting, sustainability indicators with a more 'social' face, and by the excited enthusiasm of inter-departmental communication along more integrationist lines. Maybe we will have to wait for a new breed of bureaucrat to deliver all this. But we think not. Some exceedingly committed people are already in place.

Finally there is LA21. To date this is a very mixed experience, with initiatives confined primarily to the UK and to Norway. Down in the European Union's Southern Member States, the political status of local government is still undergoing transition to a greater budgetary freedom and civic activism. In the Northern countries, the autonomy of local government remains more imagined that actual. LA21 should be a catalyst for the kind of empowerment and revelation initiatives that otherwise cannot take place. For this to be truly successful, however, the custodial agencies also have to get involved in habitat management, catchment planning, and integrated environmental protection. This is on the cards, and the new European Environment Agency may help to stimulate it. But we are not optimistic that the kind of integration of strategy and empowering procedures needed will emerge this side of the next millennium. The 'old democracy' will die hard.

REFERENCE

O'Riordan, T. (ed.) (1996), *Ecotaxation*. London: Earthscan Publications.

Acronym

LA21   Local Agenda 21